EVERYTHING®
Fondue Party Book

Dear Reader,

In my family, entertaining came as naturally as breathing. Of course, initially my Cajun parents didn't call their lively soirees "entertaining." They just cooked up giant pots of food, called family and friends, and said, "Ya'll come." The music, laughter, and eating went on until the wee hours, and it became the soundtrack of my earliest childhood memories.

Later, we moved to suburban New Orleans and my parents joined a neighborhood round robin and had potluck cocktail parties at a different house every month. I was a little older then, and those affairs struck me as so very elegant. The moms on our block got all dolled up; the men told jokes and shared workday war stories; and everyone nibbled on chips, dips, and interesting hors d'oeuvres.

The culinary star of those Wonder Years–era socials was the fondue pot—usually an enameled vessel of avocado green, poppy red, or harvest gold. Someone always contributed some variety of cheese or chocolate fondue to the table, and the ritual of skewering, dunking, cooling, and eating fascinated me. As one of the adolescents in the neighborhood, I was deemed old enough to help myself to the flame-warmed sauces. My love of all things fondue and my tendency to associate it with good times and fun people were born during this time in my life.

Now, decades later, I've had the great fortune to be able to write about fondue—in all its forms—as the centerpiece of fab parties large and small. I've had a grand time writing The Everything® Fondue Party Book, testing recipes, and building on all my childhood fondue memories. I truly hope the menus will inspire you to fire up the fondue pot and call a few friends and say, "Ya'll come!"

Belinda Hulin

THE EVERYTHING® FONDUE PARTY BOOK

Cooking tips, decorating ideas, and over 250 crowd-pleasing recipes

Belinda Hulin

Adams Media
Avon, Massachusetts

To my husband Jim Crissman and our children Dylan and Sophie,
with gratitude for their love and well-tested palates.

Publishing Director: Gary M. Krebs
Associate Managing Editor: Laura Daly
Associate Copy Chief:
Brett Palana-Shanahan
Acquisitions Editor: Kate Burgo
Development Editor: Jessica LaPointe
Associate Production Editor: Casey Ebert

Director of Manufacturing: Susan Beale
Associate Director of Production: Michelle Roy Kelly
Cover Design: Paul Beatrice, Matt LeBlanc
Layout and Graphics: Colleen Cunningham,
Jennifer Oliveira, Brewster Brownville

An Everything® Series Book.
Everything® and everything.com® are registered trademarks of F+W Publications, Inc.

Published by Adams Media, an F+W Publications Company
57 Littlefield Street, Avon, MA 02322 U.S.A.
www.adamsmedia.com

ISBN 10: 1-59337-702-9
ISBN 13: 978-1-59337-702-1
Printed in The United States of America.

J I H G F E D C B A

Library of Congress Cataloging-in-Publication Data
Hulin, Belinda.
The everything fondue party book / Belinda Hulin.
p. cm. -- (The Everything series)
Includes index.
ISBN-10: 1-59337-702-9
ISBN-13: 978-1-59337-702-1
1. Fondue. 2. Chafing dish cookery. I. Title.

TX825.H85 2006
641.8'1--dc22

2006019733

This book is available at quantity discounts for bulk purchases.
For information, call 1-800-872-5627.

Contents

Acknowledgments ix

Introduction x

Chapter 1: FONDUE PARTY BASICS 1
A Little History 1
Fondue Pots 3
The Dips 5
The Dippers 6
Libations 7
Fon-Dos and Fon-Don'ts: Health and Safety 8

Chapter 2: CLASSIC SWISS AND OTHER EUROPEAN CHEESE FONDUES ... 11
Before-Theater Champagne Party 12
Après-Ski Sunset Supper Menu 15
Red Hat Luncheon Menu 19
Fondue-a-Deux Dinner Menu 23
Martinis and Fondue Mixer Menu 26
Fondue Trio Matinee Menu 31
A Night at the Opera Fondue Supper 35

Chapter 3: CHEESE FONDUES FROM THE GREAT AMERICAN
MELTING POT 43
St. Patrick's Day Pots o' Gold Brunch 44
Pennsylvania Dutch Quilting Party 55
South of the Border Queso Party 62
Tailgate Supper Menu 70
Grown-Up Princess PJ Party 76

Cool Kids' Fall Party Menu 81

Neighborhood Block Party Potluck 87

Fondue-for-All Party Menu 90

Chapter 4: BOILED IN OIL: FONDUE BOURGUIGNON AND
OTHER OIL-BASED FONDUES 99

Dinner at Eight 100

Celebration of Summer Fondue 106

Southern Fried Fondue 111

Veggie Feast Fondue 118

Caribbean Swing Fondue Party 125

Shish Kebab Social 132

Chapter 5: HERE'S TO BACCHUS: WINE AND BEER-BASED
FONDUES 139

Tapas Fondue Party Menu 140

Sake Fondue for Two 147

Napa Valley Wine Fondue and
Cheese Reception 152

Mardi Gras Madness Fondue 156

Octoberfest Beer Fondue Menu 164

Chapter 6: SOUP'S ON! BROTH, SAUCE, AND COURT BOUILLON
FONDUES: HOLIDAYS AND FAMILY GATHERINGS 169

Tabletop Seafood Boil for a Crowd 170

Holiday Matzo Ball Fondue 174

Southern Italian Feast Fondue 179

Play-Offs Boiled Beef Pot Fondue 183

Patio Luncheon Fish Fondue 187

Sweet Sixteen Tropical Chicken Curry 191

Chapter 7: ASIAN FONDUES: HOT STUFF FROM HOT POTS 195

Mongolian Hot Pot Affair 196

Spicy Summer Soiree 200

Beefy Hot Pot Potluck 203

Asian New Year Dumpling Fete 207
Shabu-Shabu to Share 213
Harvest Moon Hot Pot Party.........................217
After Practice Hot Pot 221

Chapter 8: WARM AND WONDERFUL CHOCOLATE FONDUES 225
Sophisticates' Chocolate Tasting Menu
Fondues 226
Box of Chocolates Fondue Fun Party 229
Mocha Madness Fondue Buffet 232
Favorite Flavors Chocolate Fondues 236
Dipping and Dunking Fondue Party 239
Favorite Fruits Chocolate Fondue................. 243
Chocolate Candy-Making Party 247

Chapter 9: DESSERT PARTY FONDUES: BEYOND CHOCOLATE 259
Sweet Southern Nights................................ 260
Fruity Brunch Fondues 264
Creamy, Dreamy Fondue Desserts 268
Fondue Shortcake Dessert Party.................... 272
Dessert Fondue for Two 277
Cheese Course Fondue................................. 280

Chapter 10: GOOD CARBS, GOOD FATS, GREAT FONDUE:
HEALTHY CELEBRATIONS 285
Game Night Supper Fondue......................... 286
Olé Mole Fondue 292
Cine-Fest Fondue di Napoli 297
After-Hours Ginger Lemongrass Hot Pot 301
Rustic Impromptu Fondue Dinner Party........ 305
Bloody Mary Brunch Fondue 310

Appendix A: SOURCES FOR PARTY SUPPLIES 317
Appendix B: ARTISANAL CHEESE PRODUCERS...........................319
Index 321

Acknowledgments

Many thanks to the talented, creative minds at Adams Media for their guidance and support. In particular, I'd like to thank acquisitions editor Kate Burgo, development editor Jessica LaPointe, copy editor Tracie Telling Barzdukas, and managing editor Laura Daly. I also want to toss virtual rose petals to agent June Clark, who served as a catalyst for this book.

Of course, a book about food and fun can't happen in a vacuum. I owe a huge debt to my parents, Audrey Hulin and my late father A.J. Hulin, for teaching me to trust my instincts in the kitchen and for showing me the importance of gathering loved ones together for nurturing and nourishment. My in-laws, Roberta and Jim Crissman, have offered moral support, for which I'm truly grateful. My undying thanks also go to the friends and family members who, over the years, have graced my table and enriched my life.

Finally, hugs and kisses to my husband and children. They make every meal a labor of love.

Introduction

A bubbling fondue pot is a party waiting to happen. A simmering vessel of savory or sweet sauce, platters of dip-worthy victuals, a basket of long forks or skewers—add guests to the mix, and pretty soon they're shoulder-to-shoulder, dipping, sipping, munching, and laughing. With this book and a few well-chosen implements, you can make the party a reality.

Fondue, a centuries-old Swiss dish with culinary cousins in many countries, likely started as peasant food. Melting cheeses together, with a splash of wine or spirits and herbs and spices, offered a way to reclaim and share leftovers from the summer larder. One can imagine family and neighbors savoring the aroma of the hot, intensely flavorful melts during cold Alpine winters. Swirling chunks of crusty bread in the communal pot warmed hearts as well as stomachs. Of course, as with many worthy peasant dishes, fondue also found favor with people of means. Embellished with quality ingredients and more refined implements, fondue—from the French *fondre,* which means "to melt"—took on the trappings of an elegant hors d'oeuvre.

On the other side of the globe, communal cooking over a hot pot of broth had equally practical origins. More than a thousand years ago, Mongolian nomads prepared meals in a bubbling cauldron heated by campfire. This practice of creating a portable feast every night evolved into a rich, diverse network of hot pot cooking traditions throughout Asia. Each province or country highlights its own lively flavors and ingredients in sociable meals that often have cultural as well as culinary significance.

Fondue purists can recite a litany of fondue rules ranging from the proper ingredients and perfect dippers to the preferred cooking vessels. There are rituals appropriate to specific European fondues and Asian hot pot meals, plus variations that apply to dishes starring cheese, oil, broth, wine or beer, sauces, chocolate, or other sweets. All of that historic etiquette and trivia is well and good, and certainly interesting to learn. But here's the important thing to remember: A fondue is a way to bring people together to share a meal. By all means, learn as much as you can about classic fondue cooking (this book will help you!), but don't be afraid to experiment. Party fare should never be intimidating to the cook, or the guest.

So, add a soupçon of your favorite sauce or spice to melted cheese. Turn your signature party dip into a fondue masterpiece. Go ahead and dip Grandma's special fruitcake into a warm caramel–cream cheese bath for dessert. All the so-called classic fondue dishes started with ingredients on hand and a creative cook—feel free to start your own fondue traditions. If you need a little inspiration, start with the menus and recipes offered in this book.

Whether you're planning a fabulous fete, a little holiday hoopla, or just a casual, sociable supper, *The Everything® Fondue Party Book* will give you everything you need to succeed. Learn fondue basics—including different types of fondue pots, fondue styles and techniques, fondue party planning, and more—in the first chapter. Subsequent chapters will offer themed menus for large and small gatherings, recipes for fondues and accompaniments, and a primer on different fondue and hot pot cooking traditions from around the world.

Chapter 1

Fondue Party Basics

The elements of fondue—even in all of its various forms—remain fairly simple: a simmering pot of seasoned liquid, a platter of foods worthy of dipping, and perhaps a few condiments or garnishes. A fondue dish can stand alone, with libations, as a hearty snack or a small meal, or it can star in a larger menu. Either way, a fondue course makes the host's job easier. With all of the prep work done in advance, there's nothing left to do but join the party and bask in your guests' compliments.

A Little History

Most food historians track the first fondues to Neuchâtel, a canton in Switzerland, in the 1600s. The basic Neuchâtel dish was embellished by different cooks according to their tastes and available ingredients, and before long the recipe traveled to other Swiss cantons and beyond. Servants introduced this dish to Switzerland's merchant and noble classes, who in turn offered it to visiting dignitaries from surrounding countries.

European Traditions

Traditional Swiss fondue includes the variations served in each of the cantons of the country. Most versions use two or more types of cheese—balancing flavor with fat content for the best taste and texture—plus wine, cider, or milk and other flavorings.

ESSENTIAL

The best fondue cheeses are high-fat, low-moisture. Look for hard cheeses with a 45 percent fat content as the primary player in the fondue pot. After that, a semi-hard or semi-soft cheese can be added for flavor.

Asian Traditions

Mongolian barbecue, or firepot, is a feature in many Chinese restaurants around the world. The setup, which hasn't changed much over the centuries, usually consists of a doughnut-shaped fondue pot heated by a central chimney. In the chimney are hot coals. Beef broth simmers in the outer ring, and diners use chopsticks to dunk slivers of beef and scallions. Soy sauce, hoisin sauce, and mustard and chili sauces might accompany the dish.

FACT

In many Chinese families, hot pot is a popular dish to celebrate the Chinese New Year. In northern cities, noodles and flour dumplings are a likely accompaniment. In the south, steamy bowls of white rice will be passed around the table.

However, this is only one style of hot pot. A few hundred years into the first millennium the hot pot, or "steamboat," tradition moved south, with homes and gathering places in many regions of Asia embracing the concept of a steamy copper kettle of broth, sometimes in a chimney pot, sometimes situated in a recessed coal pit at the center of a table, ready to provide a hot meal.

Swinging Sixties Fondue Americana

Jean Anthelme Brillat-Savarin is credited with serving the first fondue in America. The nineteenth-century author of *The Physiology of Taste* spent some time in the fledgling United States fleeing the French Revolution. His version was more of an egg-and-cheese casserole than a true fondue, but no matter. The word *fondue* made its way onto the party circuit of the day.

The next round of fondue fever came in the late 1950s. Konrad Egli, chef of New York's Swiss Chalet restaurant, added Fondue Bourguignon to his menu and introduced Americans to the practice of communal cooking and the exquisite flavor of ultra-tender beef cooked in hot oil. At the same time, post-World War II jet-setters and corporate climbers were busy traveling the world. After sampling cheese fondues at Swiss lodges, the businesspeople developed a taste for it, so they brought the recipes back to their estates and newly minted subdivisions.

Chocolate fondue is America's very own indigenous fondue dish. In 1964, Konrad Egli melted Swiss chocolate with cream in his New York restaurant and served it as a fondue-style dessert. From then on, hosts in the United States began to serve every sort of cheese fondue, from authentic Swiss recipes to Velveeta dip, then brought out another pot for angel food cake dipped in chocolate fondue.

Fondue Pots

Although fondue pots come in a variety of shapes and sizes, there are two basic categories for the container portion of the apparatus: ceramic and metal.

Ceramic

The traditional cheese fondue pot is the *caquelon*, a heavy, wide, not-too-deep pottery vessel that holds and distributes heat evenly. The *caquelon* is a good choice for cheese and other dairy-rich fondues as well as most chocolate and dessert fondues. It can be warmed in the microwave, if need be, and cooled leftovers can be covered and refrigerated in the pot. Ceramic pots are designed for low, consistent heat. For that reason, they are not suitable for broth or oil fondues that have to be heated to higher temperatures.

Metal

A metal fondue pot is essential for oil- and broth-based fondues that have to remain hot enough to cook meats and vegetables. Stainless steel pots, some with nonstick coatings, are available in a wide range of styles, weights, and prices. These pots can be used for all types of fondue, although some come with ceramic inserts to use for cheese and chocolate. (Generally the inserts work as a double-boiler. You pour a little water in the stainless steel pot, then place the insert over simmering water instead of directly onto the hot metal.)

ALERT

Very inexpensive, very thin metal fondue pots may not be stable enough to use for oil fondues. Make sure you have a sturdy pot before moving it from the stove to the heat source on the table.

The very best all-purpose fondue pots are made of enamel-coated cast iron. These jewels go from stove burner to tabletop heating source, keeping oil hot and broth bubbling. The cast iron can take direct heat at high temperatures and can hold heat for long periods of time. That means less reheating of fondue broths and oils during your parties. The enamel coating, which keeps the iron from discoloring foods, makes the pots acceptable for cheese and chocolate.

The Asian fondue pots, which have a doughnut-shaped vessel for broth and a central heating chimney, are available at many Asian markets and specialty cookware stores. These pots are usually made of stainless steel or heavy-gauge aluminum. Some versions are quite small, suitable for preparing a hot pot for two (or one).

The Dips

There aren't many hard-and-fast rules when it comes to fondue. Use the freshest, best-quality ingredients you can find. Beyond that, if you can cook it in oil or broth, or if you can melt it into a smooth sauce, it's likely a good candidate for the fondue pot. Use the recipes in this book and elsewhere as guidelines, then experiment with your own favorite flavors.

Cheese and Chocolate

These fondues work best when a few simple guidelines are followed. Cheese fondues generally blend two cheeses for best flavor. At least one cheese should be a firm, aged cheese with a relatively high fat content and low moisture content. The other can be an aged, high fat cheese or a semi-hard or semi-soft cheese. Look for complementary flavors—sharp and mild, salty and buttery, tart and creamy. The classic combination is Gruyère and Emmenthaler; however, you might choose an especially sharp Cheddar with a mild Monterey Jack, an aged Asiago with semi-soft Havarti, a dry Manchego with Queso Blanco, or a crumbly Parmesan with a smooth Mozzarella.

FACT

One pound of cheese or chocolate prepared fondue-style will feed four guests as a primary or dessert course. For big parties, keep another batch of fondue warming on the stove to replenish the pot as needed.

Chocolate fondue is, essentially, warm chocolate ganache. Ganache is a creamy, thick mixture of chocolate and hot cream. The two ingredients can be mixed together in different proportions. Flavorings, such as liqueurs, fruits, nuts, and extracts, can be added. Thick, warm ganache is often poured over cakes and pastries to create a glaze. Cooled ganache can be whipped into truffle centers or used as flexible chocolate sheets in architectural desserts.

Cooking Liquids

Aside from the traditional cheese and chocolate fondues, there are a variety of other dipping liquids you can try, including wine, stock or broth, and hot oil.

The Dippers

Bread is the classic fondue dipper, and the earliest fondues probably employed slightly stale loaves of hearth-baked breads. Don't attempt to serve fondue with fresh, squishy white bread or even soft wheat. You'll wind up with a limp mess, assuming the bread makes it out of the hot fondue at all. Instead, use sturdy or crusty breads such as rye, pumpernickel, multi-grain, or sourdough. White breads should be the hearth-baked types with hard crusts and a coarse crumb, or fine-grained but slightly dry focaccia and ciabatta. Plan on providing 18 to 22 bread cubes or bread portions (i.e., one hard pretzel) per guest. A standard French baguette will likely provide enough bread to serve three people at the fondue table.

Meats and Seafood

Raw meats and fish should be cut into small cubes or paper-thin slices for quick cooking. This keeps the flow going at the table, giving guests quick gratification. It also ensures proper cooking. If you're serving meatballs or seafood balls, either make them tiny or serve them precooked, ready to be warmed and crisped in the fondue pot.

ALERT Never attempt to dip raw meats into cheese fondue—the pot may not be hot enough to cook the meat, and dipping the raw food could add bacteria to the pot. Cooked or cured meats, such as sausage, and cooked shrimp are fine in any fondue.

Allow 6 to 8 ounces of raw meat, poultry, or seafood per guest. At a buffet or cocktail party where many foods compete for attention, guests will likely eat less of any one dish than they will at a sit-down dinner party.

Sweet Stuff

Buttery croissant rolls, cut in small pieces and dipped in very dark chocolate fondue, are a gourmet treat. Ladyfingers, biscotti, angel food cake, toasted pound cake spears, cookies, graham crackers, pretzels, and fresh or dried fruits are all fine for the fondue dessert table. If you're a candy maker, consider whipping up a batch of truffle centers, freezing them, then having guests coat their own truffles with chocolate fondue.

Libations

It's always a good idea to have a signature drink for the evening—a special tea or punch, a wine flight built around a theme, a blender full of some tropical cocktail, fun-tinis, or coffee drinks. If you are serving alcohol, always remember to have a good nonalcoholic option available for guests who choose not to drink.

For classic Swiss fondues, think of Sauvignon Blanc, Pinot Grigio, Pouilly-Fuisse, Muscadet, and Chardonnay. These wines should be your standbys, although you'll find different vintages—say a full-bodied Chardonnay—might be perfect for your Brie-laced fondue. More intensely flavored cheese (like bleu cheeses and Chevre) could be paired with such dry reds as Pinot Noir and Shiraz. Then there are regional affinities. For example, Soave or Sangiovese might be a good match for Asiago or Parmesan-flavored melts. Bold aged Cheddars, Manchego, and herb-laced cheeses can stand up to a fruity Beaujolais, a Bordeaux or Merlot, or even a dry sherry.

Bold European and Mexican cheese fondues, as well as very spicy hot pots, beg to be paired with beer. Welsh Rarebit, Pub-style Cheddar fondues, and German-inspired melts go very well with rich ales and dark lagers. Dry, pale Caribbean and Mexican lagers are the logical choice for queso fondues and spicy jerk dishes. Asian lagers have a crisp, floral taste that's quite refreshing with salty and peppery hot pot dishes.

When entertaining, allow ½ of a 750-ml bottle of wine per person. Your guests may drink more or less, depending on personal taste and whether you're serving cocktails before the wine. When serving beer, allow two 12-ounce bottles per person.

FACT

Fon-Dos and Fon-Don'ts: Health and Safety

Fondue is by nature a communal experience. No matter how exclusive your guest list, or how pricey your ingredients, a fondue meal has a casual air. Still, there are a few rules to ensure everybody's safety and comfort:

- Never fill a pot more than ⅓ full for oil fondue. If oil must be reheated or more oil added, move the fondue pot away from the heating source and away from your guests. Handle refreshing the oil in the kitchen, then carefully return the pot to the table.
- Never refuel an alcohol-fueled pot while it's still hot. The burner attachment must be completely cool before fuel is added.
- Always carefully read the instructions that come with your fondue set. Different heating sources have slightly different requirements and procedures.
- Have enough plates, skewers, forks, and dipping bowls on hand to discourage your guests from redipping already nibbled items into the fondue pot or sauce bowls.

- Keep raw meats and seafood away from breads, vegetables, and other ready-to-eat items. Meats and seafood should be prepared, then either served immediately or covered and refrigerated until ready to serve.
- Have antibacterial wipes ready to mop up spills or dropped ingredients.
- Raw eggs carry a risk of salmonella. Some Asian hot pots call for a dipping sauce of raw egg. You may want to consider using pasteurized eggs or skipping raw egg sauces altogether.
- Oil and broth fondue mixtures must stay hot enough to cook meats and shellfish thoroughly.

Finally, to avoid the problem of double dipping, put a large basket of skewers next to the fondue pot. Put regular forks at everyone's place, or a basket of regular or disposable forks next to buffet plates. Your guests will quickly get the idea—dunk with the skewers, move the food onto a plate, and eat with the regular fork. In the case of vegetables, fruits, or long chunks of bread, guests can just dip one end into the pot, much as they might help themselves to chips and salsa. Remember these simple health and safety tips, and have fun fondue-ing!

Chapter 2

Classic Swiss and Other European Cheese Fondues

Before-Theater Champagne Party

Invite friends to a light supper before a play or concert. You'll have a lively, easy-to-plan social hour followed by great entertainment. Best of all, you'll eliminate the rush to find an early dinner reservation before the show.

MENU

Neufchatel Cheese Fondue

Mixed Breads

Cold Seafood Platter

Raw Vegetables

Grapes, Strawberries, and Pineapple Spears

Champagne

Neufchatel Cheese Fondue

Serves 8

2 cups Sauvignon Blanc

2 small cloves garlic

Juice of 2 lemons

1 pound Gruyère cheese

1 pound Emmenthaler cheese

1½ tablespoons cornstarch

3 tablespoons Kirsch

½ teaspoon white pepper

¼ cup parsley, minced

½ teaspoon nutmeg

Cubed bread, including French, rye, wheat, and pumpernickel

> Emmenthaler is the original hole-filled Swiss cheese. For this dish, you'll want to splurge on authentic Emmenthaler rather than a generic Swiss cheese.

1. Pour wine into heavy saucepan over medium heat. Put garlic cloves through a press. Add pressed garlic to wine along with lemon juice. Bring mixture to a simmer.
2. Shred cheeses in a food processor. Add ¼ of the cheese to the simmering liquid and stir in a figure-eight pattern. Once that cheese has melted, add another ¼ of the cheese to the saucepan. Keep stirring. Repeat until all cheese is melted and mixture is hot, but not boiling.
3. Dissolve cornstarch in Kirsch. Stir into cheese mixture. Cook until just bubbly, then reduce heat and simmer for 1 minute.
4. Add white pepper, parsley, and nutmeg to the melted cheese and stir well.
5. Pour liquid into fondue pot and keep warm over heating source. Serve with assorted bread cubes.

Bread Basics

Always serve hearty breads that can stand up to dunking. For variety, try tossing bread cubes in olive oil, sprinkle with sea salt or herbs, and bake in a single layer at 350°F until crisp.

Cold Seafood Platter

Serves 8

Romaine lettuce
2 pounds large shrimp,
  cooked and peeled
3 pounds clams, steamed in the shell
2 pounds steamed mussels, in the shell
1 pound sea scallops
3 lobster tails, shelled and cut in 1-inch pieces
⅔ cup extra-virgin olive oil
1 teaspoon fresh thyme
2 teaspoons fresh basil, chopped
1 green onion, trimmed and finely chopped
1 tablespoon fresh parsley, chopped
Fresh-ground black pepper

> Save time and energy—buy seafood already steamed from your local fish market. If you do prepare shellfish yourself, be sure to allow time for chilling.

1. Line a chilled platter with lettuce leaves. Pile sea scallops and lobster pieces in the center in matched semicircles. Arrange shrimp, clams, and mussels around the edge of the platter.
2. Whisk together olive oil, thyme, basil, green onion, and parsley.
3. Drizzle herb-oil mixture over seafood. Generously grind black pepper over everything.
4. Place on the serving table with tongs and plates large enough to hold seafood and fondue-dipped bread cubes.

. . . .

Herbal Magic

Herbed olive oil allows the seafood flavor to shine through and eliminates the need for heavy cocktail or tartar sauce. Of course, don't be surprised if your guests start dunking shrimp in the fondue pot!

Après-Ski Sunset Supper Menu

Even if you can't get to the slopes, this hearty, casual meal is perfect for cool-weather entertaining. Stoke the fireplace and invite friends to drop in for board games and fondue.

MENU

Garlicky Vaud Fondue

Whole Wheat Baguette Rounds

Mixed Sausage Platter

Radish Slaw with Balsamic Dressing

Cranberry Apple Tart with Cinnamon Cream

Coffee with Frangelica

Garlicky Vaud Fondue

Serves 6

1 small head garlic
1 tablespoon olive oil
1½ cups dry white wine
Juice of 2 lemons
1 pound Gruyère cheese, shredded
½ pound Emmenthaler cheese, shredded
½ teaspoon black pepper, coarsely ground
2 teaspoons cornstarch
1 tablespoon brandy
1 slender whole wheat baguette, cut into 1-inch rounds

> Roasting turns pungent fresh garlic into a sweet, mellow paste.

1. Remove outer skin from garlic head, leaving head intact. Rub garlic with olive oil and wrap in heavy foil. Bake at 350°F for 1 hour. Set aside until cool enough to handle. Pull cloves apart and squeeze garlic from cloves into a dish.
2. Heat wine and lemon juice in a saucepan over medium heat until hot, but not boiling.
3. Add cheese to liquid in 4 batches, stirring in a figure-eight motion, until each addition is melted. Add roasted garlic to the cheese and mix until well blended. Sprinkle in black pepper. Heat fondue until bubbly.
4. Dissolve cornstarch in brandy and stir into fondue. Simmer for 2 minutes, then pour fondue into fondue pot and place over heating source.
5. Serve with baguette rounds and mixed sausages.

· ·

More Than a Hint of Garlic

The original Vaud garlic fondue uses minced fresh garlic. Roasted garlic offers a more complex flavor profile. However, in a pinch, chopped raw or sautéed garlic can be substituted for roasted garlic.

Mixed Sausage Platter

Serves 6

½ pound chicken-and-apple
   smoked sausage
½ pound smoked chorizo sausage
½ pound andouille sausage
½ pound portobello mushroom
   sausage

1 large sweet onion
1 large red bell pepper
1 large green bell pepper
4 ears corn

1. Cut sausage links into 1-inch pieces.
2. Cut onion into 8 sections, then separate the layers. Cut peppers into 1-inch pieces.
3. Blanch corn on the cob until just tender, then use a sharp knife to cut into 2-inch slices.
4. In a large skillet or Dutch oven, sauté the sausages over high heat for 1 minute. Add onion and peppers and cook until sausage is just heated through and veggies are still crisp.
5. With a slotted spoon, move sausage mixture to a large, shallow serving bowl or platter. Mix in corn slices and serve.

Radish Slaw with Balsamic Dressing

Serves 6

2 cups daikon radish, shredded
2 cups jicama, shredded
1 cup red radish, shredded
1 cup purple cabbage, finely shredded

½ cup balsamic vinegar
¼ cup light olive oil
1 teaspoon sesame oil

1. Combine daikon and red radish, jicama, and cabbage.
2. Whisk together balsamic vinegar, olive oil, and sesame oil.
3. Toss radish mixture with balsamic dressing. Cover and let stand in the refrigerator for at least 1 hour, mixing occasionally. Toss and drain before serving.

Cranberry Apple Tart with Cinnamon Cream

Serves 8

Crust

1 cup all-purpose flour, sifted
Pinch of salt
½ cup chilled shortening
¼ cup ice water

Dried cranberries are available in a range of flavors. For variety, try orange- or cherry-infused cranberries in this recipe.

Filling

5 Granny Smith apples, peeled,
   cored, and sliced
1 cup dried cranberries
⅔ cup sugar
3 tablespoons flour
1 teaspoon cinnamon
1 teaspoon vanilla extract
2 tablespoons butter

Topping

1 cup brown sugar
⅓ cup granola
1 cup all-purpose flour
⅓ cup butter

1. To make the crust, combine flour and salt in a bowl. Add chilled shortening and cut with knives or pastry cutter until mixture resembles small peas. Add ice water and work mixture with fingers until water is incorporated. Form dough into a soft ball. Place ball in the center of a 9-inch greased quiche or tart pan. Press dough evenly across bottom and up sides of pan.
2. Place apples and cranberries in a large bowl. Mix together sugar, flour, and cinnamon and toss with apples and cranberries. Sprinkle with vanilla. Spread mixture evenly over crust and dot with butter.
3. In a bowl, combine brown sugar, granola, and flour. Work in butter with fingers until mixture is crumbly. Sprinkle over the apple mixture.
4. Place pan on a foil-lined baking sheet. Bake at 350°F for 40 minutes, or until top is browned and apple mixture is bubbly.
5. Serve with cinnamon-spiked whipped cream.

Red Hat Luncheon Menu

Let the chatter and laughter commence! The best thing about being a woman of a certain age is the freedom to let loose with other like-minded women. Even if you aren't (or aren't yet) a member of the Red Hat Society, this fondue and salad luncheon menu will fuel a fabulous girlfriends' get-together.

MENU

Appenzeller Cider Fondue

Challah and Sunflower Seed Bread

Red Hat Salad

Chardonnay

Raspberry Jelly Roll

Hazelnut Coffee

Appenzeller Cider Fondue

Serves 6

1½ cups dry hard cider
1 pound Appenzeller cheese,
    shredded
½ pound Emmenthaler or
    Fribourg Vacherin, shredded
Pinch of nutmeg or cinnamon
¼ teaspoon white pepper
2 teaspoons cornstarch
1 tablespoon Kirsch
3 cups challah, toasted and diced
3 cups sunflower seed bread, toasted and diced

When your party includes children or non-drinkers, use regular apple cider or apple juice in place of hard cider. If you want the flavor of alcohol without the kick, use a mixture of half apple juice, half alcohol-free white wine.

1. In a saucepan over medium heat, bring cider to a simmer. Add shredded cheese in 4 batches, stirring in a figure-eight motion until each batch is melted.
2. Add nutmeg or cinnamon and pepper.
3. Dissolve cornstarch in Kirsch. Heat fondue until bubbly and stir in cornstarch mixture. Reduce heat and simmer for 2 minutes.
4. Pour mixture into a fondue pot and keep warm over low heat.
5. Serve fondue with challah and sunflower seed bread.

. . . .

Fribourg Vacherin

This is a semi-soft, slightly acidic cow's milk cheese with a high fat content. Remove the dull yellow rind before melting.

Red Hat Salad

Serves 6

10 cups mesclun salad mix

2 cups lean ham, finely diced

1 cup red apples, diced

1 cup pears, diced

1½ cups beets, cooked and
shredded

1 cup whole baby green beans, blanched

1 cup raspberry vinaigrette

1 cup toasted pecans

A colorful, crisp salad makes a perfect accompaniment to a luncheon fondue. The fondue and salad menu is fun, elegant, and oh, so easy to prepare. Dessert can be baked the night before, or, in a real pinch, ordered from a favorite bakery.

1. Combine salad greens, ham, apples, pears, green beans, and beets in a large salad bowl.
2. Pour a small amount of raspberry vinaigrette over salad and toss to coat. Add more if desired.
3. Sprinkle toasted pecans over the top.

Raspberry Vinaigrette

Makes 1½ cups

1 cup vegetable oil

⅓ cup almond oil

¾ cup raspberry vinegar

1 teaspoon sugar

¼ teaspoon vanilla

¼ teaspoon black pepper

Raspberry vinaigrette, once the province of gourmet delis and restaurants, is now readily available in supermarkets. Buy a favorite brand, or make your own with this easy recipe.

1. Combine all ingredients in a small bowl. Whisk briskly.
2. Pour into a serving bottle or pitcher. Stir or shake well before serving.

Raspberry Jelly Roll

Serves 8

3 eggs
¼ cup cold water
1 cup sugar
1 cup all-purpose flour
2 teaspoons baking powder
Pinch of salt
1 teaspoon vanilla extract
1 cup seedless raspberry preserves or jelly
Confectioners' sugar or Turbinado sugar
Berries for garnish

A jelly roll may be an old-fashioned dessert, but it never seems to go out of style. The elegant pinwheel slices look festive, and fillings can include a wide range of jams, creams, and custards. Try chocolate-hazelnut spread for a different treat.

1. In a large bowl, combine eggs with cold water and sugar. Beat on medium speed until thick and frothy.
2. Combine flour, baking powder, and salt. Sift into the egg mixture and beat until blended well. Mix in vanilla.
3. Grease a baking sheet, line with waxed paper, and butter paper. Pour batter over paper and bake at 400°F for 15 minutes.
4. While cake is baking, spread a clean, lint-free tea towel on a clean surface. Cover the towel with waxed paper. Sprinkle confectioners' sugar or Turbinado sugar over the paper. Remove cake from oven and let stand for 1–2 minutes. Carefully turn the hot cake onto sugared waxed paper.
5. Spread cake with preserves or jelly. Using towel and paper as rolling aids, slowly roll cake over on itself into a log. Leave rolled cake wrapped in towel and paper until cooled. Remove towel and waxed paper carefully and trim ends if needed to make neat appearance. Place on a platter and garnish with berries.

. . . .

Sugar, Sugar

You choose. Confectioners' sugar gives finished cake a delicate "frosted" appearance. Turbinado crystals add a slightly crunchy texture to your jelly roll.

Fondue-a-Deux Dinner Menu

Kindle a flame with an informal but sensual fondue repast for two. This menu works for the first time you entertain a new belle or beau—it's fun, nonthreatening, and gives you something to do during awkward pauses. It's also a nice way for already married moms and dads to break out of their routines. After all, the kids have to sleep sometime.

MENU

Fribourg-Style Fondue

Ciabatta Bread

Pan-Seared Sea Scallops

Steamed Red Potatoes with Asparagus and Peppers

Grapes

Chocolate Truffles

Pinot Grigio

Fribourg-Style Fondue

Serves 2

½ pound Fribourg vacherin cheese,
   shredded or finely chopped
½ cup half-and-half
3 tablespoons Kirsch or brandy
1 loaf ciabatta bread, sliced and quartered

Cornstarch isn't necessary to stabilize a fondue of ripe Fribourg cheese with cream. Even the alcohol is optional in this rich fondue.

1. Combine cheese with half-and-half over low heat.
2. Stir, using a figure-eight motion, until cheese is melted and smooth.
3. Stir in Kirsch or brandy. Serve with ciabatta.

Pan-Seared Sea Scallops

Serves 2–3

3 tablespoons unsalted butter
1 tablespoon extra-virgin olive oil
1 pound sea scallops
3 tablespoons all-purpose flour
¼ teaspoon each salt, black pepper, red pepper
¼ cup parsley, finely chopped
Drizzle of white truffle oil, optional

Scallops have a wonderfully delicate flavor and moist texture. However, if you're not a seafood fan, this recipe works equally well with cubes of boneless chicken breast. To serve at a dinner party, double quantities and add a pound of fresh, sliced mushrooms to the pan.

1. In a large skillet, heat butter and olive oil over high heat until hot.
2. Mix flour with salt and peppers and toss scallops in flour mixture.
3. Add scallops to skillet in a single layer and cook for 2 minutes on each side.
4. Sprinkle with parsley.
5. Drizzle with white truffle oil and move to a serving platter.

Steamed Red Potatoes with Asparagus and Peppers

Serves 2

12 small new red potatoes

12 fresh asparagus spears

1 large orange sweet pepper

Salt and pepper to taste

Although prepared separately, these veggies can be served together on a platter for an aesthetic affect. Because these items are destined to be dipped in fondue, a light sprinkle of salt and pepper is the only dressing required.

1. Wash and trim potatoes, but do not peel. Place on a steamer basket in a pot and add water until level reaches just below basket. Cover and cook over medium-high heat, checking water level occasionally, for 15 minutes or until potatoes are tender. Move potatoes to a platter.
2. Wash and trim asparagus. Bring a skillet full of water to a boil. Place asparagus in the skillet and cook just until spears begin to turn bright green. Use tongs to remove still-crisp asparagus to platter with potatoes.
3. Wash sweet pepper and cut into strips. Add to platter with potatoes and asparagus. Mix veggies together (potatoes and asparagus will warm, not cook, pepper strips) and sprinkle with salt and pepper.
4. Serve alongside fondue pot with bread and scallops.

. . . .

Asparagus in a Snap

You could spend a fortune on special pots and attachments for cooking asparagus. However, the real trick to great fresh asparagus is to remove spears from boiling water before they're actually cooked. The spears will continue to cook outside the pot and will be crisp and tender for eating. To stop the cooking process, drop blanched asparagus in cold water.

Martinis and Fondue Mixer Menu

Credit the resurgence of the martini—that hallmark of James Bond, the Rat Pack, and swanky 1950s-era night-clubs—for bringing cocktail parties back into vogue. The original martini recipe has been variously credited to several late-nineteenth-century American bartenders. There's no telling who actually invented it, but in recent years, it has definitely evolved. A martini can be a dry gin-and-vermouth cocktail, or it can be offered in a kaleidoscope of colors and flavors. Either way, martini sampling is as good an excuse for a party as a bubbling fondue pot is.

MENU

Geneva-Style Fondue

Bread Basket

Vegetable Platter

Duck Breast and Chutney Pinwheels

Smoked Salmon and
Dilled Cream Cheese Pinwheels

Fruit Platter

Classic and Flavored Martinis

Geneva-Style Fondue

Serves 12

3 cups dry white wine
1 pound Gruyère cheese, shredded
1 pound Emmenthaler cheese,
*   shredded*
1 pound Walliser Bergkase, grated
1 cup morel mushrooms, finely chopped
1 small clove garlic, minced
2 tablespoons cornstarch
½ cup Kirsch
½ teaspoon nutmeg
Black pepper to taste

> This recipe will make enough fondue to keep two fondue pots bubbling. With a cocktail party, it's best to try to set up two fondue stations to keep from creating a bottleneck.

1. In a large saucepan over medium heat, bring wine to a simmer. Add shredded cheese in several batches, stirring each batch in a figure-eight motion until the cheese has melted.
2. When all the cheese has been incorporated, add the morels and garlic. Simmer, stirring, for 2–3 minutes.
3. Dissolve cornstarch in Kirsch. Add to fondue mixture. Turn up heat and cook fondue until bubbly. Stir in nutmeg and black pepper.
4. Remove from heat. Pour fondue into 1 or more fondue pots and set over heat source.
5. Place fondue forks, bread basket, and veggie platter nearby.

. . . .

The Staff of Life

Nothing says abundance like a big basket of mixed breads. Line a basket with large colorful napkins and place soft pretzels, breadsticks, crisp flatbreads, and mini baguettes around the edge. Fill the center with cubes of sourdough, marble rye, multi-grain, pumpernickel, and hearth-baked Italian breads.

Duck Breast and Chutney Pinwheels

Serves 12

6 10-inch tomato-flavored wraps

2 cups prepared apple or mango
  chutney

6 cups duck breast, cooked and
  shredded

4 cups cabbage, finely shredded

1 cup sour cream

Duck adds a rich note to these easy pinwheels. However, if your budget can't accommodate duck breast for a crowd, substitute shredded smoked turkey or roasted chicken. For a vegetarian dish, used diced smoked or marinated tofu or oven-roasted asparagus, eggplant, or zucchini.

1. Separate wraps onto a clean work surface. Spread wrap faces lightly with chutney, stopping ¼ inch from the edge.
2. Sprinkle shredded duck breast evenly over chutney.
3. Place a line of shredded cabbage down the center of each wrap.
4. Put a line of sour cream over the cabbage.
5. Pick up one edge of one wrap and tightly roll into a tube. Leave seam side down. Repeat procedure with remaining wraps. Trim edges. With a sharp knife, slice each roll across into 1-inch pinwheels. Place on a serving platter.

. . . .

It's a Wrap!

Wraps—part tortilla, part Middle Eastern flatbread—are the party giver's friends. Virtually any combination of meats, spreads, and vegetables can be placed, sliced, and served in a wrap for quick canapés. Best of all, most supermarkets carry a wide range of wrap sizes and flavors.

Smoked Salmon and Dilled Cream Cheese Pinwheels

Serves 12

6 10-inch herb or plain wraps
12 ounces cream cheese
3 tablespoons sour cream
3 tablespoons fresh dill, chopped
Fresh-ground black pepper
½ pound Nova Scotia smoked salmon, sliced
½ cup red onion, finely chopped
3 cucumbers

Sliced smoked salmon makes a beautiful pinwheel filling. It is pricey, however. If you're trying to save money, mix a small amount of salmon with cream cheese in a food processor and spread that mixture over wraps.

1. Separate wraps and spread over a clean work surface.
2. In a food processor, combine cream cheese, sour cream, and dill. Process until smooth. Spread mixture over wraps, stopping ¼ inch from the edge.
3. Grind black pepper over cream cheese mixture to taste.
4. Place smoked salmon sliced in a line at the center of each wrap. Sprinkle salmon with red onion.
5. Peel cucumbers and cut each into 4 spears. Arrange 2 spears in a line at the center of each wrap.
6. Lift each wrap and roll tightly. Trim edges and cut each roll into 1-inch slices. Place pinwheels on a serving platter.

. . . .

Spread the Wealth

It's important to have easily accessible noshes at your cocktail parties. While the fondue stations will be the main attraction, make sure to have platters of goodies strategically placed around the room.

Classic Martini

Serves 2

Ice
5 ounces gin, preferably chilled
1 ounce dry vermouth
2 twists lemon peel
2 olives

A classic martini is made with icy gin—although some folks prefer vodka—and dry vermouth. An olive and a twist of lemon peel are standard garnishes. Substitute a cocktail onion for the olive and you've got a Gibson.

1. Fill a cocktail shaker with ice.
2. Pour gin and vermouth into the shaker, cover, and shake vigorously.
3. Strain mixture into two martini glasses and garnish each with a skewered olive and lemon twist.

Flavored Martini

Serves 2

Ice
5 ounces flavored rum or vodka,
*   preferably chilled*
1 ounce sweet liqueur
1 ounce fruit juice
2 tablespoons heavy cream, optional
Spears of fruit, candy canes, or cinnamon sticks for garnish

Sweet, flavored martinis are all the rage these days. Most have little in common with real martinis, but they're fun nevertheless. Here's a template for making your own fun-tini.

1. Fill a cocktail shaker with ice.
2. Pour in flavored rum or vodka—add apple, lime, banana, mango, or another fave—and a complementary liqueur. Add an ounce of fruit juice. Shake vigorously.
3. Strain into 2 martini glasses. Swirl a tablespoon of cream into each, if desired. Garnish with fruit or other goodies.

Fondue Trio Matinee Menu

Entertaining friends doesn't have to be a major production. In fact, you could all just park yourselves in front of the television. Design your own film festival with a triple-feature of videos built around your favorite director, actor, or genre. Or treat friends to an afternoon of old *I Love Lucy* episodes or vintage *Star Trek*. Whatever you decide to watch, you'll need sustenance. This three-pot fondue menu ought to do the trick.

MENU

French Brie Fondue

Baguette Cubes

Raw Vegetables

Welsh Rarebit

Toast Triangles

Apple Slices

Kaasdoop

Rye Bread Cubes

Diced Ham

Grapes or Fresh Cherries

Chardonnay or Light Lager Beer

French Brie Fondue

Serves 6

3 tablespoons butter
3 tablespoons all-purpose flour
1½ cups half-and-half
16 ounces Brie, rind removed
1 clove garlic, peeled
½ cup fresh parsley
2 green onions, trimmed and cut in thirds
2 tablespoons fresh tarragon
Fresh-ground black pepper

This recipe can be made without the garlic-herb mixture. Just add a pinch of nutmeg to the fondue and serve with bread and fresh fruit or use dried apricots, papaya, and pineapple for dippers.

1. Melt the butter in a saucepan. Add flour and stir until blended.
2. Slowly whisk in half-and-half. Cook over medium heat until mixture is smooth and slightly thickened.
3. Dice Brie and stir into the milk, using a figure-eight motion. Stir frequently until cheese is completely melted.
4. Place garlic, parsley, green onions, and tarragon leaves in a food processor. Process until herbs are all finely minced. Stir into cheese mixture.
5. Cook over medium-high heat until bubbly. Pour into fondue pot, place over heating source, and serve with baguette cubes and raw vegetables.

Brie Alternatives

For variety, use a mixture of Brie with Camembert and other soft cheeses. For a less expensive dish, use 8 ounces of full-fat cream cheese with 4 ounces of bleu cheese in place of the Brie. Although these are all high-moisture cheeses, the roux in the recipe helps produce a good, thick fondue.

Welsh Rarebit

Serves 6

3 tablespoons butter

3 tablespoons all-purpose flour

1 cup ale

12 ounces extra-sharp Cheddar cheese,
    shredded

½ cup heavy cream

1 teaspoon English mustard, prepared

Cayenne pepper to taste

This dish is usually served as a meatless entrée with the cheese poured over toast points. Old cookbooks call it "Welsh Rabbit," and the story goes that it was what one ate when the family hunter failed to bag the prey.

1. Melt butter in a saucepan over medium heat. Add flour and stir until well-blended.
2. Whisk in ale. Continue cooking over medium heat until ale is hot. Add shredded Cheddar in 4 batches, stirring in a figure-eight pattern. Wait until each addition is melted before adding more cheese.
3. Stir in cream, mustard, and pepper.
4. Cook, stirring constantly, until mixture is bubbly.
5. Pour into fondue pot and place over heat source. Serve with toast points.

. . . .

A Toast to Rarebit

To make uniformly crispy toast, lightly brush good-quality white bread with butter and place on a baking sheet. Bake at 350°F until browned on top. Turn slices over and bake until that side is browned. Place on a platter and cut diagonally into quarters.

Kaasdoop

Serves 6

1½ cups milk
12 ounces Gouda cheese, diced
1½ tablespoons cornstarch
3 tablespoons brandy
¼ teaspoon nutmeg
Black pepper to taste

No mystery here. The name of this Dutch fondue dish means "cheese dip." For variety, stir in smoked Gouda or a mixture of Gouda and Edam cheeses.

1. Bring milk to a simmer in a saucepan over medium heat.
2. Add cheese in 4 batches, stirring in a figure-eight motion. Wait until each batch is melted before adding more cheese.
3. Combine cornstarch and brandy, stirring until smooth. Add to cheese mixture.
4. Cook, stirring constantly, until mixture is thick and bubbly. Add nutmeg and pepper.
5. Pour mixture into a fondue pot and place over heating source. Serve with rye bread.

A Night at the Opera
Fondue Supper

Make room on the couch for a couple of friends and set an Italian-inspired fondue feast on the coffee table. Then pick your entertainment. Go highbrow with a recording of *Tosca* at the Met from your favorite PBS broadcast, or settle in for some Marx Brothers slapstick with a DVD of that 1930s favorite, *A Night at the Opera*.

MENU

Northern Italian Fonduta

Focaccia

Raw Vegetable Tray

Gnocchi

Basil Shrimp

Chicken-Spinach Croquettes

Sautéed Baby Artichokes

Melon and Prosciutto

Amaretto Cheesecake with Sliced Peaches

Cavalleri Rose or Cavalleri Brut

Espresso or Decaf Espresso

Northern Italian Fonduta

Serves 6

6 tablespoons butter

2 tablespoons all-purpose flour

2 cups cream

4 egg yolks

1½ pounds Fontina cheese,
    finely chopped or shredded

½ teaspoon white truffle oil

White pepper to taste

> This ultra-rich fondue recipe is based on a classic dish from the mountains of northwest Italy. Buy authentic Fontina cheese rather than a sliced, packaged brand. If you like, sprinkle a little grated Asiago cheese into the mix to deepen the flavor.

1. In a large saucepan over medium heat, melt butter. Sprinkle in flour and stir with a wooden spoon until roux is smooth and bubbly. Slowly add cream and cook, stirring, until mixture is hot and thickened.
2. In a large bowl, whisk egg yolks together. While whisking, slowly pour a ladle of hot cream into the eggs. When it's blended, quickly whisk it into the saucepan.
3. Working in batches, stir Fontina into the cream mixture using a figure-eight motion. Wait until one batch has completely melted before adding the next. When mixture is completely melted and bubbly, pour in white truffle oil and pepper.
4. Remove from heat. Pour fonduta into fondue pot and set over heat source.

Truffle Trivia

Every fall, trifalau—that is, Italian truffle hunters—work the hillsides of the Piedmont region of Italy in search of white truffles. These prized fungi grow under soft ground at the base of oaks and other clustered trees. The trifalau use trained dogs to sniff them out. When in season, truffle-scented dishes permeate the region. Imported truffles are dear, selling for more than $1,000 a pound in the United States. Oregon-cultivated truffles sell via mail-order for about one-fourth the price of Italian truffles. If you can afford a splurge, by all means shave a few slices of fresh truffles in your fonduta—otherwise, use the far more affordable truffle-flavored oil.

Focaccia

Serves 6

½ cup lukewarm water

2 ounces dry yeast

7 cups plus a few tablespoons
all-purpose flour

½ cup olive oil

2 teaspoons salt

1 small sweet onion, thinly sliced

1 tablespoon fresh rosemary leaves

Whether you think of it as thin bread or thick pizza crust, a well-seasoned focaccia makes a great dipper for fondue. Or slice it horizontally and add dry cured ham or salami and provolone for a flavorful sandwich.

1. Dissolve yeast in lukewarm water.
2. Place 6 cups flour on a board. Make a well in the center. Pour yeast mixture in the center of the well, along with half the olive oil. Slowly work the flour into the liquid until a sticky dough begins to form. Before flour is completely combined, mix salt into the remaining cup of flour and add it to the mixture.
3. Sprinkle enough additional flour over the dough to make it easy to handle. Knead lightly, then place dough in a large bowl and place a damp towel over the top. Let rise for 2 hours or until doubled in size.
4. Punch dough down. Place on a baking sheet and spread into a large oval, slightly more than ½-inch thick. Dimple the top with a spoon. Brush liberally with olive oil. Separate onion slices and arrange over the top of the dough. Sprinkle with rosemary leaves.
5. Bake at 425°F for 20–25 minutes or until golden brown. While baking, use a water bottle to spray mist into the oven once or twice to create a moist heat. Slice with a serrated bread knife.

Gnocchi

Serves 6

2½ pounds baking potatoes
1 egg
2 cups plus a few tablespoons all-purpose flour
¼ cup Parmesan cheese, grated
Salt to taste
½ cup melted butter

These potato dumplings can be served plain as a side dish or sauced with fonduta.

1. Wash potatoes and boil, unpeeled, just until tender.
2. Cool potatoes until safe to handle, then peel. Grate potatoes or push through a ricer into a large bowl. Beat egg and quickly stir into potatoes. Add 2 cups flour and Parmesan and work mixture into a soft dough, using a hand mixer on slow speed. Add salt to taste.
3. Divide dough into 3 or 4 portions and roll each into a tube about 1-inch in diameter. Slice tubes into 1-inch pieces.
4. Flatten each piece of dough lightly with your finger, then roll the disk back over itself with a fork. The result should be a small shell-shaped dumpling with ridges on the outside.
5. Lightly dust formed gnocchi with flour. Bring a large pot of water to a boil and drop gnocchi, a small batch at a time, into the water. When gnocchi float, they're done. Scoop gnocchi from water with a slotted spoon or small strainer. Place cooked, drained gnocchi in a single layer in a baking dish and drizzle with melted butter. Keep warm until ready to serve.

. . . .

Gnocchi Varieties

Although potato-based gnocchi are most common, these tender little dumplings can be made with a mixture of ricotta cheese and flour as well. Some cooks flavor their gnocchi with puréed spinach or herbs. Once boiled, gnocchi can be served in broth with tomato sauce or lightly coated with butter.

Basil Shrimp

Serves 6

6 tablespoons butter
2 tablespoons olive oil
2 cloves garlic, minced
2 pounds large shrimp, peeled and deveined
⅓ cup fresh basil ribbons
Salt and pepper to taste

The secret to this delicious, super-simple dish is fresh, high-quality ingredients cooked quickly.

1. In a large, heavy skillet or flat-bottomed wok, melt butter. Add olive oil and heat until a drop of water skips over the surface of the butter.
2. Add garlic and shrimp and sauté over high heat just until shrimp turn opaque.
3. Add basil ribbons and toss to combine. Sprinkle with salt and pepper and serve.

· ·

Splurge a Little

Basil shrimp makes a great topping for baked or pan-seared flounder, red snapper, or salmon. To really gild the lily, toss ½-pound of lump crabmeat into the skillet with the shrimp.

Chicken-Spinach Croquettes

Serves 6

1½ pounds ground chicken
½ cup fresh spinach, finely chopped
3 green onions, minced
¼ cup parsley, minced
2 eggs
Salt and pepper to taste
1–1½ cups soft bread crumbs
1 cup dry seasoned bread crumbs
Vegetable oil for frying

These little meatballs should nicely round out your selections of fonduta dippers.

1. In a large bowl, combine chicken, spinach, green onions, parsley, and eggs. Mixed together with hands until all ingredients are blended.
2. Add 1 cup soft bread crumbs and combine until mixture is slightly stiff. Add more soft bread crumbs if necessary.
3. Form mixture into 30 small meatballs. Roll each lightly in dry bread crumbs.
4. Pour vegetable oil 2 inches deep into a pan. Warm oil over medium-high heat until hot, but not smoking. Fry chicken balls a few at a time, until each is golden brown. Drain on paper towels and keep warm until ready to serve.

Sautéed Baby Artichokes

Serves 6

24 baby artichokes
Juice of 1 lemon
6 tablespoons butter
2 tablespoons olive oil
4 cloves garlic, minced
⅓ cup parsley, minced
Salt and pepper to taste

Baby artichokes take a little preparation, but the rewards are worth it. Look for bags of these tiny artichokes at produce counters in the spring and fall. If baby artichokes aren't available, substitute fresh or frozen artichoke hearts.

1. Rinse baby artichokes. Peel away outer green leaves until artichokes leaves are yellow on the bottom, green on top. With a sharp knife, cut off the green tops. Cut stems even with the base of the artichokes and cut artichokes in half lengthwise.
2. As artichokes are trimmed and cut, place them in a bowl of water mixed with the lemon juice.
3. In a heavy skillet, heat butter and olive oil until butter is melted and hot. Drain baby artichokes and add to hot skillet with minced garlic. Sauté artichokes until halves are fork-tender.
4. Add parsley, salt, and pepper to the artichokes. Serve warm.

Amaretto Cheesecake with Sliced Peaches

Serves 6

Crushed amaretto cookies give this cheesecake an unusual, flavorful crust.

2 cups amaretto cookies, finely ground
8 tablespoons butter, melted
1½ cups sugar, divided
1 pound cream cheese, cut in chunks
1 tablespoon sour cream
2 tablespoons amaretto liqueur
½ teaspoon vanilla extract
Pinch of salt
2 eggs
2 cups slivered almonds, toasted
3 fresh peaches, peeled, pitted, and sliced
Whipped cream

1. Combine cookies, butter, and 1/3 cup sugar. Mix well and press mixture into a deep 8-inch pie pan or springform pan. Cover bottom evenly and press mixture up sides as far as possible.
2. In a food processor bowl, combine 1 cup sugar, cream cheese, sour cream, 1 tablespoon amaretto, vanilla, and salt. Pulse until mixture is smooth. Add eggs and process until mixture is creamy and eggs are fully incorporated.
3. Pour cream cheese mixture into the pie crust and bake at 350°F for 40 minutes.
4. Toss toasted almonds with remaining sugar and sprinkle over the cheesecake. Bake for an additional 10 minutes, or until almond topping is browned.
5. Remove from oven and refrigerate until chilled. Serve with peaches tossed with remaining tablespoon of amaretto and whipped cream.

Chapter 3

Cheese Fondues from the Great American Melting Pot

St. Patrick's Day
Pots o' Gold Brunch

Green beer isn't the only way to tip your tam-o-shanter to the Emerald Isle. Invite a few friends over for a warming, hearty mid-March brunch featuring two rich cheese fondues, plus a few updated Irish favorites.

Menu

Dubliner Cheddar Fondue

Carrigaline Blue Fondue

Irish Brown Soda Bread

Corned Beef Hash Cakes with Eggs

Sautéed Cabbage with Bacon and Parsley

Sliced Tomatoes

Green Apple Salad

Currant Scones with Lemon Curd

Bread Pudding with Bailey's Irish Cream Sauce

Guinness Stout

Iced Mint Tea

Irish Coffee

Dubliner Cheddar Fondue

Serves 8

2 cups ale

2 small cloves garlic, pressed

1 small onion, finely chopped

1½ pounds Dubliner cheese

½ pound sharp Cheddar cheese

1½ tablespoons cornstarch

3 tablespoons heavy cream

½ teaspoon white pepper

¼ cup parsley, minced

Brown soda bread cubes (see page 47)

> Dubliner cheese adds a mellow, complex flavor to this fondue. Keep a few ladles ready—your guests will want to drizzle a bit over their corned beef cakes.

1. Pour ale into a heavy saucepan over medium heat. Add garlic and chopped onion to ale. Bring mixture to a boil, then reduce heat to keep ale simmering.
2. Shred cheeses in a food processor. Add ¼ of the cheese to the simmering liquid and stir in a figure-eight pattern. Once that cheese has melted, add another ¼ to the saucepan. Keep stirring. Repeat until all cheese is melted and mixture is hot, but not boiling.
3. Dissolve cornstarch in cream. Stir into cheese mixture. Cook until just bubbly, then reduce heat and simmer for 1 additional minute.
4. Add white pepper and parsley to the melted cheese and stir well.
5. Pour liquid into 1 or more fondue pots and keep warm over heating source. Serve with bread cubes.

. . . .

The All-American St. Patrick's Day

In Ireland, St. Patrick's Day is primarily a religious holiday, observed in churches and with a family dinner at home. Irish immigrants in the United States get credit for turning the feast day of their homeland's patron saint into an all-out celebration of Irish culture.

Carrigaline-Blue Fondue

Serves 8

2 cups dry white wine

2 small cloves garlic, pressed

Juice of 2 lemons

1 pound Cashel Blue cheese

1 pound Carrigaline farmhouse
　　cheese

1½ tablespoons cornstarch

3 tablespoons Kirsch

½ teaspoon white pepper

¼ cup parsley, minced

½ teaspoon vanilla extract

Brown soda bread cubes

Cashel Blue is an Irish blue-veined cheese that's a little milder than other European blues. In this fondue, we pair it with buttery-tasting Carrigaline. If you can't find these cheeses at your local supermarket, substitute a Danish blue cheese and a good Havarti.

1. Pour wine into heavy saucepan over medium heat. Add garlic and lemon juice to wine. Bring mixture to a simmer.
2. Shred cheeses in a food processor. Add ¼ of the cheese to the simmering liquid and stir in a figure-eight pattern. Once that cheese has melted, add another ¼ to the saucepan. Keep stirring. Repeat until all cheese is melted and mixture is hot, but not boiling.
3. Dissolve cornstarch in Kirsch. Stir into cheese mixture. Cook until just bubbly, then reduce heat and simmer for 1 additional minute.
4. Add white pepper, parsley, and vanilla to the melted cheese and stir well.
5. Pour into fondue pots and serve with bread cubes.

· ·

Not-So-Plain Vanilla

Pure vanilla extract adds a warm, caramel-like richness to savory dishes. In fondues, fragrant vanilla enhances the buttery flavor of the cheese. It's also been famously added to cream and reduction sauces for lobster, duck, and veal. Make sure to use pure vanilla extract in savory recipes—artificial vanilla and flavoring blends could give your dish an undesirable sweet or "off" flavor.

Irish Brown Soda Bread

Serves 4

2 cups unbleached white flour

1½ cups stone-ground whole wheat flour

⅓ cup rolled oats

2 tablespoons toasted wheat germ

3 tablespoons brown sugar

1 teaspoon salt

1 teaspoon baking soda

3 tablespoons cold unsalted butter

2 cups buttermilk

A mix of grains and flours gives this coarse, country-style soda bread a distinctive flavor. The batter isn't yeast raised, which makes it pretty fail-safe for tentative bakers.

1. Preheat oven to 400°F. Grease and flour a 9" × 5" loaf pan or a 9-inch round cake pan.
2. In a large bowl, combine unbleached white flour, whole wheat flour, oats, wheat germ, brown sugar, salt, and baking soda. Stir with a whisk to break up any lumps.
3. Chop chilled butter into pieces and work into the flour mixture with hands or a fork until blended.
4. Add buttermilk in small amounts, stirring to combine, until mixture forms a sticky dough. Knead briefly, then place dough in prepared pan.
5. Bake until browned and a tester comes out clean, about 40 minutes. Cool on a wire rack.

· ·

Densely Delicious

Soda breads have the same dense texture as quick breads like date-nut bread and banana bread. Also like those breads, soda bread tends to get stale and crumbly quickly. Try to bake soda breads the same day you plan to serve them, or plan on toasting bread cubes in the oven before serving.

Corned Beef Hash Cakes with Eggs

Serves 8

4 *white baking potatoes, peeled*

2½ *pounds corned beef brisket,*
    cooked and trimmed

1 *medium onion, finely chopped*

⅓ *cup parsley, finely chopped*

¼ *teaspoon thyme leaves*

½ *teaspoon mustard, prepared*

2 *eggs*

Salt and pepper to taste

2 *cups dry bread crumbs*

If you're serving this dish for family or a very small group, feel free to make the eggs poached. However, for do-it-ahead ease, a fan of boiled egg slices makes a nice presentation without the last-minute hassle of turning out 16 poached eggs.

Vegetable oil for frying

16 *boiled eggs, peeled*

2 *cups sour cream*

4 *tablespoons horseradish*

1. Cut baking potatoes in half lengthwise and boil until just tender. Do not overcook. Rinse potatoes in cold water, drain well, and shred in a food processor.
2. Shred or finely chop corned beef. In a large bowl, combine potatoes, corned beef, onion, parsley, thyme, mustard, and raw eggs. Knead ingredients together until mixture is well-blended. If mixture seems too wet, work in 1–2 tablespoons of bread crumbs. Add salt and pepper.
3. Lightly shape mixture into 16 patties and coat each in bread crumbs.
4. Pour oil 1 inch deep in a large skillet. Heat over high heat and add patties, 2 or 3 at a time. Cook, turning once, until patties are well-browned on each side. Place cooked patties on a baking sheet and keep warm in the oven until ready to serve.
5. Before serving, slice eggs and place an overlapping circle of egg slices on top of each corned beef hash cake. Mix sour cream and horseradish and place a dollop on each cake.

Sautéed Cabbage with Bacon and Parsley

Serves 8

½ pound meaty bacon

1 tablespoon butter

1 large head cabbage, cored
   and chopped

1 cup fresh parsley, minced

1 tablespoon raspberry vinegar

Salt and pepper to taste

> In an Irish kitchen, this dish would most likely feature a thick white sauce spiked with parsley. Since we're pairing our cabbage with a rich fondue course, we've added the parsley without sauce.

1. In a large skillet or flat-bottomed wok, cook bacon until crisp. Drain on paper towels. Remove all but 2 tablespoons of bacon drippings from the skillet.
2. Add butter and cabbage to skillet and cook over high heat, stirring frequently, until cabbage is crisp and tender. Add parsley. Drizzle raspberry vinegar over the cabbage and toss well.
3. Crumble cooked bacon over cabbage and add salt and pepper to taste. Serve with corned beef hash cakes.

. . . .

Cabbage Patch Facts

Inexpensive, plentiful cabbage is packed with vitamin C as well as other antioxidants and heart-healthy fiber. Although often considered too common for company, cultivated cabbage has been nourishing humans for more than 4,000 years. It also stars in beloved dishes of many cuisines, from coleslaw to sauerkraut to kimchee.

Green Apple Salad

Serves 8

4 tart green apples, unpeeled
1 seedless cucumber, unpeeled
1 cup seedless green grapes
½ cup fennel bulb, finely diced
½ cup sultanas
½ cup plain yogurt
½ cup mayonnaise
1 tablespoon orange zest
2 teaspoons sugar or sugar substitute equivalent

This crunchy, refreshing salad makes a nice counterpoint to the rich foods normally served at breakfast or brunch.

1. Core and dice apples. Trim ends off cucumber and cut into small cubes.
2. In a bowl, toss together apples, cucumber, grapes, fennel, and sultanas.
3. Whisk together yogurt, mayonnaise, orange zest, and sugar. Pour dressing over apple mixture and stir to coat.

Fennel Facts

Fennel looks a little like celery and can be used in place of celery in salads, stuffings, and other dishes. However, unlike somewhat bland celery, fennel has a pronounced licorice flavor. Most cooks are familiar with fennel seeds—which are available on any supermarket spice rack—but fresh fennel is worth trying.

Currant Scones

Serves 8

2 cups all-purpose flour

⅓ cup sugar

2 teaspoons baking powder

¼ teaspoon salt

½ cup unsalted butter

2 eggs

1 teaspoon vanilla extract

½ cup plus 1 tablespoon heavy cream

1 cup currants

Use a small biscuit cutter to make these mini-scones. If you prefer large triangle-shaped scones, roll the dough into a circle and cut eight triangles.

1. In a large bowl, combine flour, sugar, baking powder, and salt. Whisk to combine and break up any lumps.
2. Add butter. Blend with 2 knives or a pastry blender until mixture resembles coarse meal.
3. Whisk together 1 egg, vanilla, and ½ cup cream. Add to flour mixture and stir until wet and dry ingredients are just blended. Stir in currants.
4. Turn dough onto a floured board and lightly knead a few times. Roll out until dough is about 1½ inches thick. Using a small circle-shaped biscuit or cookie cutter, cut out 16 scones. Place on a lightly greased baking sheet.
5. Whisk together remaining egg with remaining tablespoon of cream. Brush scone tops with egg mixture. Bake at 350°F for 12–15 minutes. Serve with lemon curd and butter or clotted cream.

Time for Tea?

Not-too-sweet scones are a favorite teatime treat. The recipe above can be varied by adding raisins, dried cranberries, dried apricots, or other fruits. Some cooks like to glaze scones by dusting the tops with confectioners' sugar, then briefly putting scones under a broiler. The sugar caramelizes quickly, leaving a shiny brown glaze.

Lemon Curd

Serves 8

⅔ cup freshly squeezed lemon juice

1½ cups sugar

4 eggs

2 tablespoons lemon zest, grated

8 tablespoons butter

The trick to making great lemon curd is bringing the mixture to a temperature just below simmering. Too hot, and the eggs will curdle; too cool, and the mixture won't thicken. Use a double boiler (and patience) to get it right.

1. In the top half of a double boiler, whisk together lemon juice, sugar, and eggs until well blended.
2. Place water in the bottom of the double boiler so the level falls below—and does not touch—the bottom of the top pan when it is put in place. Bring water to just simmering and put top pan in place.
3. Whisk constantly until mixture is thick enough to coat a spoon, which should take about 10–12 minutes. Add zest and remove from heat. Stir in butter, 1 tablespoon at a time, until it is melted and completely blended into the curd. Set aside to cool. Cover and refrigerate for up to 2 weeks.

. . . .

Sweet Tart Citrus Curds

Although lemon curd is the most common version of the creamy spread, fruit curd can be made with any tart citrus fruit or berry. Try lime, grapefruit, and cranberry (pure, not sweetened) juices in your recipe for variety. Fruit curd can be used as a cake or pastry filling as well as a spread.

Bread Pudding

Serves 8

16 slices white bread, torn in pieces
1½ cups milk
½ cup cream
4 eggs
4 tablespoons butter, melted
1 cup sugar
1 tablespoon vanilla extract

Every family has a favorite bread pudding recipe—some very moist, some firm, some laced with spices and fruit. This recipe makes a simple, rich, slightly firm bread pudding.

1. In a large bowl, combine bread and milk. Mix with a spoon until all bread is moistened, then let stand for 15 minutes.
2. Add cream and eggs. With an electric mixer on low speed, beat mixture until eggs and cream are blended. Drizzle in butter and add sugar. Increase mixer speed and beat until mixture forms a thick batter. Mix in vanilla.
3. Pour batter into a 7" × 11" glass baking dish. Bake at 325°F for 25 minutes or until a knife inserted in the center of the pudding comes out nearly clean. Set aside to cool slightly before cutting. Serve warm or at room temperature with Bailey's Irish Cream Sauce (page 54).

. . . .

A Good Soak

The best bread puddings start with bread that's well soaked with milk. Depending on the type of bread used, it could take more or less milk. Trust your judgment. If your bread pudding batter seems dry, add a little more milk or cream to the mix.

Bailey's Irish Cream Sauce

Serves 8

1 cup heavy cream
½ cup Bailey's Irish Cream
3 cups confectioners' sugar

If you prefer a nonalcoholic sauce, substitute an Irish cream flavoring designed for coffees and teas.

1. Combine heavy cream and Bailey's Irish Cream.
2. Add confectioners' sugar, a little at a time, whisking until sugar is dissolved and sauce is smooth. Spoon over bread pudding.

Irish Coffee

Serves 8

1½ cups Irish whiskey
8 6-ounce cups dark roast coffee
12 teaspoons brown sugar
1 cup heavy cream, whipped

This coffee, with a kick, is a perfect meal-ender for windy March weekends. In the summertime, try it blended with vanilla ice cream for a coffee dessert.

1. Pour 1½ ounces of whiskey in each of 8 footed Irish coffee mugs. Stir in 1½ teaspoons sugar in each mug, then pour 6 ounces of freshly brewed coffee in each. Stir well.
2. Top each mug with a generous spoonful of whipped cream and serve immediately.

Pennsylvania Dutch Quilting Party

Whether your friends are expert quilters turning out Double Wedding Band patterns or just crafters making memento squares with glue guns, this homey menu of fondue, roasted chicken, and salads will fuel creative conversation.

MENU

Cup Cheese Fondue

Soft Pretzels and Whole Wheat Bread

Rosemary Roasted Chicken

Potato Salad

Pepper Slaw

Corn Salad

Bread and Butter Pickles

Shoo-Fly Pie

Old School Pie Crust

Lemonade

Coffee

Cup Cheese Fondue

Serves 6

½ pound cottage cheese

4 ounces goat cheese, in pieces

2 ounces Limburger cheese, in pieces

1 tablespoon butter

1 cup heavy cream

2 teaspoons cornstarch

2 tablespoons apple brandy

¼ cup chives, finely chopped

Salt and pepper to taste

Authentic Amish cup cheese is a fresh cheese made with raw cow and goat milks, eggs, cream, butter, and herbs. This fondue offers some of the flavor without the hard-to-find ingredients.

1. In a heavy saucepan over medium heat, combine cottage cheese, goat cheese, Limburger cheese, butter, and 1 cup of cream. Stirring constantly with a wooden spoon, bring mixture to a simmer.

2. Continue cooking and stirring until cheeses are melted and well-blended with the cream. Combine cornstarch with apple brandy and add to simmering fondue. Keep stirring until mixture is thickened and bubbly.

3. Add chives, salt, and pepper to taste. Pour mixture into 1 or more fondue pots and place over heating source. Serve with soft pretzels and whole wheat bread cubes.

About Curds and Whey

Cottage cheese adds a zippy, fresh flavor to cheese fondues. However, cottage cheese, because of its low-fat content, doesn't always melt seamlessly into other ingredients. Expect your cottage cheese-based fondues to be tasty but a bit grainy or lumpy in texture.

Rosemary Roasted Chicken

Serves 6

1 chicken, about 3½ pounds
2 tablespoons olive oil
2 cloves garlic, pressed
1 tablespoon rosemary leaves
Salt and pepper
1 lemon, quartered

Sometimes a simple oven-roasted chicken is the most satisfying entrée you can prepare. For best flavor, buy fresh farm-raised chicken or additive-free chicken.

1. Wash chicken and pat dry. Remove giblets, if any. Coat chicken with olive oil and garlic.
2. Place chicken in an open roasting pan. Sprinkle with rosemary, salt, and pepper. Put quartered lemon inside chicken cavity. Roast at 350"F for 1 hour. Remove from oven and let stand for 15 minutes before carving.

Safe Poultry Handling

Chicken and turkey should be cooked to an internal temperature of 180°F in order to kill any harmful bacteria that might be lurking in the raw meat. Never place raw poultry next to foods that will be consumed raw—like salad veggies and fruit. Always give utensils and platters that have come in contact with raw poultry a good wash with soap and water.

Potato Salad

Serves 6

7 *large white potatoes*

4 *hard-boiled eggs*

1 *small onion, diced*

2 *tablespoons bacon fat or*
    vegetable oil

1 *tablespoon apple cider vinegar*

1 *tablespoon sugar*

1 *cup mayonnaise*

2 *teaspoons prepared mustard*

⅔ *cup celery, finely chopped*

Salt and pepper to taste

> Remind your guests what real homemade potato salad tastes like. This version is both simple and delicious.

1. Peel and dice potatoes. Place in a pot of cold water and bring to a boil. Reduce heat slightly and cook, stirring occasionally, until potatoes are just tender, about 10–15 minutes. Pour potatoes into a colander and rinse with cold water.
2. Peel eggs and separate whites and yolks. Grate yolks into a medium-size bowl. Chop egg whites and set aside.
3. In a heavy skillet, combine onion and fat or oil. Sauté until onion is soft, but not brown. Remove from heat and add vinegar to the skillet, stirring quickly. With a slotted spoon, place onion in a large serving bowl. Add cooled potatoes and chopped egg whites to the bowl and mix well.
4. Whisk together sugar, mayonnaise, and mustard. Add to grated egg yolks and mix until smooth. Fold dressing into potato mixture. Add chopped celery, salt, and pepper and mix until blended. Add more mayonnaise if desired. Cover and refrigerate until ready to serve.

Marinated Potato Salad

For an alternative, crunchy potato salad, combine halved and sliced boiled potatoes with sliced celery, carrots, radishes, and chopped onion. Place in a glass bowl and pour a bottle of vinaigrette-type salad dressing over all. Cover and refrigerate for 8 hours, turning mixture occasionally. When ready to serve, drain off excess salad dressing and toss potatoes and veggies with a small amount of mayonnaise.

Pepper Slaw

Serves 6

½ head cabbage, chopped
1 red bell pepper, chopped
1 green bell pepper, chopped
1 small onion, chopped
1 cup apple cider vinegar

1 ⅓ cups sugar
⅛ teaspoon turmeric
1 teaspoon mustard seed
⅛ teaspoon cloves
½ teaspoon salt

1. In a food processor, finely chop (but do not purée) cabbage, peppers, and onion. Place in a large glass bowl.
2. In a saucepan, combine vinegar, sugar, turmeric, mustard seed, cloves, and salt. Bring to a boil and stir until sugar is completely dissolved. Set aside to cool slightly.
3. Pour vinegar mixture over the vegetables. Cover and refrigerate for 24 hours. Move vegetables to a serving dish with a slotted spoon.

Corn Salad

Serves 6

4 cups corn kernels, blanched
2 cups zucchini, diced
1 red bell pepper, diced
1 small onion, minced
1 tablespoon sugar

½ cup tarragon or white
   balsamic vinegar
½ cup vegetable oil
Salt and pepper to taste

1. Combine corn, zucchini, bell pepper, and onion in a glass bowl.
2. Whisk together sugar, vinegar, and oil. Pour over vegetables.
3. Cover and let stand a few hours or overnight in the refrigerator. Season with salt and pepper before serving.

Shoo-Fly Pie

Serves 6

1 9-inch *Old School Pie Crust*
    (see page 61)
1 cup light molasses
1 egg
⅔ cup boiling water
1 teaspoon baking soda
1 cup all-purpose flour
⅔ cup sugar
4 tablespoons butter or shortening
Pinch of salt

Although Dinah Shore made Shoo-Fly Pie famous in her 1946 hit record, few people outside Pennsylvania have enjoyed this traditional, molasses-based dessert.

1. Place pie crust in a pie dish. Whisk molasses and egg. Slowly add boiling water while continuing to whisk. Stir in baking soda. Pour molasses mixture into a pie shell.
2. In a bowl, combine flour and sugar. Cut in butter or shortening with 2 knives or a pastry cutter until mixture forms coarse crumbs. Work in salt.
3. Sprinkle crumb mixture over molasses. Bake at 350°F for 40 minutes or until molasses filling starts bubbling through the crumbs. Cool and serve.

. . . .

About Molasses

Derived primarily from boiling sugar cane, molasses is a long-lasting staple and can be fermented into rum, which made it a valuable commodity during colonial times. Before sugar refining became cost-effective, molasses was the chief sweetening agent in many dishes.

Old School Pie Crust

Serves 8

4 cups all-purpose flour
Pinch of salt
2 cups lard, chilled
1 cup ice water

Country cooks will tell you that nothing compares to lard when it comes to making flaky, tender pie crusts. This recipe makes 2 9-inch crusts.

1. Combine flour and salt in a bowl. Add lard in pieces and combine with the flour using 2 knives or a pastry blender until mixture resembles coarse meal.
2. Slowly add ice water, very lightly working it into the flour mixture with your fingers until a soft dough forms. Divide dough into 2 pieces.
3. On a marble or floured board, roll out dough to form 2 9-inch circles.

Crusty Alternatives

Some cooks prefer a thicker, more cakelike pie crust. To accomplish this, just whisk an egg and ½ teaspoon of vinegar into the ice water before adding the water to the flour-lard mixture. Flour hands well before handling the soft dough.

South of the Border Queso Party

Invite the gang over for Cinco de Mayo, a patio party, or just to watch the World Series on television. This menu—which offers a range of colors, textures, and flavors—works well for multi-generation parties and casual gatherings of all kinds. Each recipe serves 12 as a single course. However, taken together, the menu can easily accommodate a party of 20.

MENU

Queso Fundido

Queso Chili Con Carne

Favorite Ro-Tel Dip

Tortilla Chips

Plantain Chips

Raw Vegetables

Fajita Chicken

Fajita Beef

Roasted Corn Salsa

Mango Salsa

Fresh Tomato Salsa

Easy Frozen Margaritas

Soft Corn and Flour Tortillas

Sour Cream

Black Olives

Guava and Pineapple Petit Fours

Queso Fundido

Serves 12

1 pound Queso Monterey Jack
8 ounces Mexica Cotija
1½ cups heavy cream
1 tablespoon cornstarch
1 tablespoon water or tequila
2 tablespoons onion, minced
2 green onions, finely chopped
¼ cup cilantro, finely chopped
1 jalapeño pepper, finely chopped
¼ teaspoon cumin

For variety, add chopped spinach, black olives, or chopped mushrooms to this basic hot cheese dish. For a mild queso, replace the jalapeño with chopped bell pepper.

1. Chop the Queso Monterey into small pieces. Crumble the Mexica Cotija.
2. In a saucepan over medium heat, bring the heavy cream to a simmer. Add the cheeses in 4 batches, stirring each addition in a figure-eight motion until completely melted. Dissolve cornstarch in water or tequila. Stir into cheese mixture.
3. Add onion, green onions, cilantro, and pepper to the mixture. Stir in cumin.
4. Heat cheese mixture until bubbly.
5. Pour into 1 or more fondue pots and place over heating source. Serve with tortilla chips and other dippers.

. . . .

Mexican Cheese Choices

Queso Monterey is a semi-soft cheese—softer than the more familiar Monterey Jack—and is excellent for melting. Mexica Cotija is a sharp, dry, crumbly cheese favored for toppings. Together, they make a very flavorful queso.

Queso Chili Con Carne

Serves 12

This hearty fondue also can be ladled over hot tortilla chips for a kind of quick-fix nacho snack.

1 cup half-and-half
12 ounces Monterey Jack cheese, shredded
12 ounces Manchego cheese, shredded
4 ounces sharp Cheddar, shredded
1 15-ounce can chili-seasoned tomato sauce
1 pound ground beef, cooked and drained
2 green onions, chopped
Cayenne pepper to taste

1. Heat half-and-half in a saucepan. Add cheeses in 4 batches, stirring each batch in a figure-eight motion until melted.
2. Stir in chili-seasoned tomato sauce and ground beef.
3. Add green onions and cayenne. Cook over medium heat until thick and bubbly.
4. Spoon into fondue pot and place over heating source. Serve with chips and other dippers.

Favorite Ro-Tel Dip

Serves 12

1 pound Velveeta cheese
1 10-ounce can Ro-Tel tomatoes and green chilies, undrained

1. Cut Velveeta into cubes.
2. In a medium saucepan over medium-low heat, combine cheese and can of tomatoes and green chilies.
3. Cook, stirring constantly, until cheese is melted and dip is bubbly.
4. Pour into a fondue pot and place over heating source.
5. Serve with chips and other dippers.

Fajita Chicken

Serves 12

8 boneless chicken breast halves
½ cup lime juice
1 cup olive oil
4 cloves garlic, pressed
2 teaspoons salt
1 teaspoon black pepper
1 teaspoon cumin

1 teaspoon dried oregano
2 bell peppers, preferably
    different colors
2 large onions

> This recipe calls for searing chicken in a hot skillet. If you prefer grilled chicken breasts, by all means fire up the barbecue—but be careful not to overcook the boneless chicken.

1. Place chicken breasts in a resealable plastic bag. Combine ½ cup lime juice, ½ cup of the olive oil, and garlic. Pour into bag over chicken, seal, and place bag in a baking dish in the refrigerator for 4 hours or overnight. Turn bag occasionally.
2. Remove chicken from marinade, shaking off excess liquid. Discard marinade.
3. Combine salt, black pepper, cumin, and oregano. Sprinkle seasoning mix over chicken breasts.
4. Trim onions and bell peppers and cut into strips.
5. Heat a large, heavy skillet on high. When the skillet is just hot, pour some of the remaining olive oil in the skillet, add chicken breasts, and sear for 2 minutes on each side. Reduce heat and continue cooking until chicken breasts are no longer pink, about 5–7 minutes, depending on the thickness. Place chicken on a platter. Slice across the grain into thin strips.
6. Turn up heat and stir-fry onions and peppers over high heat for 2 minutes. Spoon over chicken strips and serve.

. . . .

It's All in the Bag

Resealable plastic bags take the mess out of marinating, making it easy to turn ingredients and distribute marinades evenly. If you don't have time to make marinade from scratch, just pour a bottle of store bought vinaigrette over meats.

Fajita Beef

Serves 12

4 pounds sirloin steak
⅓ cup olive oil
2 cloves garlic, pressed
2 teaspoons salt
1 teaspoon black pepper
1 teaspoon cumin
¼ teaspoon cayenne pepper
½ teaspoon dried oregano
2 bell peppers, preferably different colors
2 large onions

Flank steak or London broil can be used in place of sirloin steak, but these less expensive cuts should be marinated overnight before grilling.

1. Coat steak generously with olive oil. Rub garlic on both sides.
2. Combine salt, black pepper, cumin, cayenne pepper, and oregano. Sprinkle over steak.
3. Grill steak over hot coals or sear in a hot skillet, starting with 2 minutes on each side. Cook as desired, being careful not to overcook. Remove to a platter.
4. Trim bell peppers and onions and cut into strips. Add a small amount of oil to skillet and stir-fry onions and peppers for 2 minutes. Or coat onions and peppers with oil and place in a grill basket over hot coals until just crisp and tender.
5. Slice steak across the grain into thin strips. Arrange peppers and onions over steak and serve.

Time Saver

Here's an entertaining tip: Grill and slice fajita ingredients in advance. Just before serving, heat a cast-iron skillet over high heat. Add a little oil and stir-fry the fajita ingredients quickly, just enough to heat through and fill the house with wonderful aromas. Bring the chicken or beef to the table still sizzling.

Roasted Corn Salsa

Serves 12

6 cups corn kernels
2 cups plum tomatoes, chopped
1 jalapeño pepper, minced
½ cup sweet onion, finely chopped
⅓ cup fresh cilantro, chopped
Juice of 2 limes
Salt to taste

Skillet roasting gives corn a rich, smoky-sweet flavor. Substitute bell pepper for jalapeño pepper if a mild salsa is desired.

1. Place fresh or thawed corn kernels in a hot skillet over high heat. Toss until kernels begin to brown. Remove kernels from skillet and let cool.
2. In a bowl, combine corn, tomatoes, pepper, onion, cilantro, and lime juice. Mix well.
3. Add salt to taste and refrigerate until needed.

Mango Salsa

Serves 12

4 mangoes
2 cucumbers
2 jalapeño peppers, minced
¼ cup green onion, finely chopped
¼ cup fresh cilantro, finely chopped
Juice of 2 limes

For this recipe, pick just-ripe mangoes that are still firm. Mangoes and jalapeños combine to create a sweet-hot treat.

1. Peel and seed mangoes. Dice fruit. Peel and dice cucumbers.
2. Combine all ingredients in a bowl and mix well.
3. Refrigerate until needed.

Fresh Tomato Salsa

Serves 12

6 ripe tomatoes, diced
1 medium onion, finely chopped
1 jalapeño pepper, minced
⅓ cup cilantro, finely chopped
2 cloves garlic, minced
¼ cup parsley, finely chopped
2 tablespoons balsamic vinegar

Balsamic vinegar gives a touch of sweetness to this otherwise classic salsa. For variety, add a little fresh oregano to the mix.

1. Combine all ingredients in a large bowl. Mix well.
2. Cover and refrigerate at least 1 hour before serving.

Easy Frozen Margaritas

Serves 4

1 6-ounce can of frozen limeade
6 ounces tequila
2 ounces Triple Sec
Ice
Coarse salt
Lime wedges

This recipe is super-easy and a party favorite. Save the juicing of fresh limes for nonfrozen margaritas.

1. Put frozen limeade in the blender. Fill can with tequila and pour into blender. Fill the can 1/3 full with Triple Sec and add that to the limeade mixture.
2. Fill the blender container with cracked ice. Process until smooth.
3. Run lime wedges over the rims of four tequila glasses to moisten, then dip glass rims in a plate of coarse salt. Pour frozen margarita mixture into glasses.

Guava and Pineapple Petit Fours

Serves 12

1 cup butter, softened

2 cups sugar

4 eggs

3 cups cake flour, sifted

1 tablespoon baking powder

½ teaspoon salt

1 cup milk

2 teaspoons vanilla extract

1½ cups guava jelly

1½ cups pineapple preserves

Confectioners' sugar

Flaked coconut

A layer cutter—a kind of saw with a wire "blade" for slicing cake layers in half horizontally—would come in handy here. If you don't have one, try using dental floss or a serrated knife. Prepare the cake a day in advance to make cutting easier.

1. Cream butter and sugar together in a large bowl. Beat with mixer on medium speed until fluffy. Add eggs 1 at a time, beating each until incorporated.
2. Add cake flour, baking powder, and salt. Add flour alternately with milk, beating well after each addition. Mix in vanilla.
3. Pour batter into a greased and floured 9" × 13" pan. Bake at 350°F for 25–30 minutes or until tester inserted in the center comes out clean. Allow cake to cool slightly, then turn onto a baking sheet that has been lined with wax paper. Cover loosely and let stand for at least 24 hours.
4. Cut cake into 2 9" × 6½" portions. Trim off edges. Holding 1 portion firmly but gently, cut the cake horizontally into 2 even layers. Spread guava jelly over one layer and carefully top with the other layer. Very carefully spread jelly over top of cake. (If jelly is too stiff, warm in a microwave.) Sprinkle confectioners' sugar over top of cake. Repeat with the other portion, using pineapple preserves. Sprinkle coconut over the top of the pineapple cake.
5. Cut each cake into 24 squares. Place petit fours on doily-lined dessert platters.

Tailgate Supper Menu

Fans of the toughest gridiron rivals will be able to agree on one thing: Rich Cheddar fondue is a great way to start a fall meal. Serve this menu from the back of a truck—all your fondue pot needs is a level surface—or from the kitchen counter. Even if your tailgate gatherings take place in front of the television, this hearty fare will fuel the most passionate cheers.

Menu

Ale-Spiked Cheddar Fondue

Soft Pretzels

Sourdough Cubes

Marble Rye Cubes

Grilled Bratwurst

German-Style Potato Salad

Ranch Beans

Texas Sheet Cake

Sparkling Apple Juice

Medium Ale or Stout Beer

Ale-Spiked Cheddar Fondue

Serves 12

2 cups ale

1 pound sharp Cheddar cheese,
* shredded*

1 pound medium Cheddar cheese,
* shredded*

1 small onion, finely chopped

1 teaspoon Worcestershire sauce

1½ tablespoons cornstarch

2 tablespoons milk

Cayenne pepper to taste

Use nonalcoholic beer in place of ale when serving a crowd that includes nondrinkers. The fondue can be made at home, transported in a heat-safe dish to the tailgate site, then warmed in a fondue pot.

1. In a saucepan over medium heat, heat ale until simmering. Add cheese in 4 batches, stirring in a figure-eight motion until each batch is melted.
2. Stir in onion and Worcestershire sauce. Increase heat slightly.
3. Dissolve cornstarch in milk and add to cheese mixture. Cook until smooth, thick, and bubbly.
4. Add cayenne pepper to taste.
5. Pour into fondue pot and place over heating source. Serve with hearty breads and pretzels.

Getting Cheesy

A bold Cheddar fondue will add just the right amount of variety to your tailgate menu. For the main course, stick with something substantial and familiar. We suggest sausages, but grilled burgers, steaks, or chops would work as well.

Grilled Bratwurst

Serves 12

24 *bratwursts*
4 *cans beer*
6 *whole cloves*
1 *onion, chopped*
Spray bottle filled with water or beer

Parboiling bratwurst in beer or seasoned water before grilling adds flavor and ensures that brats remain plump and juicy after grilling.

1. Place bratwurst, beer, cloves, and onion in a large pot and bring to a boil.
2. Reduce heat and simmer for 25 minutes.
3. Heat charcoal or gas grill to medium-hot (coals should be white, not flaming).
4. Place bratwurst on grill and cook for 10 minutes, turning often. Spraying with water or beer a few times while cooking will make brat skins crispy.
5. Remove from heat and serve with brown mustard.

. . . .

Brats 101

Bratwurst can be boiled at home, then grilled at your tailgate party location. Of course, you can always cook brats completely on the grill, but do be careful to avoid flare-ups, and turn them often.

German-Style Potato Salad

Serves 12

5 pounds white potatoes

1 pound bacon

1 large onion, diced

1 tablespoon all-purpose flour

3 tablespoons sugar

2 teaspoons salt

½ teaspoon black pepper

⅔ cup white or apple cider vinegar

1 cup water

⅓ cup green onion, chopped

¼ cup fresh parsley, chopped

2 teaspoons celery seeds (optional)

> Your friends will love this departure from ordinary potato dishes. Tart German potato salad, served warm, makes a wonderful foil for sausages or grilled meats of any kind.

1. Scrub potatoes and boil, unpeeled, until tender. Drain and set aside until cool enough to handle. Peel potatoes and slice thinly. Place in a large serving dish.
2. In a large skillet, fry bacon until crisp. Drain and crumble.
3. Add onion to bacon drippings and cook over medium heat until just softened.
4. Combine flour, sugar, salt, and black pepper. Add vinegar and water, stirring until smooth. Pour mixture into skillet with bacon drippings and onion. Bring to a simmer, stirring constantly, until mixture thickens slightly. Add crumbled bacon to the pan.
5. Pour dressing over potatoes and toss to mix well. Add green onion and parsley, plus celery seeds, if desired.

. . . .

Thrifty and Nifty

Go to your nearest dollar store to stock up on paper plates, plastic table covers, and cups. Most carry a range of solid colors or seasonal patterns. You'll be able to put together a festive table without breaking the bank.

Ranch Beans

Serves 12

1½ cups black beans, cooked
1½ cups red kidney beans, cooked
1½ cups white cannellini beans, cooked
1½ cups pinto beans, cooked
1½ cups pork roast or beef brisket, cooked and shredded
2½ cups beef broth
2 cups barbecue sauce
1 large onion, chopped
1 green bell pepper, chopped
2 cloves garlic, minced
Salt and hot pepper sauce to taste

Canned beans work just fine for this dish. Figure one 15- or 16-ounce can for each 1½ cups of beans.

1. Combine all ingredients in a Dutch oven and stir well.
2. Bake at 350°F, uncovered, for 1 hour, stirring occasionally.
3. Remove from oven and keep warm until ready to serve.

Texas Sheet Cake

This quick scratch cake from the Lone Star State features a fudge-like topping that goes on the hot cake, eliminating the need to wait for the cake to cool before frosting.

Serves 12

2 cups all-purpose flour

2 cups sugar

½ teaspoon salt

1 stick butter

½ cup vegetable shortening

1 cup water

6 tablespoons cocoa powder

½ cup sour cream

2 eggs

1 teaspoon vanilla extract

Dash of cinnamon

1 teaspoon baking soda

Frosting

1 stick butter

5 tablespoons cocoa

6 tablespoons milk

1 box confectioners' sugar

1 teaspoon vanilla extract

1 cup pecans, chopped

1. Combine flour, sugar, and salt in a bowl. Stir with a whisk to blend and break up any lumps.
2. In a large saucepan, combine butter, shortening, water, and cocoa powder. Cook, stirring, over medium-high heat until mixture comes to a boil. Remove from heat and let cool until just warm.
3. Pour cocoa mixture over flour and sugar. Beat with a mixer until smooth. Add sour cream, eggs, vanilla, cinnamon, and baking soda. Mix well. Pour into a buttered 11" × 16" sheet pan and bake at 350°F for 20 minutes.
4. When cake is halfway done, make frosting. Melt butter, cocoa, and milk in a saucepan over medium heat. Bring to a boil and remove from heat. Add confectioners' sugar, vanilla, and pecans. Mix until blended.
5. Pour frosting over hot cake and carefully smooth over the top. Cool, cut, and serve.

Grown-Up Princess PJ Party

Sometimes you just need to let your inner princess shine. The best way to do that—without real-world consequences—is to invite your gal pals over for a no-holds-barred gabfest. This menu is both decadent and elegant, perfect for an all-night sweatpants-and-tiaras affair.

MENU

Lump Crab and Cream Cheese Fondue

Artichoke Bottoms with Chicken Salad

Crudités

Mini Spinach Quiches

Strawberries

Meringue Tarts

Dark Chocolate

Lump Crab and Cream Cheese Fondue

Serves 12

12 ounces cream cheese

1¼ cups heavy cream

½ cup mayonnaise

1 pound lump crabmeat

¼ cup Parmesan cheese, grated

¼ cup green onion, finely chopped

¼ cup parsley, finely chopped

Coarsely ground black pepper

2 tablespoons sherry (optional)

This fondue variation on a favorite hot dip will satisfy your royal court. For a twist, just add 1 9-ounce pack of frozen artichoke hearts, finely chopped, to the mix.

1. In a saucepan, warm cream and cream cheese over low heat until cream cheese is melted and mixture is smooth. Increase heat to medium. When mixture is bubbly, quickly whisk in mayonnaise. Reduce heat.
2. Stir in crabmeat, Parmesan, green onion, parsley, and black pepper.
3. Stir in sherry, if desired.
4. Pour mixture into a fondue pot and place over heating source.
5. Serve with pieces of brioche and croissant and raw vegetables.

. . . .

An Extravagant Gesture

The fastest way to make guests feel indulged and coddled is by showcasing luxury ingredients (lump crabmeat, lobster, filet mignon) on your table. Prepare them simply and wait for the compliments.

Artichoke Bottoms with Chicken Salad

Serves 12

24 *artichoke bottoms, chilled*
Juice of 1 lemon
6 *chicken breast halves, poached*
     and chilled
1 *cup celery, chopped*
1 *cup mayonnaise*
2 *tablespoons fresh tarragon, chopped*
Salt and pepper to taste
1 *cup pecans or walnuts, chopped*

> Artichoke bottoms make a wonderful base for canapés. Use them for low-carb hors d'oeuvres, or when another dish at the same meal—like fondue—calls for a generous helping of bread.

1. Place artichoke bottoms on a serving platter. Dilute lemon juice with 2 tablespoons of water. Brush tops of artichoke bottoms with lemon water.
2. Trim chicken breast halves of any fat or cartilage. Cut into small pieces.
3. Place chicken in a bowl with celery, mayonnaise, and tarragon. Fold until well blended. Add salt and pepper to taste.
4. Mound chicken salad on artichoke bottoms. Sprinkle nuts over chicken salad and serve.

The Culinary Garden

Fresh herbs add layers of flavor to even the most basic dishes. Save money by growing your own. Most common herbs can be easily cultivated in a backyard garden or even in patio containers.

Mini Spinach Quiches

Serves 12

1 pound fresh spinach leaves

1 clove garlic, peeled

2 cups mild Cheddar, shredded

8 eggs

1 cup cream

Pinch of nutmeg

½ teaspoon salt

¼ teaspoon pepper

This recipe makes a crustless quiche using nonstick muffin pans. Substitute chopped mushrooms, bell peppers, or asparagus for the spinach.

1. Rinse spinach and place with garlic in a saucepan. Cover and cook over medium heat until spinach is just wilted. Set aside to cool.
2. Press excess moisture from spinach and place with garlic in a food processor. Pulse once or twice until spinach is just chopped, not puréed.
3. Butter cups of a muffin pan, preferably a nonstick pan. Divide spinach among cups and top spinach with shredded cheese.
4. In a blender, place eggs, cream, nutmeg, salt, and pepper. Process until well blended. Pour egg mixture over spinach and cheese in muffin cups.
5. Bake at 350°F for 20–25 minutes. Let stand for a few minutes, then remove quiches from pan, using a knife to loosen edges if necessary.

Meringue Tarts

Serves 12

4 egg whites, room temperature
¼ teaspoon salt
¼ teaspoon cream of tartar
1 cup sugar
1 teaspoon vanilla or almond extract
½ cup lemon curd
½ cup raspberry preserves
½ cup apricot preserves
½ cup cherry preserves

Crunchy, airy meringue shells make these dessert tarts unique. Fill with a mix of brightly colored preserves or citrus curd for a beautiful presentation.

1. Beat egg whites with a mixer at medium speed until foamy. Add salt and cream of tartar. Add sugar, a spoonful at a time, beating well after each addition. Add vanilla or almond extract.
2. When all ingredients have been incorporated, turn mixer to high speed and beat egg whites until glossy. Mixture should form stiff peaks when beaters are pulled from the bowl.
3. Line a baking sheet with nonstick foil. Spoon meringue onto the foil, making 24 mounds. With the back of a spoon, make an indentation in the center of each mound.
4. Bake meringues at 250°F for 1 hour or until opaque and firm. Turn off oven, but do not open oven door. Leave meringues in oven for 2–3 hours after baking.
5. Carefully remove meringues to a serving platter. Just before serving, spoon lemon curd and preserves into the indentations, making 6 of each flavor.

Meringue Art

If you're handy with cake-decorating bags and tips, you can always pipe meringue circles onto the foil, being careful to fill the bottom and build up the sides. Bake as directed in the recipe for beautiful, professional-looking shells.

Cool Kids' Fall Party Menu

Whether you're hosting the neighborhood Halloween bash, the playground soccer club celebration, or a school birthday party, this menu is full of flavors kids love. The fondue will be a big hit with cheese-loving youngsters, so make sure to have more than one station. For safety's sake, avoid open flames. Use an electric fondue pot or a small low-heat slow cooker to keep the cheese warm.

MENU

Cheddar-ama Fondue

Assorted Chips, Pretzels, and Breads

Baked Chicken Fingers

Baked Potato Wedges

Pigs in Blankets

Apple Slices

Chocolate Chip Marshmallow Fluff Cookie
Sandwiches

Hot Chocolate

Cheddar-ama Fondue

Serves 12

2 cups half-and-half
2 pounds mild Cheddar cheese,
    shredded
1 teaspoon sugar
1½ tablespoons cornstarch
2 tablespoons milk
Pinch of white pepper

As a rule, children want to eat food that's fun but familiar. If your children balk at fondue, just call it melted cheese.

1. Heat half-and-half in a saucepan over medium heat. Add cheese in 4 batches, stirring in a figure-eight motion until each addition is melted.
2. Stir in sugar.
3. Combine cornstarch and milk, stirring until smooth. Add to cheese mixture.
4. Add a pinch of pepper. Heat mixture until bubbly.
5. Pour into fondue pot and place pot over heating source. Serve with chips, pretzels, and other dippers.

Food and Fun

To keep young children from getting restless, set up three activity stations, each featuring a different craft or game. Rotate groups of children among the tables, then direct them all to the fondue table.

Baked Chicken Fingers

Serves 12

8 chicken breast halves
2 eggs
½ cup milk
2 cups Italian seasoned bread crumbs
Vegetable oil spray

Oh sure, you could fry these chicken fingers in a skillet. But this baked version comes out crispy with much less of a mess, and it's healthier.

1. Trim chicken breast halves of fat and cartilage. Slice each half lengthwise into 3 strips.
2. Combine eggs and milk in a bowl and mix with a fork until combined.
3. Pour bread crumbs onto a plate. Dip each chicken strip into egg mixture, then turn in bread crumbs to coat.
4. Line a baking sheet with nonstick foil. Place chicken fingers on sheet and spray lightly with vegetable oil.
5. Bake at 350°F for 20 minutes, turning once. Chicken fingers should be brown and crisp on both sides.

Crumb Control

Kids love to dip and dunk their foods. If you'd like to keep the fondue pot crumb-free, provide small bowls of Chedder-ama fondue for each child. Then they can dip chicken fingers and pigs in blankets in their own little pots.

Baked Potato Wedges

Serves 12

8 medium white potatoes, scrubbed
    and trimmed
½ cup olive oil
1 teaspoon salt
½ teaspoon garlic powder
½ teaspoon black pepper
½ teaspoon cumin

Bake these seasoned potato wedges alongside the chicken fingers.

1. Slice potatoes in half lengthwise, then slice each half into 4 wedges. Place potatoes into a bowl.
2. Pour olive oil over potato wedges and toss well. Each wedge should be lightly coated.
3. Line a baking sheet with nonstick foil. Spread potato wedges over foil.
4. Combine salt, garlic powder, black pepper, and cumin. Sprinkle over potato wedges.
5. Bake at 350°F for 20 minutes, turning once.

Pigs in Blankets

Serves 12–16

48 cocktail wieners or sausages
3 tubes crescent roll dough

This will never be confused with gourmet fare, but kids absolutely love them. And you'll find more than a few parents at the platter indulging their inner child.

1. Remove wieners or sausage from package and pat dry with paper towels.
2. Open crescent roll tubes one at a time, split dough in half at perforation, and unroll each half. There should be perforations for 4 rolls on each half. Separate rolls and cut each in half diagonally, making 16 wraps per can.
3. Place a wiener or sausage on each wrap and slightly stretch dough to encase the meat. Place wrapped pigs on a non-stick or lightly greased baking sheet.
4. Bake at 350°F for 10–12 minutes or until dough is browned.
5. Cool slightly before removing from baking sheet with a spatula.

Chocolate Chip Marshmallow Fluff Cookie Sandwiches

Serves 12

½ cup butter, softened
1½ cups confectioners' sugar
1 7-ounce jar of marshmallow crème
24 large chocolate chip cookies

This dessert treat is both easy to make and portable. If you prefer, substitute oatmeal cookies for the chocolate chip cookies.

1. Combine butter and sugar in a bowl. With a mixer on medium speed, beat until creamy. Add marshmallow crème and beat until ingredients are well combined and fluffy.
2. Place 12 cookies face up on a work surface. Drop a generous tablespoon of marshmallow mixture onto each cookie. Top with remaining 12 cookies to make sandwiches. Cover until ready to serve.

Hot Chocolate for a Crowd

Combine ¾ cup unsweetened cocoa powder with 1 cup sugar. Bring 3 quarts of milk to a simmer in a large pot. Stir two cups of hot milk into the cocoa mixture, then add the resulting paste to the pot. Stir until chocolate has dissolved in the milk. Ladle into 12 mugs and top with marshmallows. For adult palates, use dark chocolate cocoa powder or add a couple of tablespoons of instant coffee to the cocoa and sugar mix.

Neighborhood Block Party Potluck

Meet and greet the neighbors! Organize a potluck and offer to provide the main attraction: a bubbling fondue pot of rich, tomato-kissed Alfredo sauce surrounded by bowls of ready-to-skewer meatballs, artichoke hearts, and chicken tortelloni. Let everyone else bring a salad or dessert, and you've got a party.

MENU

Rosy Alfredo Fondue

Ciabatta Cubes

Ready-to-Dip Chicken Tortelloni

Cocktail Meatballs

Artichoke Hearts

Chianti

Potluck Salads and Desserts

Rosy Alfredo Fondue

Serves 12

4 tablespoons butter

4 tablespoons all-purpose flour

2 cups heavy cream

2 cloves garlic, pressed

1 pound fontina cheese, shredded

12 ounces Parmesan, grated

4 ounces Romano, grated

½ cup tomato-basil pasta sauce (jarred)

Splash of Chianti (optional)

Fresh-ground black pepper to taste

This recipe is just a tad richer than your garden-variety Alfredo sauce. It's perfect for coating a plump tortelloni, ravioli, or crusty bread cube.

1. In a heavy saucepan over medium heat, melt butter. Add flour and stir until roux is bubbly and blended well. Add cream and garlic.
2. Increase heat slightly and cook, stirring, until roux is dissolved and cream is hot.
3. Add cheese in 4 batches, stirring each addition in a figure-eight motion until completely melted. When cheese mixture is thick and bubbly, whisk in tomato-basil sauce and, if desired, a bit of Chianti.
4. Add pepper to taste and ladle mixture into a fondue pot. Place pot over heating source. Serve with stuffed pasta and dense bread.

Viva Italiano!

Italian fare is so well assimilated into the North American menu that you can always feel confident serving Italian dishes to a crowd. Use quality ingredients like aged, freshly grated cheeses to give your creations an authentic flare.

Cocktail Meatballs

Serves 12

1 cup soft bread crumbs

½ cup ice cold milk

2 eggs

1 small onion, finely chopped

½ cup parsley, finely chopped

1 pound ground beef

1 pound ground pork or veal

1 teaspoon salt

½ teaspoon black pepper

⅓ cup ice water

Try this recipe for light, tender meatballs. If you prefer your own meat mixture, feel free to use it. But use a light hand when shaping the meatballs. Too much rolling makes them tough and hard.

1. Combine all ingredients except ice water in a large bowl. Mix well.
2. Using ⅓–½ of the mixture at a time, place seasoned meat in a food processor. Pulse once or twice, then add a small amount of ice water to the mixture. Process until everything is blended well and fluffy.
3. With damp hands, lightly roll meat mixture into 1-inch meatballs. Place meatballs on a baking sheet.
4. Bake at 350°F for 15–20 minutes, turning occasionally.
5. Remove meatballs to a tray lined with paper towels. Cool slightly, then place in a serving dish.

· ·

Bread Basics

Ciabatta means "slipper shaped," and these slightly flat, oval loaves are found in many regions of Italy and, increasingly, in bakeries and supermarkets in the United States. Most U.S. versions feature a substantial crust and a soft, slightly dense interior.

Fondue-for-All Party Menu

Pick any one of these three menus for a dinner party, or make an event of the evening by creating three themed fondue tables. Here we have Louisiana Cajun, Chicago-style Greek, and California coastal menus that will set any office party or family reunion apart.

MENU

<><><><><><><><><>

LOUISIANA CAJUN

Cajun Hot Pepper Cheese Fondue

Andouille Sausage

Boiled Shrimp

Crawfish Balls

Mirliton Slices

Hot Pickled Okra

French Bread Slices

Dixie Beer

CHICAGO-STYLE GREEK

Spiced Feta-Spinach Fondue

Grilled Lamb Bites

Cucumber Spears

Cherry Tomatoes

Red Pearl Onions

Olives

Mini Pita Loaves

Greek or Spanish Red Wine

CALIFORNIA COASTAL

Gorgonzola Fondue

Seared Tuna Bites

Blanched Asparagus Spears

Stir-Fried Pattypan Squash

Raw Snow Peas, Broccoli, and Carrots

Fresh Figs

Sourdough Bread Cubes

Pinot Noir

Cajun Hot Pepper Cheese Fondue

Serves 12

2 cups beer

1 pound smoked Gouda cheese,
    shredded

8 ounces white Cheddar, crumbled

8 ounces Gruyère cheese, shredded

2 cloves garlic, pressed

1 onion, finely chopped

½ cup green onion, finely chopped

½ cup parsley, finely chopped

1 small bell pepper, finely diced

1 tablespoon cornstarch

2 tablespoons water

1–2 tablespoons Tabasco sauce

> This fondue isn't for the faint of heart—or stomach. Make sure there's plenty of bread available.

1. Heat beer in a saucepan. Add cheese in 4 batches, stirring in a figure-eight motion until each batch is completely melted.
2. Add garlic, onion, parsley, and bell pepper to the mix. Heat until bubbly.
3. Combine water and cornstarch, stir until smooth. Add to cheese mixture.
4. Continue cooking and stirring for 1–2 minutes. Add Tabasco.
5. Remove cheese mixture to a fondue pot. Place on heating source and serve with crusty bread, sausages, and vegetables for dipping.

. . . .

Shopping Savvy

Andouille is a coarse, spicy, smoked sausage once available only in Louisiana. It's now widely available under several brand names. Savoie's and Richard's are both authentic Louisiana brands. Fresh mirlitons can be found in the produce section of most supermarkets. They're also called chayotes.

Crawfish Balls

Serves 12

3 slices white bread

1 medium onion, peeled
   and quartered

1 small bell pepper, quartered

1 rib celery, trimmed and sliced

½ cup fresh parsley

2 pounds crawfish tails, peeled

2 eggs

1 teaspoon salt

½ teaspoon cayenne powder

½ teaspoon garlic powder

1 cup all-purpose flour

Oil for frying

Blanched frozen crawfish tails are available in many cities year-round. If you can't find crawfish, just substitute shrimp that's been dipped in boiling water for 1 minute.

1. Break up bread slices and place in a food processor. Pulse until bread forms soft crumbs. Set aside. Place onion, bell pepper, celery, and parsley in food processor. Pulse until finely chopped and place in a large bowl.
2. Working in 2 batches, put drained crawfish tails in the food processor. Pulse until coarsely chopped. Put crawfish in the bowl with onion mixture.
3. Add eggs, salt, black pepper, cayenne, and garlic powder to the crawfish. Mix with hands until well combined. Add soft bread crumbs a handful at a time, mixing after each addition. Use only enough bread crumbs to get a firm mixture that will hold together when rolled.
4. Roll mixture into small balls. Coat each ball lightly with flour.
5. Pour oil into a skillet or Dutch oven to a depth of 2 inches. Heat oil until hot but not smoking. Fry crawfish balls, turning often, until brown and crispy, about 5 minutes. Drain on paper towels and serve warm.

Crawfish on the Menu

In South Louisiana, crawfish seasons come in the spring and fall. During those months, these freshwater lobster cousins turn up in everything from appetizers and soups to entrées and vegetable blends. It takes 6–8 pounds of whole crawfish to make one pound of peeled crawfish tails.

Spiced Feta-Spinach Fondue

Serves 12

2 cups milk
1 pound feta cheese, crumbled
1 pound whole milk ricotta cheese
2 cloves garlic, pressed
1 pound fresh spinach, cooked
½ cup fresh parsley
2 green onions, chopped
1 tablespoon cornstarch
2 tablespoons water
¼ teaspoon nutmeg
¼ teaspoon cinnamon
Black pepper to taste

Authentic feta is made from sheep's milk, although many supermarket versions are made from cow's milk. Either type will work here.

1. Heat milk in a large saucepan until just scalded. Add feta and ricotta cheese to hot milk in batches, stirring in a figure-eight motion until the cheese is melted and the mixture is smooth. Add pressed garlic.
2. Press excess moisture from spinach. Place in a food processor with parsley and green onions. Pulse until chopped, but not puréed.
3. Combine cornstarch and water. Stir until smooth and add to cheese mixture. Heat until cheese is bubbly. Add spinach mixture and stir well.
4. Add nutmeg, cinnamon, and black pepper.
5. Ladle into a fondue pot and place over heating source. Serve with bread, vegetables, and lamb cubes.

Grilled Lamb Bites

Serves 12

*4 pounds boned leg of lamb,
    cut into 1-inch cubes*
1 cup olive oil
½ cup lemon juice or red wine vinegar
1 tablespoon Worcestershire sauce
4 cloves garlic, minced
1 onion, coarsely chopped
¼ cup dried rosemary leaves
1 tablespoon dried oregano
Salt and black pepper to taste

Buy leg of lamb as a roast. Then ask your butcher—or the manager of the meat department of your favorite supermarket—to bone, trim, and cube the meat for you.

1. Place lamb cubes in a large resealable plastic bag.
2. Combine olive oil, lemon juice or wine, Worcestershire sauce, garlic, onion, rosemary, and oregano. Mix well and pour into bag over lamb cubes. Seal well.
3. Place on a platter and refrigerate 8 hours or overnight, turning bag occasionally.
4. Remove from refrigerator, drain off marinade, and push lamb cubes onto skewers. Sprinkle with salt and pepper.
5. Cook on a grill over medium-high heat for 15 minutes, turning frequently. Push lamb from skewers onto a platter and serve.

Substitutions

Lamb today is a much milder-tasting product than many older folks remember. However, if you prefer, beef or pork can be substituted for the lamb.

Gorgonzola Fondue

Serves 12

2 cups cream

1 pound Gorgonzola cheese,
  crumbled

1 pound cream cheese

1 shallot, minced

1 clove garlic, minced

1 tablespoon cornstarch

2 tablespoons milk or water

Fresh-ground black pepper to taste

Crumbled Gorgonzola cheese adds a rich, pronounced flavor to dishes. In this recipe, cream and cream cheese give this sharp, blue-green veined cheese a smoother edge.

1. Heat cream in a saucepan over medium heat until hot, but not boiling. Add Gorgonzola crumbles by the handful, stirring in a figure-eight motion until each addition is melted.
2. Add cream cheese, 1 tablespoonful at a time, stirring well after each addition.
3. Add shallot and garlic, then increase heat slightly.
4. Combine cornstarch and water or milk, stirring until smooth. When cheese mixture begins to bubble, add cornstarch mixture. Reduce heat and simmer, stirring, until mixture is thick and smooth.
5. Ladle hot mixture into a fondue pot and place over heating source. Serve with crusty sourdough bread, tuna, and vegetables.

Shopping Adventures

Farmers' markets and supermarkets offer a treasure trove of unusual produce. Make your table a conversation starter with multi-colored, bite-size sweet peppers, purple fingerling potatoes, and orange cauliflower.

Seared Tuna Bites

Serves 12

6 1-inch-thick sushi-grade
    tuna steaks
½ cup vegetable oil
2 tablespoons sesame oil
½ cup maple syrup
⅓ cup soy sauce
2 tablespoons fresh ginger, grated
⅓ cup lemon juice
Black pepper to taste
Sesame seeds

> Buy sushi-grade tuna and don't overcook it. Meaty, red fresh tuna is at its best when it's still tender and pink in the center.

1. Place tuna steaks in a baking pan. Combine ⅓ cup vegetable oil (reserve remaining), sesame oil, maple syrup, soy sauce, ginger, and lemon juice. Pour over steaks.
2. Refrigerate and let marinate for ½ hour, turning once.
3. Pour remaining oil into a skillet over high heat.
4. Remove steaks from marinade and drain. Sprinkle with black pepper. Sear each steak for 2 minutes on each side.
5. Cut seared steaks into 1-inch cubes, sprinkle with sesame seeds, and serve immediately.

Red Wine with Fish

Although delicate fish calls for a crisp white wine, hearty tuna pairs best with dry, light-bodied reds or full-bodied roses. Think Pinot Noir and Beaujolais.

Stir-Fried Pattypan Squash

12 servings

1 tablespoon dark sesame oil
2 tablespoons vegetable oil
2 cloves garlic, minced
½ teaspoon fresh ginger, minced
1 sweet onion, halved vertically
    and thinly sliced
3 dozen baby pattypan squash,
    halved vertically
3 tablespoons soy sauce or to taste
Salt and pepper to taste
2 tablespoons fresh cilantro, minced

Baby pattypan squash is available in most large supermarkets. It's a squat little summer squash with the flavor of zucchini. It's great in sautés, or toss whole squash in a little olive oil and throw it on the barbecue grill for a few minutes.

1. In a large, flat-bottom wok or Dutch oven, heat sesame and vegetable oils until hot but not smoking. Add garlic, ginger, and onion and sauté for 1 minute.
2. Add pattypan squash and sauté until squash is crisp-tender, about 3 to 5 minutes. Sprinkle with soy sauce and salt and pepper to taste. Add cilantro just before serving.

Chapter 4

Boiled in Oil: Fondue
Bourguignon and Other
Oil-Based Fondues

Dinner at Eight

Basic meat and potatoes become haute fare in this easy-to-prepare dinner party menu. Just make sure guests have a fondue pot within reach—you may want to plan on one pot for every three or four guests.

MENU

Endive Stuffed with Salmon Tartare

Chardonnay

Fondue Bourguignon

Roasted Fingerling Potatoes with Garlic
and Rosemary

Sautéed Baby Green Beans

Warm Baguettes with Garlic-Parsley Butter

Cabernet Sauvignon

Coffee Crème Brûlée with Chocolate Shortbread

Endive Stuffed with Salmon Tartare

Serves 8

4 heads endive
1 pound skinless sushi-grade salmon
⅓ cup red onion, finely chopped
2 tablespoons parsley, minced
1 tablespoon lemon zest, grated
2 tablespoons extra-virgin olive oil
Salt and fresh-ground pepper to taste
Capers

Crisp, fresh endive leaves make great edible spoons!

1. Trim endives and separate leaves. Allow 3–4 large leaves per person.
2. Finely chop salmon and toss together with onion, parsley, lemon zest, and olive oil. Sprinkle with salt and pepper.
3. Spoon a small amount of tartare into the base end of each endive leaf. Garnish each with a caper.

Fishy Business

Raw fish dishes must be made with high-quality, super-fresh fish. If you're squeamish about serving raw salmon, substitute smoked salmon or cooked lump crabmeat for this dish.

Fondue Bourguignon

Serves 8

4 pounds beef tenderloin
Salt and fresh-ground black pepper,
    to taste
1 pound small white button mushrooms
5–6 cups peanut oil
2 cups Béarnaise sauce
2 cups tomato-basil sauce

Real beef tenderloin is a splurge, but definitely worth the cost!

1. Cut tenderloin into 1-inch cubes. Sprinkle lightly with salt and pepper and place in 1 or 2 serving bowls. Keep chilled until ready to serve. Wash mushrooms and place in bowls.
2. Add oil to 1 or more fondue pots, making each pot no more than ⅓ full. Heat oil to 325°F–350°F.
3. Guests should skewer beef cubes with fondue forks and deep fry in oil for 2–3 minutes, depending on desired level of doneness. Mushrooms should be dipped just long enough to heat through.
4. Spoon Béarnaise and tomato sauces into individual bowls for dipping.

. . . .

Make a Classic Béarnaise

Place one stick of softened butter, 4 egg yolks, and 4 tablespoons tarragon vinegar in the top of a double boiler. Whisk over simmering water until butter is melted and ingredients are well combined. Add another stick of butter, 1 tablespoon at a time, whisking until each addition is melted and mixture is thick. Whisk in a few tablespoons of chopped fresh herbs and serve immediately.

Roasted Fingerling Potatoes with Garlic and Rosemary

For a lively dish, mix red, white, and purple fingerling potatoes together.

Serves 8

5 pounds fingerling potatoes
⅓ cup olive oil
4 cloves garlic, pressed
3 tablespoons rosemary leaves
Salt and pepper to taste

1. Scrub fingerling potatoes. Trim obvious blemishes, but do not peel.
2. Combine garlic and olive oil. Place potatoes in a bowl or baking dish. Drizzle oil-garlic mixture over potatoes and toss to coat.
3. Sprinkle potatoes with rosemary, salt, and pepper and place in a shallow baking dish. Bake at 350°F for 30 minutes, or until tender.

For Garlic Lovers Only

Giant elephant garlic cloves caramelize and become buttery soft as they roast. For a variation on this dish, skip the pressed garlic. Instead, add 8–10 peeled elephant garlic cloves to the pan with the potatoes. Coat with olive oil and rosemary and bake as directed.

Coffee Crème Brûlée

Serves 8

4 egg yolks
2 whole eggs
⅓ cup superfine sugar
3 cups heavy cream
1½ tablespoons instant espresso powder
1 tablespoon Kahlua
1 cup light brown sugar

Nothing elicits "oohs" and "aahs" like a silken crème brûlée.

1. In a large bowl, whisk together egg yolks, eggs, and sugar.
2. Place heavy cream and espresso powder in a heavy saucepan over medium heat. Stir until powder is dissolved and mixture just comes to a boil. Stir in Kahlua.
3. Slowly pour hot cream into egg mixture in a steady stream, whisking constantly. Pour mixture back into saucepan and cook over low heat, stirring, until mixture coats the back of a wooden spoon.
4. Pour the mixture into 8 ramekins. Place ramekins in a roasting pan and fill pan with water to reach at least halfway up the sides of the ramekins. Bake at 300°F for 40 minutes, or until crème brûlées are set but still jiggly.
5. Remove the ramekins from the water and allow to cool slightly. Then cover the ramekins and chill for 4 hours. Just before serving, sprinkle brown sugar over ramekins and place under a hot broiler for 2–4 minutes—just long enough for the sugar to caramelize. Serve immediately.

· ·

Carrying a Torch

If you plan to make crème brûlée often, it's worth investing in a small kitchen torch. They're relatively inexpensive and operate on butane. With a torch, you can caramelize the sugar coating quickly, without turning on the broiler.

Chocolate Shortbread

Serves 12

1 cup butter
1 cup confectioners' sugar
2 cups all-purpose flour
Pinch of salt
1 tablespoon vanilla extract
3 ounces bittersweet chocolate, melted
3 tablespoons white or Turbinado sugar

Crumbly, rich shortbread makes a perfect foil for custards and frozen desserts.

1. With a hand-held mixer, cream together butter and confectioners' sugar until light and fluffy.
2. Whisk together salt and flour, stirring to break up any lumps in the mixture. Slowly stir flour into the butter and sugar. Stir in vanilla and melted chocolate and mix until blended.
3. Roll mixture into a ball, wrap in plastic wrap, and refrigerate for 1 hour.
4. Spread mixture onto waxed paper and cut into 2 dozen large cookies, using a heart or circle-shaped cookie cutter. Sprinkle each cookie with sugar and place on a greased cookie sheet. Bake at 300°F for 15–20 minutes.

. . . .

Shortbread Shortcut

If you're in a hurry, don't bother with cookie cutters. Just press the shortbread mixture into a greased baking pan, cook for 25–30 minutes, then cut the shortbread into bars.

Celebration of Summer Fondue

A sunset cocktail party on the patio or deck starts with platters of colorful produce, a fragrant pot of Bagna Cauda or "hot bath" for dipping, good wine, and good friends.

MENU

Fresh Vegetable Basket

Bagna Cauda Fondue

Antipasto Roll-Ups

Hot Peppered Olives

Ciabatta Bread

Barolo and Pinot Grigio Wines

Miniature White Peach Tarts

Italian Roast Coffee

Bagna Cauda Fondue

Serves 12

6 ounces anchovies, drained

4–5 large cloves garlic, peeled

1½ cups butter

⅔ cup olive oil

Fresh-ground black pepper to taste

This classic Italian dish hails from the gastronomically rich Piedmont region, home of white truffles, great wines, and wonderful antipasti. Veggies aren't actually cooked in this fragrant fondue— merely coated and warmed.

1. Place anchovies and garlic in a food processor and pulse until mixture forms a paste.
2. Heat butter and oil together in a pan until butter is melted and mixture is hot. Remove from heat and whisk anchovy-garlic paste into the hot oil, stirring until well blended. Add pepper to taste.
3. Pour hot mixture into a fondue pot and set over heating source. Dip bread and fresh vegetables into mixture.

. . . .

Summer Cornucopia

Serve Bagna Cauda with an overflowing basket or platter that speaks to the color and abundance of the season. Combine broccoli and cauliflower florets, strips of colorful peppers, blanched asparagus and artichoke hearts, cucumbers, carrots, celery, radishes, grape tomatoes, summer squash, mushrooms, and celery for a beautiful mix.

Antipasto Roll-Ups

Serves 12

12 10-inch wraps in assorted flavors
1 cup mayonnaise
¼ cup pesto sauce, prepared
1 pound Genoa salami, thinly sliced
1 pound prosciutto, sliced
1 pound mortadella, sliced
1 pound hard salami or pepperoni, sliced
1 pound provolone cheese, sliced
1 pound mozzarella cheese, sliced

Flatbread "wrappers" turn traditional meat and cheese rolls into mini sandwiches.

1. Arrange flatbread wraps—preferably 4 each of spinach, tomato, and wheat—on a large work surface. Mix together mayonnaise and pesto sauce and lightly coat the center of each wrap with pesto-mayonnaise.
2. Cover 3 wraps with Genoa salami, 3 with prosciutto, 3 with mortadella, and 3 with hard salami or pepperoni. Divide mozzarella and provolone over wraps as desired.
3. Tightly roll each wrap into a long tube. Place 8 colorful toothpicks along each roll, evenly spaced. Slice each roll between toothpicks and place skewered spirals on a service platter.

Hot Peppered Olives

Serves 12

3 cups mixed olives, drained
½ cup extra-virgin olive oil
2 large cloves garlic, minced
3 tablespoons hot pepper flakes
½ teaspoon lemon zest, grated

A variety of black and green olives make this dish both colorful and flavorful. For a less piquant version, substitute fresh chopped herbs for some of the pepper flakes.

1. Place olives in a glass or china bowl.
2. Heat oil over medium heat until just warm. Add garlic, pepper flakes, and lemon zest. Pour flavored oil over the olives. Toss until well mixed.
3. Cover bowl and refrigerate for at least 24 hours, stirring occasionally. Uncover and serve.

Small Dishes, Big Flavor

Punctuate your table with bowls of spiced or pickled vegetables, caramelized onions, marinated artichokes and mushrooms, pan-roasted pine nuts, olives, sesame crisps, and dried apricots. These little palate zingers will add interesting colors and textures to your buffet.

Miniature White Peach Tarts

Serves 12

3 cups all-purpose flour
1 teaspoon salt
4 tablespoons sugar
1 cup shortening
1 egg, beaten
⅓ cup cold water
3 cups white peaches, peeled and finely chopped
2 cups sweetened whipped cream

> Sweet-dough pie crust makes these super-simple morsels distinctive.

1. Combine flour, salt, and sugar in a large bowl. Add shortening and cut with 2 knives or a pastry cutter until mixture resembles coarse meal.
2. With a fork, mix in egg. Then add water and work dough until all liquid is absorbed and mixture holds together in a ball. Wrap dough and refrigerate for 2 hours.
3. Press small bits of dough into a nonstick mini-muffin pan, making 24 miniature pie shells. Bake at 350°F for 10–15 minutes or just until crust is browned.
4. Remove muffin pans from oven and allow to cool. Remove tart shells from pan and place on a serving platter. Using a slotted spoon, distribute chopped peaches among miniature tart shells. Just before serving, place a dollop of sweetened whipped cream on each tart.

A Sweet Balance

Juicy, ripe summer fruits can shine on the dessert table with very little gilding. Sweet pie crust, meringue shells, or plain cake usually provides all of the "sweetening" required for a bowl of berries, sliced peaches, chopped plums, or nectarines. Top the fruit with lightly sweetened whipped cream, sweetened vanilla yogurt, or caramel-laced crème fraiche for an extra flourish.

Southern Fried Fondue

Whether your laid-back fish feast takes place on a coastal cottage dock or an uptown patio, this menu will evoke memories of shade trees and lazy summer afternoons.

MENU

Fried Fish Fondue

Tartar Sauce

Corn Salsa

Spicy Boiled Potatoes

Coleslaw

Field Peas

Cheesy Corn Bread Muffins

Cantaloupe

Lemon Pound Cake

Iced Tea with Mint

Fried Fish Fondue

Serves 8

3 pounds catfish or grouper fillets

2 cups all-purpose flour, divided use

1 tablespoon salt

1 teaspoon cayenne pepper

1 teaspoon black pepper

½ teaspoon garlic powder

2 eggs

3 tablespoons half-and-half

½ cup cornmeal

1 cup corn flour

1 cup panko bread crumbs

5 cups peanut oil

A combination of coatings—cornmeal, flour, and panko bread flakes—gives fish a flavorful, crunchy coating that can't be achieved with flour or cornmeal alone.

1. Rinse fillets and pat dry. Cut into 1-inch cubes.
2. In a bowl, combine 1 cup flour with salt, cayenne pepper, black pepper, and garlic powder. Stir with a whisk. Toss fish cubes in seasoned flour and lightly coat.
3. In large bowl, whisk together eggs and half-and-half. In a deep baking dish, mix together cornmeal, corn flour, bread crumbs, and remaining cup of flour.
4. Dip fish cubes in egg mixture, then coat with flour-crumb mixture and place in a shallow casserole or serving platter. Cover and refrigerate until ready to use.
5. Fill 1 or 2 fondue pots with oil no more than 1/3 full. Heat to 350°F. Guests should skewer fish with fondue forks, then place in oil until brown and crispy, about 3–4 minutes.

Corn Salsa

Serves 8

*6 cups yellow and white corn
    kernels*
1½ cups zucchini, diced
1 cup grape tomatoes, halved
1 red bell pepper, diced
1 jalapeño pepper, minced
1 small sweet onion, finely chopped
¼ cup cilantro, minced
Juice of 2 limes
½ teaspoon cumin
Salt to taste

Corn freshly cut from the cob and blanched makes this dish taste amazingly sweet and fragrant. However, if you're pressed for time, thawed frozen corn will do.

1. If corn is fresh, cook until just crisp and tender. If frozen, thaw.
2. Toss together corn, zucchini, tomatoes, bell pepper, jalapeño pepper, onion, and cilantro.
3. Drizzle lime juice over mixture and fold until blended.
4. Sprinkle with cumin and salt to taste. Cover and refrigerate.

Salsa Savvy

Black beans or black-eyed peas can be substituted for corn in this salsa recipe. To make fruit salsa, toss diced peaches or mangoes with minced onion, peppers, cilantro, and lime juice.

Spicy Boiled Potatoes

Serves 8

1 *head garlic*
1 *tablespoon olive oil*
3 *pounds small red creamer potatoes*
1 *tablespoon Old Bay Seasoning*
1 *tablespoon cayenne pepper*
1 *tablespoon black pepper*
1 *tablespoon salt*
5 *tablespoons butter*

If you can't find small creamer potatoes, use red potatoes, halved or quartered.

1. Remove the outer layers of peelings from the garlic head. Coat head with olive oil and wrap in foil. Bake at 350°F for 1 hour. (This step can be done in advance.)
2. Place washed, unpeeled potatoes, Old Bay, peppers, and salt in a large pot. Cover with cold water and bring to a boil. Cook until potatoes are tender, about 15–20 minutes.
3. Drain potatoes in a colander.
4. Place butter in the empty boiling pot. Heat until melted. Press soft garlic from cloves and whisk into butter. Toss potatoes in garlic butter and serve.

Coleslaw

Serves 8

1 *medium head cabbage*

2 *carrots*

1 *green onion*

1 *cup mayonnaise*

1 *tablespoon sour cream*

3 *tablespoons sugar*

¼ *cup vinegar*

¼ *teaspoon poppy or celery seeds (optional)*

Black pepper to taste

> Coleslaw is a Dutch dish (*kool* is Dutch for cabbage) that appeared in North America during colonial days and has remained a favorite ever since.

1. Trim and finely shred cabbage, carrots, and green onion. Place in a bowl.
2. Whisk together mayonnaise, sour cream, sugar, and vinegar.
3. Toss mayonnaise dressing with cabbage mixture, sprinkle with seeds and black pepper. Cover and refrigerate until ready to serve.

Slaw Smarts

Shredded radishes, broccoli stems, firm apples, jicama, and raw turnips can all be used in addition to, or instead of, cabbage to make interesting slaws. And for a low-carb version of the popular salad, replace sugar with your favorite sugar substitute.

Cheesy Corn Bread Muffins

Serves 8

1½ cups stone ground cornmeal
1½ cups flour
1 tablespoon baking powder
1½ teaspoons salt
⅓ cup sugar
2 eggs
1 ⅓ cups milk
⅓ cup melted butter
1 14-ounce can creamed corn
1½ cups shredded Cheddar cheese

There's virtually no difference between white and yellow corn meal. One is made from dried and milled white corn, the other from yellow corn. Yet many cooks vehemently defend using one over the other. White cornmeal, they say, is smoother and sweeter. Yellow corn meal has a more pronounced flavor and better visual appeal. Either can be used in recipes calling for cornmeal.

1. In a large bowl, combine cornmeal, flour, baking powder, salt, and sugar. Whisk to remove any lumps.
2. In another bowl, whisk together eggs, milk, butter, and creamed corn. Add wet mixture to dry mixture and stir until just blended. Stir in shredded cheese.
3. Divide mixture over 2 dozen well-buttered muffin cups. Bake at 350°F until muffin tops are just starting to brown, about 15 minutes. Serve with butter.

Lemon Pound Cake

Serves 12

1 pound unsalted butter, softened

3 cups sugar

6 eggs

½ cup plus 2 tablespoons lemon juice

1 cup buttermilk

1 teaspoon vanilla extract

2 teaspoons baking powder

4 cups all-purpose flour

½ teaspoon salt

1 cup confectioners' sugar

Every Southern cook has a great pound cake recipe in his or her repertoire.

1. In a large mixing bowl, blend butter and sugar with a hand mixer until creamy. Add eggs one at a time, mixing well after each addition.
2. Add 2 tablespoons lemon juice to butter-sugar mixture.
3. Combine buttermilk and vanilla. In a separate bowl, whisk together baking powder, flour, and salt.
4. Add ½ of the flour mixture to the butter and eggs and beat on medium speed until blended. Slowly add the buttermilk and vanilla and mix well. Add the remaining flour mixture and beat well. Batter should be thick and perfectly smooth.
5. Pour pound cake batter into a greased and floured bundt pan. Bake at 350°F for 50–60 minutes or until tester comes out clean. Allow cake to cool in the pan for 15 minutes, then turn onto a serving plate.
6. Whisk together confectioners' sugar with ½ cup fresh lemon juice. Poke toothpick holes in the top of the warm cake. Pour lemon glaze over the top.

Veggie Feast Fondue

Serve this assortment of small bites together for a meatless meal or hot hors d'oeuvre table, or serve one or two as dinner party side dishes to a simple roast chicken.

MENU

Tempura Veggie Skewers with Ginger-Soy Sauce

Swiss Potato Balls with Herbed Crème Fraiche

Nutty Spinach Balls with Tomato Coulis

Falafel Fondue

Cucumber and Asparagus Salad

Raspberry Sorbet in Chocolate Cups

Tempura Veggie Skewers with Ginger-Soy Sauce

Serves 6

You can buy ginger-flavored soy sauce to replace the fresh ginger in this recipe.

2 cups broccoli florets
2 cups cauliflower florets
2 cups small white mushrooms
2 cups bell pepper, sliced into strips
3 large eggs
1 cup ice water
1 teaspoon salt

1 cup all-purpose flour
5 cups peanut oil
1 tablespoon sesame oil
1 cup soy sauce
2 tablespoons fresh ginger, grated

1. Arrange vegetables on skewers, with 2–3 pieces on each, separated by bell pepper strips. Place skewers on a serving platter.
2. In a bowl, beat together eggs, water, salt and flour. Cover and refrigerate until read to use. Divide batter into 2 bowls for easy dipping.
3. Heat peanut oil in 1 or more fondue pots. Pots should not be more than ⅓ full.
4. Combine sesame oil, soy sauce, and ginger. Divide into 6 dipping bowls for guests.
5. Guests should dip veggie skewers in batter, then immediately dip into hot fondue pot. Fry in hot oil until batter is brown and crispy. Dip in ginger-soy sauce and enjoy.

. . . .

The Crunch Factor

With the exception of spongy mushrooms, fondue-fried vegetables tend to remain very crisp inside. If you prefer your vegetables a little more tender (but never mushy), you can blanch them for 1 minute in boiling water. Dry and cool completely before dipping in tempura batter.

Crème Fraiche

Serves 4 to 6

1 cup heavy whipping cream
2 tablespoons buttermilk

Use pasteurized, rather than ultra-pasteurized, cream in this recipe. The ultra-pasteurized kind takes longer to thicken.

1. Combine whipping cream with buttermilk. Pour into a glass jar, cover, and let stand at room temperature for 24 hours or until thick.
2. Stir well, cover, and refrigerate. Will keep in refrigerator for up to 10 days.

Swiss Potato Balls with Herbed Crème Fraiche

Serves 6

1 cup prepared crème fraiche (above)
2 tablespoons fresh herbs, minced
2½ cups potatoes, dry and coarsely mashed
1 cup Swiss cheese, shredded

2 eggs
¼ teaspoon nutmeg
Salt and pepper to taste
1 tablespoon milk
2 cups seasoned bread crumbs
5 cups peanut oil

1. Stir fresh herbs into cold crème fraiche and set aside.
2. In a large bowl, combine mashed potatoes, cheese, 1 egg, nutmeg, salt, and pepper. Mix until blended, then shape into 1-inch balls.
3. In a small bowl, beat remaining egg with tablespoon milk. Dip potato balls in egg wash, then coat with seasoned bread crumbs.
4. Heat peanut oil in one or more fondue pots filled no more than ⅓ full. Guests can skewer potato balls or lower into the oil using a wire strainer. Cook until browned and dip in crème fraiche.

Nutty Spinach Balls with Tomato Coulis

Serves 6

Try Asiago cheese bread or herbed focaccia to make bread cubes.

2 cups stale bread, cubed

1 cup boiling broth, milk, or water

1 cup fresh spinach, cooked and drained

2 cloves garlic

¼ cup fresh parsley

2 green onions

Dash Tabasco

1 egg

Salt and pepper to taste

1 cup pecans, chopped

5 cups peanut oil

Tomato Coulis (page 122)

1. In a large bowl, pour boiling liquid over bread cubes. Cover and set aside.
2. In a food processor, combine spinach, garlic, parsley, and green onions. Pulse until ingredients are finely chopped. Add spinach mixture to moistened bread cubes, along with Tabasco, egg, and salt and pepper. Mix ingredients until blended. Form mixture into 1-inch balls.
3. Roll balls in chopped pecans, pressing gently while rolling, and set aside.
4. Heat oil into one or more fondue pots, taking care not to fill pots more than ⅓ full. Guests can skewer balls or use wire strainers to dip in hot oil.
5. Spinach balls should be dipped in tomato coulis before eating.

Tomato Coulis

Serves 4 to 6

*3 cups tomatoes, peeled, seeded,
and diced*
2 tablespoons fresh basil, chopped
Salt and pepper to taste

For a richer coulis, stir 1–2 tablespoons of
cream into the purée.

1. Use vine-ripened tomatoes or the ripest plum tomatoes available. Place tomatoes in a large saucepan and cook over medium heat, stirring frequently, for 2 minutes.
2. With potato masher, break up the tomato pieces. Cook another 3–4 minutes, or until excess liquid has evaporated.
3. For a smooth purée, pulse briefly in a food processor. Stir in chopped basil and season with salt and pepper. Makes ¾–1 cup coulis.

Getting Saucy

Colorful fruit and veggie coulises are among the simplest of sauces. All you have to do is purée, season, and strain raw, roasted or lightly-sautéed produce. Bell peppers, tomatoes, berries, peaches, nectarines, mangoes, and plums are all good candidates.

Falafel Fondue

Serves 6

2 cups chick peas, soaked overnight
1 onion, finely chopped
¼ cup fresh parsley, minced
¼ cup cilantro, minced
2 cloves garlic, pressed
1 teaspoon baking powder
½ teaspoon cumin
¼ teaspoon sesame oil
Salt and pepper to taste
5 cups peanut oil or combination vegetable and olive oil

Dried, soaked fava beans can be substituted for chick peas in this popular Middle Eastern snack.

1. Drain chick peas. Place in a food processor with onion, parsley, cilantro, and garlic. Pulse a few times.
2. Add baking powder, cumin, sesame oil, salt and pepper. Pulse until mixture forms a smooth paste.
3. Roll paste into firm 1-inch balls.
4. Heat oil into 1 or more fondue pots, taking care not to fill pots more than ⅓ full. Guests can use fondue forks to skewer firm falafel balls, or use wire strainers to dip falafel in hot oil.
5. Cook until balls are brown and crisp. Dip in tahini before eating.

. . . .

Quick Tahini Dip

Sesame tahini is a peanut butter-like paste that adds flavor to many Middle Eastern dishes. To make tahini sauce, season tahini with a clove of pressed garlic, lemon juice, salt, and pepper. Stir until smooth. For a thinner sauce, add more lemon juice or a little warm water.

Cucumber and Asparagus Salad

Serves 6

½ pound fresh asparagus spears
2 large cucumbers
3 ripe tomatoes
1 small red onion, minced
⅔ cup toasted pine nuts
⅔ cup extra-virgin olive oil
⅓ cup balsamic vinegar

½ teaspoon Dijon mustard
1 clove garlic, pressed
4 cups romaine lettuce,
    washed and torn
Fresh-ground black pepper to taste

> Fresh asparagus and toasted pine nuts make this salad extraordinary.

1. Wash asparagus and cut off tough stems. (Discard 1–2 inches depending on the size of the spears.) Blanch in boiling water for 1–2 minutes, until spears are bright green and still firm. Remove from boiling water and rinse with cold water. Drain well.
2. Slice spears into ½-inch pieces, leaving tips intact. Peel and dice cucumbers. Trim and dice tomatoes.
3. Combine asparagus, cucumbers, and tomatoes with onion and pine nuts in a large bowl.
4. Whisk together olive oil, vinegar, mustard, and garlic. Pour over asparagus mixture. Toss well, cover, and refrigerate for 15–30 minutes.
5. Arrange romaine leaves over the bottom of a shallow bowl. Stir asparagus mixture well. With a slotted spoon, pile asparagus salad over romaine leaves, sprinkle with pepper, and serve.

· ·

Warm and Toasty

Toasted pine nuts add a rich, satisfying flavor to salads and they smell heavenly while toasting. To toast, pour nuts into a dry, heavy skillet and cook over medium-high heat, shaking and turning frequently, until kernels just start to brown. Remove from pan immediately and allow to cool on a plate.

Caribbean Swing Fondue Party

The Caribbean Islands have a rich culinary heritage, combining influences from Latin America, Africa, Europe, and Asia.

MENU

Chopped Salad

Jerk Shrimp, Pork, and Chicken

Coconut Rice

Pineapple Salsa

Black-and-White Bean Salsa

Fresh Heirloom Tomato and Lime Salsa

Roasted Tomato Salsa

Pigeon Peas

Sliced Papaya

Rum Cake with Guava Glaze and Ice Cream

Chopped Salad

Serves 8

5 cups iceberg and romaine lettuce,
    chopped
1 cup red cabbage, chopped
1 cup carrots, finely diced
1 cup radishes (unpeeled), finely diced
1 cup celery, finely diced
1 cup cauliflower, finely chopped
½ cup red bell pepper, finely diced
½ cup yellow summer squash, finely diced
1 cup green peas or edamame, cooked and chilled
⅓ cup red onion, minced
1 cup extra-virgin olive oil
⅓ cup red wine vinegar
1 teaspoon Dijon mustard
1 clove garlic, minced
1 teaspoon soy sauce
2 tablespoons sugar

There's nothing fancy about these ingredients, but the bright colors and crisp textures complement the rest of the menu nicely.

1. In a large glass salad bowl, place chopped lettuces. Spread cabbage over lettuces in a single layer.
2. In a separate bowl, combine carrots, radishes, celery, cauliflower, bell pepper, squash, peas or edamame, and red onion.
3. Whisk together olive oil, vinegar, mustard, garlic, soy, and sugar. Pour over chopped vegetables and mix well.
4. Spoon chopped vegetables over lettuces in salad bowl and serve.

. . . .

Chop Shop

To turn a chopped salad into an entrée, add diced salami or ham, Swiss or provolone cheese, and chicken or turkey to the veggie mixture. Thousand Island salad dressing makes a nice accompaniment, although it does obscure the colors of the ingredients a bit.

Jerk Shrimp, Pork, and Chicken

Serves 8

1 pound boneless chicken breast

1 pound boneless pork tenderloin

1 pound medium shrimp, peeled

1 cup orange juice

2 tablespoons lime juice

6 tablespoons jerk seasoning

3 tablespoons sauce and gravy flour

5 cups peanut or other vegetable oil

Usually jerked meats would be prepared on a grill. However, frying small pieces in hot oil sears in the fragrant, spicy seasoning just as well.

1. Dice chicken and pork into 1-inch cubes. Place chicken, pork, and shrimp in separate bowls. Combine orange juice and lime juice and pour equal amounts over each bowl. Mix well and let stand 15 minutes.
2. Mix jerk seasoning with sauce and gravy flour in a shallow bowl. Drain chicken, pork, and shrimp. Coat each meat cube or shrimp with seasoning. Arrange on a serving platter.
3. Heat oil into 1 or more fondue pots, taking care not to fill pots more than ⅓ full. Guests can skewer cubes of meat or shrimp and fry in the fondue pot until morsels are browned and crisp outside, but opaque inside.
4. Serve with tomato, mango, and black bean salsas and coconut rice.

. . . .

Jerk Blends

Jerk seasonings are readily available in most supermarkets. The blends usually contain various amounts of thyme, allspice, cinnamon, nutmeg, sage, garlic powder, cayenne, black pepper, and Scotch bonnet peppers. The result is a hot-sweet flavor that's both complex and compelling.

Coconut Rice

Serves 8

3 cups jasmine rice
1½ cups coconut milk
2 cups water
1 cup unsweetened coconut, shredded
Slivered almonds

This rice smells absolutely heavenly while cooking.

1. Combine rice, coconut milk, and water in a heavy saucepan with a lid. Bring to a boil.
2. Turn heat to low, cover, and let cook for 22 minutes.
3. With a wooden spoon, stir in shredded coconut. Garnish with almonds, if desired.

Pineapple Salsa

Serves 8

4 cups fresh pineapple, finely diced
1 cup celery, minced
1 red bell pepper, diced
1 small red onion, minced
1 jalapeño pepper, minced
⅓ cup fresh parsley, minced

Use potholders to hold rough pineapple skin while peeling the fruit. Cut off the top, bottom, and peel, then slice fruit from the tough core in four wide strips. After that, strips should be easy to dice.

1. Combine all ingredients in a large bowl. Toss to combine.
2. Cover and refrigerate for at least 1 hour before serving.

Black-and-White Bean Salsa

Serves 8

2 cups white canellini beans
2 cups black beans
1 green bell pepper, diced
2 jalapeño peppers, minced
1 red onion, minced
⅓ cup cilantro, minced
⅓ cup red wine vinegar
1 teaspoon sugar

This salsa makes a colorful addition to any buffet table. Beans should be cooked until tender, but not mushy. If you use canned beans, rinse before adding to other ingredients.

1. In a large bowl, combine beans, bell pepper and jalapeño pepper, red onion, and cilantro.
2. Whisk together vinegar and sugar. Pour over remaining ingredients and mix well. Cover and refrigerate for at least 1 hour before serving.

Fresh Heirloom Tomato and Lime Salsa

Serves 8

5 large heirloom-variety
    multi-colored tomatoes
2 jalapeño peppers, minced
⅓ cup cilantro, minced
1 small onion, minced
Juice of 2 large limes
Salt and pepper to taste

To make a milder salsa, remove and discard seeds from jalapeños before adding to the mix. For a less spicy salsa, substitute sweet bell peppers for hot peppers.

1. Finely dice large heirloom tomatoes.
2. Place in a large bowl with jalapeño, onion, and lime juice.
3. Add salt and pepper to taste. Chill before serving.

Roasted Tomato Salsa

Serves 8

16 *plum tomatoes,*
  halved lengthwise
1 *green bell pepper,*
  halved lengthwise
1 *large onion, halved*
2 *cloves garlic, minced*
2 *jalapeño peppers, minced*
2 *tablespoons olive oil*
⅓ *cup balsamic vinegar*

Fire roasting gives tomatoes a rich, smoky flavor. Use this salsa as an occasional alternative to the fresh tomato version.

1. Place plum tomatoes, bell pepper, and onion in a grill vegetable basket. Roast over medium-hot coals just until tomatoes begin to soften, 5–10 minutes. Set aside to cool.
2. Finely chop tomatoes, bell pepper, and onion. Mix with garlic and jalapeños.
3. Whisk together olive oil and vinegar and add to tomato mixture. Chill before serving.

Rum Cake with Guava Glaze

Serves 12

1 pound butter, softened

2½ cups brown sugar

½ cup sugar

6 eggs

3 cups all-purpose flour

1 teaspoon baking powder

½ teaspoon salt

1 cup milk

1 cup dark rum

1 cup guava jelly

This glaze is only slightly cooked—not enough to burn off the alcohol. For a non-alcoholic version, substitute ½ cup of fruit juice with a teaspoon of rum extract for the rum.

1. In a large bowl, combine butter and sugars. Beat with a mixer on medium speed until butter is creamy and sugar is blended.
2. Add eggs, 1 at a time, and beat until mixture is light and fluffy.
3. Whisk together flour, baking powder, and salt.
4. Add ½ the flour the mixture, beat until blended. Add the milk and the remaining flour. Mix well. Add 2 tablespoons of rum to the batter and beat to incorporate.
5. Pour batter into a greased and floured tube pan. Bake at 350°F for 60 minutes. Let cool in pan for 15 minutes, then turn onto a serving plate. Let cool completely.
6. Warm guava jelly in a saucepan until liquefied. Stir in remaining rum and cook over low heat until just warmed. With a skewer, poke holes all over the top of the cake. Slowly pour guava-rum glaze over the top of the cake, allowing as much as possible to soak into the cake.

Shish Kebab Social

This easy-to-make supper offers distinctive flavors and Mediterranean dishes your guests aren't likely to encounter often.

MENU

Marinated Lamb or Beef Kebab Fondue

Raita Sauce

Pita Bread

Tomato, Black Olive, and Feta Cheese Salad

Tabbouleh

Hummus

Red and Green Grapes

Fresh Figs and Custard Sauce

Marinated Lamb or Beef Kebab Fondue

Serves 8

3 pounds boneless leg of lamb or
*   London broil*
1 cup olive oil
½ cup balsamic vinegar
6 cloves garlic, chopped
1 large onion, sliced
1 green bell pepper, sliced
3 tablespoons dried oregano
Salt and pepper to taste
5 cups vegetable oil

The oregano-laced marinade gives this dish its distinctive flavor.

1. Cut lamb or beef into 1-inch cubes. Place cubes in a large resealable plastic bag.
2. Whisk together olive oil, balsamic vinegar, garlic, onion, bell pepper, and oregano. Pour over lamb or beef cubes, carefully press out excess air, and reseal bag. Place bag on a dish in the refrigerator for 24 hours, turning occasionally.
3. Remove meat cubes from bag and discard marinade. Place beef or lamb on a platter and sprinkle with salt and pepper.
4. Heat oil in 1 or more fondue pots, making sure pots are no more than ⅓ full. When hot, skewer meat cubes with fondue forks and cook to taste.
5. Serve with raita sauce (page 134) and small pita loaves.

. . . .

Kebabs by Any Other Name

Shish Kebab means "skewered meat," and the dish originated in Turkey. However, it's now found all over the Middle East and served worldwide under a variety of spellings. Classic Shish Kebab is cooked over a fire or broiled. However, our fried fondue version tastes just great!

Raita Sauce

Serves 8

2 cups plain yogurt
1 cup sour cream
1½ cups cucumber, peeled and shredded
1 tablespoon green onion, finely chopped
½ teaspoon cumin
¼ teaspoon curry powder
¼ teaspoon turmeric
1 tablespoon sugar
Salt and pepper to taste

> This refreshingly tart sauce can double as a salad dressing.

1. Whisk together yogurt and sour cream.
2. Stir in cucumber and green onion.
3. Stir in cumin, curry powder, turmeric, sugar, salt, and pepper.
4. Cover and refrigerate until ready to use. Stir well before serving.

. . . .

Creamy Yogurt

Middle Eastern recipes often use a thick, creamy form of yogurt. To achieve a similar consistency, place plain, low-fat yogurt in a strainer lined with cheesecloth. Place strainer over a bowl and refrigerate for 24 hours. Discard liquid that collects in the bowl. Two cups of commercial yogurt will yield 1 cup of thick yogurt cream.

Tabbouleh

Serves 8

1 cup fine or medium bulgur wheat
2 cups boiling water
1 cup parsley, chopped
1 cup green onions, chopped
2 tablespoons fresh mint, minced
1 large cucumber, peeled and diced
2 very ripe tomatoes, diced
½ cup lemon juice
½ cup olive oil
Salt and pepper to taste

> This salad offers a healthy helping of whole grains, fresh veggies, and heart-smart olive oil.

1. Place bulgur wheat in a deep bowl. Pour boiling water into the bowl, cover loosely and set aside for 1 hour.
2. Drain bulgur wheat. In a large bowl, toss bulgur with parsley, green onion, mint, cucumber, and tomatoes.
3. Combine lemon juice and olive oil. Pour over tabbouleh, mix well, cover, and refrigerate for 1 hour or until chilled.

. . . .

Toasty Tabbouleh

If you have any tabbouleh left over, try this great meatless sandwich: Spread a small amount of mayonnaise inside a pita pocket, insert a slice of Swiss or provolone cheese, and fill with tabbouleh. Toast the sandwich in a press or wrap in foil and place on a cookie sheet with a heavy pie plate on top. Bake 5–10 minutes or just until warmed through.

Hummus

Serves 8

4 cups chickpeas, canned or cooked,
    drained
½ cup sesame tahini
¼ cup warm water
4 large cloves garlic
½ cup extra-virgin olive oil
Juice of 4 lemons
½ tablespoon cumin
2 tablespoons fresh parsley, chopped
Dash Tabasco
Salt and black pepper to taste

> Don't be afraid to add an extra spritz of lemon or clove of garlic to this dish.

1. Combine chickpeas, tahini, water, and garlic in a food processor. Process with a metal blade until beans are chopped and mixture is blended.
2. With processor running, slowly pour olive oil through the top chute. Turn processor off, scrape sides of bowl. Add lemon juice, cumin, parsley, hot sauce, and a small amount of salt and pepper.
3. Pulse until mixture forms a smooth paste. Adjust seasonings to taste.

Custard Sauce

Serves 8

6 egg yolks
½ cup sugar
2 cups half-and-half
1 teaspoon vanilla extract
2 tablespoons brandy (optional)

Rich custard sauce, also known as crème Anglaise, turns simple fresh or poached fruits into elegant, satisfying desserts.

1. In a large bowl, whisk together egg yolks and sugar until light-colored and thick.
2. Pour half-and-half into a saucepan and cook over medium heat until just scalded. Slowly pour hot cream into the egg mixture, whisking constantly to avoid cooking the eggs.
3. Pour egg and cream mixture into a saucepan and cook over medium heat, stirring constantly, until mixture is thick enough to coat a spoon. Stir in vanilla, and if desired, brandy. Allow to cool to room temperature, then refrigerate until ready to serve.

Chapter 5

Here's to Bacchus: Wine and Beer-Based Fondues

Tapas Fondue Party Menu

Spanish cuisine offers a nearly unlimited array of small dishes and the wonderful custom of building an early-evening meal around savory bites. Although it isn't traditional, there's no reason why fondue can't fit into a lovely evening of tapas and wine.

MENU

◇◇◇◇◇◇◇◇◇◇◇◇

Gazpacho

Sherry-Poached Chicken and Veal Fondue

Fritada Sauce

Mojo Verde

Potato Tortilla

Ham Croquettes

Garlic Shrimp

Vegetable Platter

Cava and Riojas

Marzipan Candy

Gazpacho

Serves 8

6 large ripe tomatoes, chopped
1 small red onion, chopped
1 cucumber, peeled and chopped
1 green pepper, seeded and chopped
2 cloves garlic, peeled and chopped
1 stalk celery, chopped
¼ cup fresh parsley
¼ cup red wine vinegar
¼ cup extra-virgin olive oil
1 teaspoon Worcestershire sauce
1 teaspoon sugar
3 cups tomato juice
1 large avocado, finely diced

Diced avocado adds delicious richness to this salad-in-a-cup. Also, be sure to use very ripe tomatoes for this recipe.

1. Combine all ingredients except tomato juice and avocado in a blender or food processor. Pulse until puréed.
2. Strain mixture through a coarse sieve into a glass bowl or pitcher. Press to extract all the juices. Stir in the tomato juice, cover, and refrigerate until well-chilled.
3. Just before serving, dice avocado. Pour gazpacho into soup cups and garnish with diced avocado.

. . . .

Avocado Savvy

Avocados don't ripen on the tree. They only begin to soften after picking. Very ripe avocados work well in guacamole and dips, but when dishes call for sliced or diced avocado, or for avocado halves, it's best to go with fruit that's firm but "gives" slightly when pressed.

Sherry-Poached Chicken and Veal Fondue

Serves 8

4 boneless, skinless chicken breast
    halves
8 veal cutlets, pounded thin
3 tablespoons olive oil
Salt and pepper to taste
2 cups fresh spinach leaves, stems removed
½ cup fresh parsley
6 cloves garlic, pressed
Dry Manzanilla sherry

> How much sherry you'll need depends largely on the size and depth of your fondue pots. Count on at least 3 cups per fondue pot.

1. With a sharp knife, reduce the thickness of the chicken breasts by slicing each piece in half vertically. With a stone or non-stick rolling pin, flatten each chicken slice into thin cutlets.
2. Coat top side of each chicken and veal cutlet with olive oil and sprinkle salt and pepper. In a food processor, finely chop spinach, parsley, and garlic. Sprinkle a thin layer of the spinach mixture over the top of each cutlet.
3. Working from the longest side, roll cutlets tightly into a pinwheel. Secure each pinwheel with a toothpick or skewer. Slice each pinwheel horizontally into 1-inch slices. Place alternating veal and chicken pinwheels on fondue skewers with 2 or 3 on each skewer.
4. Heat sherry on the stovetop until bubbles just start to appear around the edges. Pour hot sherry into 1 or more fondue pots. You should have enough to reach halfway up the edge of the pot. Guests can place skewers in simmering sherry until chicken and veal is thoroughly cooked. Serve with dipping sauces.

Fritada Sauce

Serves 8

½ cup olive oil
1 medium onion, finely chopped
4 cloves garlic, minced
2 medium green bell peppers, diced
3 large ripe tomatoes, diced
Salt to taste

> This simple sauce goes with chicken and veal fondue, but also with other dishes on the tapas table.

1. Heat olive oil in a heavy skillet. Add onion and garlic. Cook over medium-high heat, stirring often, until onions begin to brown.
2. Add green pepper and sauté for 5 minutes.
3. Add tomatoes and sauté for 5–7 minutes or until tomatoes are thoroughly cooked and sauce has thickened. Add salt to taste.

Mojo Verde

Serves 8

12 cloves garlic, peeled
1 cup cilantro leaves
½ teaspoon cumin
¾ cup white wine vinegar
1 cup olive oil
Salt to taste

> This herb sauce originated in the Canary Islands, where it's often served at tapas bars.

1. In a food processor, combine garlic, cilantro, cumin, and vinegar.
2. Pulse until finely chopped. With motor running, add olive oil in a thin stream until mixture is thick and blended.
3. Add salt to taste.

Potato Tortilla

Serves 8

4 large potatoes, peeled and diced
1 large onion, diced
½ cup olive oil
6 eggs
¼ cup half-and-half
Salt and pepper to taste

This Spanish dish is actually a potato omelet, or frittata, and bears no resemblance to Mexican flatbread.

1. Heat olive oil in a 10-inch skillet until hot. Add potatoes and onion and reduce heat to medium. Stir often and cook until potatoes and onions are tender, but not browned. With a slotted spoon, remove potatoes and onion from oil and place in a bowl.

2. Whisk together eggs and half-and-half. Pour over potatoes in bowl and let stand 10 minutes.

3. Remove excess oil from skillet, leaving about 3 tablespoons. Heat skillet over medium heat and pour in egg and potato mixture. Spread ingredients evenly over the skillet and reduce heat to medium-low. Cover skillet and cook for 6 minutes. Remove lid and cover skillet with a plate. Turn skillet and plate over so tortilla slides onto the plate. Add another 2 tablespoons of the reserved oil to the skillet. Slide the tortilla back into the skillet. Cover and cook for 6 more minutes. Let stand 10 minutes in the skillet, then slide onto a serving plate. Cool and cut into wedges.

Omelet Options

Sautéed peppers or tomato salsa makes great sauce for this dish, which is traditionally served at room temperature for tapas. In a pinch, the Potato Tortilla mixture can be poured into a cast-iron skillet or oiled baking dish and baked at 325°F for 20–35 minutes.

Ham Croquettes

Serves 8

¼ cup butter

¼ cup all-purpose flour

1 cup milk

¼ teaspoon black pepper

¼ cup parsley, minced

¼ cup celery, minced

¼ cup green onion, minced

½ teaspoon mustard, prepared

2 eggs, divided use

1½ cup ham, cooked and minced

1 cup fine bread crumbs

Vegetable oil for frying

> No Spanish tapas table would be complete without some form of crispy croquettes.

1. In a heavy saucepan, combine butter and flour. Stir with a whisk or wooden spoon until smooth and bubbly. Slowly whisk in milk and cook, stirring constantly, until mixture thickens. Add black pepper.

2. In a bowl, combine parsley, celery, green onion, mustard, 1 egg, and ham. Toss until blended. Stir ham mixture into thickened white sauce. Pour mixture into a shallow dish. Cover and refrigerate for 45 minutes, or until mixture can be shaped.

3. Whisk together remaining egg with a small amount of water. Pour bread crumbs onto a plate. With a small spoon, scoop up ham mixture and shape into 2-inch oblong balls. Gently dip into egg, then coat with bread crumbs. Set aside on a platter and continue forming croquettes. Mixture should yield 32–36 croquettes.

4. Heat about 2 inches of vegetable oil in a heavy frying pan. When oil is hot, slip croquettes in. Turn frequently and cook until browned on all sides. Drain on paper towel and keep warm until ready to serve.

Garlic Shrimp

Serves 8

1½ pounds medium shrimp,
    peeled and deveined
½ cup olive oil
6 cloves garlic, minced
1 tablespoon red pepper, crushed
½ teaspoon paprika
¼ cup parsley, finely chopped
2 tablespoons lemon juice
1 tablespoon brandy or sherry

Serve this dish in a hot earthenware dish or casserole while it is still sizzling.

1. Rinse shrimp and pat dry. In a large skillet, warm olive oil and garlic over medium-high heat. Add red pepper and paprika.
2. When garlic begins to brown, add shrimp. Cook on high heat, stirring occasionally for 1–2 minutes or until shrimp is just opaque. Sprinkle parsley on shrimp.
3. Combine lemon juice and brandy. Pour over shrimp and stir. Pour shrimp into a warm earthenware bowl and bring to the table immediately.

Sake Fondue for Two

This seductive supper bursts with lively, fresh flavors. It's satisfying without being too heavy, and best of all, it's very simple to prepare.

MENU

Tomato-Basil Bisque

Spinach Salad with Tangerine Vinaigrette

Savory Scallop and Sake Fondue

Zucchini and Peppers Fondue

Steamed Jasmine Rice

Wasabi Cream and Ginger-Soy Sauce

Sake or Sparkling Blanc de Blanc

Coeur a la Crème with Berries

Coffee and Grand Marnier

Tomato-Basil Bisque

Serves 2–3

1 tablespoon butter
1 shallot, minced
6 plum tomatoes, diced
1 teaspoon sugar
1 cup chicken broth
1 cup heavy cream
2 tablespoons fresh basil, chopped
Salt and fresh-ground pepper to taste

If you can't find ripe fresh tomatoes, buy a quality canned variety.

1. Melt butter over medium-high heat in a heavy saucepan. Add shallots and sauté until softened. Reserve ⅓ cup diced tomatoes. Put remaining tomatoes, sugar, and broth in saucepan. Bring to a boil, reduce heat to simmer, and cook for 30 minutes.
2. Press tomato mixture through a fine sieve. Return to saucepan, add diced tomatoes, and bring to a simmer. Add cream, mix well, and remove from heat.
3. Add fresh basil, salt, and pepper. Serve immediately.

Time-Saving Tip

Your favorite jar of spaghetti sauce can become the base for terrific soup. Just pour sauce into a pot; thin with a little broth; and add whatever fresh herbs, beans, leftover meats, or vegetables you have on hand. Simmer long enough to allow flavors to meld and voilá—homemade soup.

Tangerine Vinaigrette

Serves 2

⅓ cup fresh-squeezed tangerine juice
1 tablespoon lemon juice
⅔ cup extra-virgin olive oil
½ teaspoon Dijon mustard
1 teaspoon sugar

Prepare a no-fuss spinach salad with baby spinach leaves, sliced mushrooms, orange-flavored dried cranberries, pine nuts, and this dressing.

1. Pour all ingredients in a blender and pulse until blended. Toss with spinach salad or any fresh greens.

Savory Scallop and Sake Fondue

Serves 2–3

1 pound sea scallops
⅓ cup vegetable oil
1 tablespoon sesame oil
¼ cup soy sauce
2 tablespoons lime juice
1 tablespoon maple syrup
2 green onions, chopped
2–3 cups sake

Sea scallops are the large white scallops that sell for top price in fish markets. Bay scallops are less expensive, much smaller, and have a creamy color. For this dish, you'll want to splurge.

1. Rinse scallops and pat dry.
2. Combine vegetable oil, sesame oil, soy sauce, lime juice, maple syrup, and green onion. Pour into a resealable plastic bag. Place scallops in bag and refrigerate 6 hours or overnight.
3. Remove scallops from marinade and place on a platter with fondue forks or skewers. Heat sake to simmering and pour into a fondue pot, allowing pot to be ½ full. Skewer scallops and cook in sake until opaque.

Zucchini and Peppers Fondue

Serves 2

4 small zucchini
1 small red bell pepper
8 small white mushrooms
Salt and pepper to taste

1. Trim ends from zucchini and cut each into 3 pieces. Cut stem, seeds, and ribs from bell pepper and discard. Cut pepper into 16 squares. Wash and trim mushrooms.
2. Thread each of 4 wooden skewers with vegetable pieces as follows: Zucchini, pepper, mushroom, pepper, zucchini, pepper, mushroom, pepper, zucchini. Sprinkle with salt and pepper.
3. Place skewers on a serving platter next to scallops. Place vegetable skewers in hot sake to cook with scallops.

Wasabi Cream

Serves 2

1 teaspoon wasabi power
2 tablespoons cream
3 tablespoons sour cream
1 tablespoon mayonnaise

Wasabi powder is available at most supermarket spice displays.

1. Combine wasabi powder with cream. Stir until smooth. Whisk in sour cream and mayonnaise. If you prefer a thinner sauce, add more cream. For a spicier sauce, add more wasabi dissolved in cream.

Coeur a la Crème with Berries

Serves 2

4 ounces cream cheese, softened
¼ cup sour cream
2 tablespoons heavy cream
3 tablespoons confectioners' sugar
¼ teaspoon lemon juice
½ teaspoon vanilla extract
1 cup mixed blueberries, raspberries, and strawberries

Coeur a la Crème molds can be found at kitchen supply stores.

1. Whip together cream cheese, sour cream, heavy cream, confectioners' sugar, lemon juice and vanilla.
2. When mixture is completely smooth and free of lumps, pour into 2 damp cheesecloth-lined coeur a la crème molds. Fold extra cheesecloth over the top of the molds. Place molds in a pan and refrigerate 6 hours or overnight.
3. Carefully remove coeurs from molds and place on individual plates. Top with berries (sweetened, if desired) and serve.

. . . .

Berry Good

Sweet, fresh berries are a real treat, but if your berries are a bit tart, or if you'd prefer more of a sauce, simply add sugar to berries about 1 hour before serving. Toss well and set aside. The berries will macerate and produce a sweet, syrupy topping. Add a spritz of eau de vie or brandy to the mix if desired.

Napa Valley Wine Fondue
and Cheese Reception

Even if your abode doesn't have a view of the vineyards, you can still capture the gracious hospitality of California wine country with this menu. If you can have it alfresco around sunset, so much the better.

MENU

◇◇◇◇◇◇◇◇◇◇◇◇◇

Tomato Bruschetta

Selection of Artisanal Cheeses

Halibut and Lobster Tail Wine Fondue

Cold Grilled Summer Squash & Asparagus

Orzo Walnut Sultana Salad

Selection of California Wines

Minted Melon Balls

Ghirardelli Chocolate-Dipped Biscotti

Italian Roast Coffee

Tomato Bruschetta

Serves 8

8 ripe tomatoes, trimmed and diced
1 teaspoon salt
4 cloves garlic, cut lengthwise into paper-thin slices
2 French baguettes, cut into 1-inch slices on the diagonal
⅓ cup olive oil
Fresh-ground black pepper
⅓ cup fresh basil ribbons

The secret to intensely flavored tomato topping? Just a little salt and time.

1. In a bowl, toss tomatoes with salt, taking care to mix well.
2. Toss in garlic and spoon tomato mixture into a large colander. Place colander over a bowl, cover loosely, and refrigerate 8 hours or overnight.
3. Brush baguette slices with olive oil. Place on a baking sheet and bake at 325°F until toasted, turning once to toast both sides.
4. Discard liquid from bowl under tomatoes. Place drained tomatoes in a serving dish. Sprinkle with black pepper to taste and toss in fresh basil. Serve with toasted bread rounds.

. . . .

The Power of Salt

Over time, salt draws some of the water from tomatoes, making the tomato flavor more concentrated. The process softens the tomato texture, making it inappropriate for salads. However, it's great for adding fresh tomato flavor to lightly cooked sauces and cold salsas.

Halibut and Lobster Tail Wine Fondue

8 servings

Less expensive spiny or rockl Lobster tails can be used in this dish.

3 pounds halibut fillets
8 small lobster tails, shelled
3–6 cups Chablis
One bouquet garni
½ cup butter, melted
2 cloves garlic, pressed
2 tablespoons lemon juice
½ teaspoon fresh tarragon, chopped
Salt and pepper to taste

1. Cut halibut fillets into 1-inch cubes. Cut lobster into 1-inch slices. Place lobster and halibut on a serving plate with skewers. Encourage guests to thread 1 piece of each on skewers.
2. Heat Chablis in a saucepan with bouquet garni until just starting to bubble. Discard herbs. Pour hot wine into fondue pots. Guests can dip fish and lobster skewers in pot until seafood is just opaque.
3. Combine melted butter, garlic, lemon juice, tarragon, salt, and pepper. Pour into small dishes for dipping sauce.

. . . .

What Is Bouquet Garni?

Bouquet garni is a small cache of aromatic herbs either tied together with string or placed in a cheesecloth pouch. Usual ingredients include bay leaves, thyme sprigs, and parsley sprigs. Some cooks add celery and green onion to the mix. Make your own or buy it already packaged.

Orzo Walnut Sultana Salad

Serves 8

6 cups al dente cooked orzo pasta
1 cup celery, thinly sliced
1 cup carrots, thinly sliced
1 cup red radishes, thinly sliced
1 small red onion, minced
2 cups walnuts, toasted
1½ cups sultanas
1 cup extra-virgin olive oil
⅔ cup balsamic vinegar
Salt and pepper to taste

> Sultanas are golden raisins. Regular brown raisins or even dried cranberries can work too.

1. Combine pasta, vegetables, walnuts, and sultanas.
2. Whisk together olive oil and vinegar. Pour over pasta mixture and toss well.
3. Add salt and pepper to taste, cover, and refrigerate until ready to serve. Toss before serving.

. . . .

Cheese on Board

Your selection of artisanal cheeses—that means specialty cheeses from small producers—should include at least 3–5 different cheeses. Include one hard, crumbly cheese like an aged Cheddar or dry Jack, one creamy goat cheese, and then think in terms of a veined cheese like Gorgonzola or Blue, or a soft, buttery Brie or Camembert. Feel free to include one herb or fruit-laced cheese on your cheese plate.

Mardi Gras Madness Fondue

Banish those midwinter doldrums with an homage to Louisiana's ultimate party. Put blues, gumbo rock, and jazz in the compact disc player, get out a few bottles of Tabasco, and fire up the fondue pot.

MENU

Artichoke and Oyster Soup

Raw Vegetable Platter with Smoked Fish Dip

Mixed Beggar's Purses in Burgundy Fondue

Rice Dressing

Mini Muffuletta Sandwiches

Creole-Italian Olive Salad

Mini Roast Beef Po-Boys

Creole Mustard and Garlic Mayonnaise
(available in stores)

King Cake

Creole Cream Cheese Ice Cream

Chocolate shell ice cream topping

Artichoke and Oyster Soup

Serves 8

4 tablespoons butter

4 tablespoons all-purpose flour

2 cups chicken broth

4 cups artichoke hearts

6 green onions, finely chopped

3 cloves garlic, pressed

24 oysters, not drained

4 cups half-and-half

> The secret to this soup is fresh oysters, cooked just until done.

¼ cup parsley, finely chopped

¼ teaspoon thyme leaves

Salt and pepper to taste

1. In a large saucepan, melt the butter over medium heat. Stir in the flour. Continue stirring until mixture is smooth and bubbling, but not browned. Pour in 1 cup of chicken broth, and stir to blend.
2. Place artichoke hearts and the remaining cup of chicken broth in a blender and purée. Add mixture to saucepan with green onions and garlic. Cook for 10 minutes over medium-high heat.
3. Cut oysters in half, taking care to reserve liquid. Add half-and-half to pan. When soup is simmering, add the oysters with liquid to the pan, along with parsley and thyme. Stir well. Cook just until oysters plump and edges begin to curl.
4. Add salt and pepper to taste. Serve immediately.

. . . .

Oysters in Season

Don't believe the old adage about only eating oysters in cool-weather months. Wild oysters taste best during cooler months because oysters spawn during warmer months and may taste watery. Properly handled, they aren't any more or less safe from May to August. That said, oysters are susceptible to marine bacteria. Anyone with an impaired immune system, in addition to the older and younger folks, should avoid eating raw oysters anytime.

Smoked Fish Dip

Serves 8

*8 ounces smoked trout, mullet,
    or salmon*
8 ounces cream cheese, softened
1 cup sour cream
Juice of 1 lemon
2 tablespoons green onion, minced
2 tablespoons parsley, minced
¼ teaspoon Tabasco sauce or to taste

Use hot-smoked fish for this dish, rather than cured fish such as lox.

1. Combine all ingredients in a food processor.
2. Pulse until mixture is blended and smooth.
3. Spoon into a bowl and serve with vegetables and crackers.

Mixed Beggar's Purses in Burgundy Fondue

Serves 8

2 pounds shrimp, cooked
1 pound andouille sausage, chopped
1 pound ham, diced
1 cup green onion, sliced
1 cup red bell pepper, diced
3–5 cups of burgundy
3 bay leaves

You'll need cheesecloth squares and uncoated string for this dish.

1. Cut shrimp in half.
2. Lay out 32 2-inch squares of cheesecloth. Divide shrimp, sausage, ham, green onion, and bell pepper among the squares. Bring ends of squares together and tie with string to make closed pouches.
3. Bring burgundy to a boil in a saucepan and add bay leaves. Pour burgundy into 1 or more fondue pots and place pot over heating source.
4. Guests can lift purses into wine with forks, small tongs, or strainers. Purses should be left in the fondue just until ingredients are warmed and flavored. After, ingredients should be removed from cheesecloth onto plates.

Treasure Pockets

Beggar's purses make fun, easy-to-eat additions to any party buffet. When purses aren't being dipped in boiling wine, they can be made fully edible. In place of cheesecloth, use flexible crepes and green onion ties to wrap savory goodies.

Rice Dressing

Serves 8

1 pound ground beef
1 pound ground pork
1 large onion, chopped
1 green bell pepper, diced
1 rib celery, finely chopped
⅓ cup green onions, finely chopped
⅓ cup parsley, finely chopped
2 cloves garlic, minced
½ teaspoon sage
½ teaspoon thyme
1½ cups raw white rice
2 cups beef broth
¼ teaspoon cayenne
Salt and black pepper to taste

Don't be afraid to add more cayenne to this dish.

1. In a large Dutch oven, combine beef, pork, onion, bell pepper, celery, green onions, parsley, and garlic. Cook over medium-high heat until meat is no longer pink. Drain excess fat from the mixture.
2. Add sage, thyme, rice, beef broth, and cayenne to the pot. Stir well. Cover tightly and cook over low heat for 25 minutes, or until rice is tender.
3. Add salt and pepper to taste. Stir to blend and serve.

. . . .

Rice Is Nice

In Louisiana, there are as many recipes for rice dressing, or "dirty rice," as there are cooks. One popular variation includes chopped chicken giblets along with ground meat. In a pinch, leftover cooked rice can be mixed with cooked meats, herbs, seasonings, and a bit of liquid for a delicious side dish.

Mini Muffuletta Sandwiches

Serves 8

16 *silver-dollar rolls*
4 *slices provolone cheese*
4 *slices Genoa salami*
4 *sliced mortadella*
4 *slices ham or prosciutto*
1½ *cups Creole-Italian Olive Salad (page 162)*

> The original muffuletta is a huge sandwich built on a round loaf of sesame bread. It's big enough to serve 2–4 people.

1. Split silver-dollar rolls open.
2. Cut provolone, salami, mortadella, and ham slices into quarters. Put ¼ of each item on the bottom layer of each roll.
3. With a slotted spoon, place a small amount of olive salad mix on top of meats and cheese. Close sandwiches and serve.

. . . .

Mini Roast Beef Po-Boys

To make mini roast beef po-boys, cut open small sub rolls (preferably French-type bread) and spread with mayonnaise. Pile on sliced roast beef, a little gravy, shredded lettuce, and tomatoes. Eat with lots of napkins.

Creole-Italian Olive Salad

Serves 8

3 cloves garlic, minced
½ cup green olives, chopped
½ cup oil-cured black olives,
    pitted and chopped
½ cup kalamata olives, pitted and chopped
½ cup roasted red peppers, chopped
2 pepperoncini, finely chopped
2 tablespoons celery, minced
2 tablespoons red onion, minced
2 tablespoons parsley, minced
¼ teaspoon dried oregano
¾ cup olive oil
1 tablespoon wine vinegar

Sometimes versions of this relish-type salad appear on supermarket shelves, but it's very easy to make the authentic muffuletta topping

1. Combine all ingredients in a bowl and mix well.
2. Cover and refrigerate for several hours or overnight, stirring occasionally.
3. Bring to room temperature before making sandwiches.

. . . .

Olive Filling, Olive Topping

This olive salad can be used for bruschetta topping, as a garnish for a Fontina cheese-based fondue, or as a dressing for green salad or potato salad.

King Cake

Serves 8

2 envelopes active dry yeast

⅔ cup sugar

½ cup butter, melted

½ cup warm milk

6 egg yolks

5 cups all-purpose flour

2 teaspoons salt

1 teaspoon cinnamon

1 teaspoon vanilla

1 teaspoon vegetable oil

King cake doll or large raw bean

¼ cup cream or evaporated milk

1 cup confectioners' sugar

1 cup each purple, green, and
    gold-tinted sugar

The guest who gets the wedge with the baby or bean is king or queen of the party (and obligated to host the next King Cake bash).

1. Fit an electric mixer with a dough hook. In mixer bowl, combine yeast, sugar, butter, and warm milk. Beat on low for 1 minute. Slowly add egg yolks and beat until blended.

2. Change speed to medium-low and add flour, salt, cinnamon, and vanilla. Beat until blended and dough pulls away from the side of the bowl. Form dough into a ball, grease ball with vegetable oil, and place in a glass bowl, covered, for 2 hours or until dough doubles in size.

3. Punch dough down and divide in 2. Roll each half into a long rope, about 32 inches long. Twist ropes together and form combined length into a circle. Press ends of circle together to form a seamless ring. Place ring on a greased cookie sheet and cover with a damp, clean towel. Allow ring to double in size, which should take about 1 hour.

4. Insert doll or bean into dough from the underside of the ring. It should be completely hidden. Bake at 350°F for 25–30 minutes or until browned. Allow to cool to room temperature.

5. Mix together confectioners' sugar and cream or evaporated milk until smooth. Pour glaze over the top. In alternating bands, sprinkle purple, green and gold sugar over the glaze and allow to set. The cake should be completely covered in colored sugar. Gather guests around to cut the cake.

Octoberfest Beer Fondue Menu

You don't have to wait until October to serve this meal. In fact, our beer fondue can be set simmering over a portable grill at your favorite tailgate spot or picnic venue.

MENU

Apple and Rutabaga Salad

Mixed Sausages with Red Pearl Onions
in Beer Fondue

Honey Mustard, Hot Mustard, Coarse Mustard

Soft White Rolls and Black Bread

Sauerkraut

Boiled Potatoes

Assorted Beers and Ales

Black Forest Cherry Cupcakes

Apple and Rutabaga Salad

Serves 8

2 tart apples, peeled, cored,
   and chopped
2 large rutabagas, peeled
   and shredded
1 small sweet onion, finely chopped
1 cup raisins
6 strips bacon, cooked crisp
½ cup apple cider vinegar
2 tablespoons bacon drippings
⅔ cup vegetable oil
2 tablespoons sugar
1 tablespoon caraway seeds
4 cups baby lettuce mix

1. In a serving bowl, combine apples, rutabagas, onion, and raisins. Crumble bacon over mixture and toss to combine.
2. Whisk together vinegar, bacon drippings, oil, sugar, and caraway seeds.
3. Pour dressing over salad, mix well, cover, and refrigerate until ready to serve.
4. To serve, line salad bowl with lettuces and mound apple and rutabaga mixture on top.

Getting to the Root

Root vegetables like parsnips, turnips, and rutabagas are sweet and crisp when eaten raw. Shred them into slaws and salads for a nutritional boost, in addition to extra flavor and texture.

Mixed Sausages with Red Pearl Onions in Beer Fondue

Serves 8

1 pound knackwurst
1 pound bratwurst
1 pound smoked duck sausage
2 cups red pearl onions, peeled
3–5 cups pilsner-type beer
Juice of 1 lemon
¼ teaspoon Tabasco

Serve this classic fall dish with rolls and dark bread, crisp kraut, and mustards.

1. Cut sausages into 1-inch slices and place together on a serving platter or board.
2. Mix onions with sausage on platter.
3. In a saucepan, bring beer, lemon juice, and Tabasco to a boil. Pour hot beer into fondue pots, no more than half full.
4. Encourage guests to spear sausages with an onion and plunge into hot beer until sausage is hot and onion has begun to soften.

. . . .

One Potato, Two Potato . . .

Boiled potatoes have a wonderfully earthy, primal flavor that complements the richness of the sausages and the tartness of sauerkraut and mustards.

Black Forest Cherry Cupcakes

Serves 8

5 ounces unsweetened chocolate
1½ cups all-purpose flour
1 teaspoon baking soda
¾ cup butter, softened
2 cups sugar
1 teaspoon vanilla extract
2 eggs
1 cup buttermilk

2 cups fresh or frozen sweet
   cherries, pitted
1 tablespoon cornstarch
8 ounces cream cheese, softened
3 cups confectioners' sugar
1 cup marshmallow fluff
24 stemmed maraschino cherries

1. Melt chocolate in the microwave or with a double boiler.
2. Whisk together flour and baking soda in a small bowl. In a large bowl, combine butter and 1½ cups sugar. Beat with an electric mixer on medium speed until smooth and creamy. Add vanilla and eggs and beat on medium-high speed until light and fluffy. Reduce mixer speed to medium-low and add melted chocolate.
3. Add ½ of the flour mixture to the chocolate mixture and beat until blended. Add the buttermilk, then the remaining flour, and beat well.
4. Preheat oven to 350°F. Line 2 dozen cupcake pans with paper liners.
5. In a saucepan, combine ½ cup sugar, cherries, and cornstarch. Cook over medium heat, stirring constantly, until cherries are softened and a thick sauce forms. Remove from heat and cool slightly.
6. Fill cupcake cups halfway with chocolate batter. Drop a tablespoonful of cherries over the batter in each cup, then divide remaining batter over the cupcakes. Bake at 350°F for 20–25 minutes. Remove from oven and allow to cool completely.
7. With a mixer on medium-high speed, whip together cream cheese, confectioners' sugar, and marshmallow fluff. Spread on cooled cupcakes and garnish each with a stemmed cherry.

Chapter 6

Soup's On! Broth, Sauce, and Court Bouillon Fondues: Holidays and Family Gatherings

Tabletop Seafood Boil for a Crowd

Missing the camaraderie of summer backyard boils and barbecues? Invite the gang over for a warming midwinter seafood boil, fondue-style.

MENU

Court Bouillon Seafood Boil

Crudites with Creamy Vidalia Dressing

Boiled Potatoes

Corn on the Cob

Red Pepper Rouille

Hearth-Baked Bread

Beer and Iced Tea

Lemon Squares

Pecan Flavored Coffee

Court Bouillon Seafood Boil

Serves 12

1 pound shrimp heads and shells and
mild-flavored fish trimmings

8 cups water

2 cups dry white wine

2 29-ounce cans tomatoes with liquid

1 teaspoon crab boil seasoning

4 bay leaves

2 large onions, coarsely chopped

6 cloves garlic, pressed

1 teaspoon thyme leaves

½ cup parsley sprigs

1 teaspoon Tabasco

Salt to taste

6 pounds raw shrimp, peeled

3 pounds sea scallops

3 pounds smoked sausage, sliced

3 pounds raw grouper fillets,
cubed

> This dish takes the traditional seafood boil a step further. Not only can it be prepared indoors, but the cooking broth makes an excellent, warming soup.

1. In a large kettle, combine shrimp and fish trimmings with water. Bring to a boil, then reduce heat to medium. Simmer for 30 minutes.
2. Carefully strain seafood broth into a clean pot. Discard solids. Add wine and liquid from tomatoes. Break up tomatoes with fork or hands and add to the pot along with crab boil, bay leaves, onions, garlic, thyme, parsley, and Tabasco.
3. Bring broth to a boil over medium-high heat. Reduce heat to medium and simmer for 30 minutes. Strain again and discard solids. Ladle hot mixture into 2 or 3 fondue pots and place over heating sources.
4. Place shrimp, sausage, scallops, and grouper fillets on serving platters next to fondue pots. Encourage guests to spear seafood and sausage and cook in bubbling court bouillon. Have ladles and soup cups or bowls handy for serving court bouillon after cooking.

Creamy Vidalia Dressing

Serves 12

3 cups mayonnaise

1 cup half-and-half

2 tablespoons honey mustard

1 clove garlic

1 tablespoon sugar

1 large Vidalia onion, peeled and chopped

Salt and pepper to taste

> A Vidalia onion is a specific kind of onion that originated in Toombs county, Georgia.

1. Combine all ingredients in a food processor.
2. Pulse until mixture is blended and onion is finely chopped. Serve over mixed greens or as a dip.

Red Pepper Rouille

Serves 12

6 cloves garlic, pressed

¼ teaspoon salt

1 slice bread, toasted

1 teaspoon fresh basil, minced

½ teaspoon saffron threads

3 tablespoons hot fish stock or clam juice

1½ cups roasted red bell peppers, peeled

4 egg yolks

1¼ cups extra-virgin olive oil

¼ teaspoon Tabasco

Salt and pepper to taste

1. Put garlic, salt, bread, and basil in a food processor. Pulse until bread is reduced to crumbs. Combine saffron threads and hot stock. Mix until threads start to dissolve.
2. Add saffron mixture, red bell peppers, and egg yolks to food processor. Pulse until puréed. Then, with processor running, add olive oil in a thin stream until mixture is thick and smooth.
3. Season with Tabasco, salt, and pepper.

Lemon Squares

Serves 8

2⅓ cups all-purpose flour
⅔ cup confectioners' sugar
Pinch salt
1 cup butter, chilled
6 eggs
2½ cups sugar
½ cup lemon juice
1 tablespoon lemon zest, grated
½ teaspoon baking powder

This favorite Southern tea or dessert treat can be made with lime juice as well as lemon juice. Think of these squares as easy-to-eat tarts.

1. In a large bowl, combine 2 cups of the flour, ½ cup of the confectioners' sugar, and salt. Add butter and cut mixture with 2 knives or pastry blender until crumbly. Press dough into a greased 9" × 12" pan. Pierce holes in the pastry with a fork, then bake at 350°F for 15 minutes or until crust just begins to brown. Remove from oven.
2. Whisk together ⅓ cup flour plus eggs, sugar, lemon juice, lemon zest, and baking powder until thick and blended. Pour mixture over crust and spread evenly.
3. Bake at 350°F for 20–25 minutes or until lemon filling is set. Remove from oven and let cool. Sprinkle remaining confectioners' sugar over top before cutting into 16 squares.

Versatile Shortbread

Sweet shortbread crusts—like the one used for lemon squares—can serve as a base for a variety of bars. Top the baked crust with a favorite cheesecake filling or thick custard, or just pour melted chocolate over the shortbread and sprinkle with nuts.

Holiday Matzo Ball Fondue

Invite the family over for a Passover menu diversion, or just to enjoy a twist on some old favorites.

MENU

Charosets in Orange Shells

Mixed Green Salad with Cranberry Vinaigrette

Deviled Eggs

Matzo Ball Fondue with Chicken

Red Horseradish Mayonnaise

Mango Sorbet

Yarden Blanc de Blancs and Cranapple Spritzers

Charosets in Orange Shells

Serves 8

4 large navel oranges
4 large, tart apples
1 1/3 cups almonds, blanched
1 teaspoon cinnamon
Pinch of ginger
2 tablespoons honey

Orange shells give Charosets—a tasty but generally beige dish—a shot of color and a heavenly scent.

1. Wash oranges well and cut in half horizontally. Cut a small slice off the bottom of each orange half so it will stand without wobbling. With a spoon, carefully scoop about ½ of the orange pulp from each shell and set aside.
2. Peel and core the apples. In a food processor, combine apples, almonds, cinnamon, ginger, and honey. Add 2–3 tablespoons of orange pulp. Pulse until ingredients are blended and finely chopped, but not puréed.
3. Spoon Charosets into orange halves. Chill until ready to serve.

Wandering Recipes

This Charosets recipe—minus the oranges—is similar to ones used in most Jewish families of European descent. However, Jewish people whose ancestors came from the Mediterranean lands tend to make chopped Charosets featuring dates and figs in place of apples. In modern-day Israel, some families use local fruits like oranges, dates, and even bananas to make this fruit relish.

Matzo Ball Fondue with Chicken

Serves 8

10 cups strong chicken broth

3 tablespoons fresh dill, chopped

2 cloves garlic, pressed

2 cups carrots, sliced

1 cup celery, sliced

Salt and pepper to taste

32 Mini Matzo Balls (page 177)

8 chicken breast halves

1 cup minced fresh parsley

Chicken soup with matzo balls is often called "Jewish Penicillin." It's comfort food, and this version makes it good for company.

1. Bring chicken broth to a boil in a large kettle. Add dill, garlic, carrots, and celery. Return broth to boiling, then simmer until carrots are tender, about 10 minutes. Season with salt and pepper to taste.
2. Pour broth into 2 or 3 fondue pots, keeping any leftover broth warm on the stove. Place fondue pots over heating sources.
3. Arrange matzo balls in shallow bowls near fondue pots. Slice raw chicken breast halves and arrange on platters. Provide each guest with a soup bowl. Have guests skewer chicken and cook in broth, then warm matzo balls in broth. When cooking has been completed, ladle a portion of broth from the fondue pots into each bowl, over the cooked chicken and warmed matzo balls. Pass around parsley and red horseradish mayonnaise.

. . . .

Mayo with a Kick

Red horseradish, which is colored and flavored with beets, is a favorite condiment in many Jewish households. To make a hot-and-tangy mayonnaise for chicken, combine 1¼ cups mayonnaise with ½ cup of red horseradish. Stir until the mixture is evenly pink and serve immediately.

Mini Matzo Balls

Serves 8

1 cup matzo meal

4 eggs

½ cup seltzer or club soda

⅓ cup margarine, softened

2 tablespoons parsley, minced

Salt and pepper to taste

Matzo balls expand greatly when cooked, so make sure to roll these marble sized before dropping in water. If the cooked matzo balls break in a fondue pot, just ladle them out with the soup!

1. Pour matzo meal in a cup and stir with a fork to break up any lumps.
2. In a bowl, beat eggs with a fork. Add seltzer, margarine, and parsley and mix well. Sprinkle in salt and pepper to taste.
3. Slowly stir in matzo meal. Keep stirring until mixture is smooth. Cover and refrigerate for at least 1 hour or until batter has stiffened.
4. Bring a large pot of salted water to a boil. Roll dough into small balls—about 36 of them—and drop into boiling water for 15 minutes. Remove with slotted spoon to a shallow serving bowl or baking dish and serve with broth fondue.

Heavy or Light?

Every Jewish family has a favorite matzo ball recipe, a favorite matzo ball cook, and an ongoing discussion about whether the best matzo balls are heavy or light. Here's one secret to making lofty or leaden balls: How much the dough is handled when rolling the balls is more important than the recipe itself. Quickly, barely shaped balls hold more air and will be fluffier when cooked. For fondue, it's best to use a little more pressure when rolling the matzo balls so they hold together in the broth.

Mango Sorbet

Serves 8

1½ cups sugar
1 cup water
6 ripe mangos
Juice of 1 lime

To make this tropical dessert creamy, but still non-dairy, add a can of coconut milk to the mix and reduce the mango purée slightly.

1. In a saucepan, combine sugar and water. Bring to a boil, stirring until sugar is dissolved. Cool sugar syrup to room temperature, then refrigerate until chilled.
2. Cut mangoes on either side of the center seed. Scrape fruit from the peel into a blender container or food processor. Pour in chilled syrup and add lime juice. Process until puréed.
3. Prepare sorbet in a sorbet or ice-cream maker according to manufacturer's instructions. Keep on ice or in the freezer until ready to serve.

Refreshing Desserts

Sorbets are incredibly easy to make—just purée fruit, sugar, and water. And although they're fat-free and relatively low in calories, these frozen treats make impressive looking and tasting desserts.

Southern Italian Feast Fondue

Southern Italian fare—the slightly-sweet red sauce, hearty meats and sausage, pastas and antipasti—is the Italian food most of us grew up loving. This fondue will bring back childhood memories, while still giving your guests an out-of-the-ordinary dining experience.

MENU

Antipasto Platter

Sicilian Red Gravy Fondue

Meatballs, Sausage, Shrimp

Fried Calamari

Penne Pasta

Sautéed Flat Green Beans

Pane Paisano or other crusty bread

Valpolicella

Tiramisu and Coffee

Sicilian Red Gravy Fondue

Serves 6

¼ cup olive oil

1 onion, chopped

3 cloves garlic, minced

1 green bell pepper, diced

1 teaspoon dried oregano

1 teaspoon dried basil

6 ounces tomato paste

1 32-ounce can diced tomatoes

1 16-ounce can tomato sauce

1 teaspoon hot pepper flakes

¼ cup fresh parsley, finely
  chopped

Salt and pepper to taste

1 tablespoon sugar

1. In a large, heavy saucepan or Dutch oven, heat the olive oil over medium-high heat. Add onion, garlic, and bell pepper. Cook, stirring, until onion turns translucent, about 5 minutes. Add oregano and basil. Stir well.

2. Stir tomato paste into the oil for 1 minute. Add 1 cup of water and mix until blended. Add tomatoes, tomato sauce, and pepper flakes. Pour 1½ quarts of water (or a mixture of water and red wine) into the sauce and reduce heat to medium.

3. Simmer sauce for 2 hours, stirring occasionally and adding water if sauce becomes too thick. When sauce reaches desired consistency, season with salt, pepper, and parsley. Stir in sugar and bring to a boil.

4. Remove sauce from heat and ladle into 1 or more fondue pots. Place pot over heating source. Serve with meatballs, shrimp, and sausage.

Tomato Sauce Dippers

In theory, you could cook meatballs, Italian sausage, and shrimp in the sauce, but in reality, it would take a long time to get the meat cooked through. Better to have cooked meatballs (count on 6 cocktail-sized meatballs per person), shrimp, and sausage ready for warming in the sauce and eating over hot, oil-tossed penne pasta.

Fried Calamari

Serves 6

*1 pound small squid, cut in
    1-inch pieces*
1 cup all-purpose flour
1 teaspoon cayenne pepper
½ teaspoon paprika
Olive oil for frying
2 lemons, halved and sliced

This recipe makes a classic, lightly breaded calamari. For more thickly coated calamari, dip the floured squid pieces in beaten egg and again in flour or bread crumbs before serving.

1. Rinse squid and pat dry. Mix together flour, cayenne, and paprika.
2. Dust squid pieces with seasoned flour. In a deep skillet over medium-high heat, add oil about 1 inch deep. Carefully drop calamari into hot oil, a few pieces at a time. Cook just until golden brown and crisp.
3. Remove calamari from oil with a slotted spoon and drain on paper towels. Serve with lemon wedges and tomato sauce.

Tender Squid

To ensure tender calamari, either cook it very quickly in hot oil, or allow it to simmer for hours in sauce. Slightly overcooking it will result in the tough rubber-band rings that should be avoided. If you can find fresh, tiny squid, buy them! If you can acquire them, the Spanish batter fingertip sized calamari, fry them, and eat them like popcorn. Delicious!

Tiramisu

Serves 6–8

1 cup brewed espresso coffee

¼ cup coffee liqueur

¼ cup brandy

8 ounces bittersweet chocolate

6 egg yolks

½ cup sugar

1 pound mascarpone cheese

1 teaspoon vanilla extract

28 Italian-type (crisp) ladyfingers

1 pint heavy cream

2 teaspoons espresso powder or
    powdered instant coffee

⅓ cup confectioners' sugar

1. In a wide bowl, combine espresso, liqueur, and brandy. Using a food processor or hand grater, grate chocolate and set aside.
2. Combine egg yolks and sugar in the top of a double boiler. Using an electric mixer on medium, beat until just fluffy. Place the pan over hot water, not bubbly, and continue to beat until egg mixture is pale yellow and leaves a trail in the mixer's path. Remove from heat and keep beating for 2 minutes. Set aside to cool.
3. In a large bowl, stir vanilla into the mascarpone. Add egg mixture to mascarpone, folding until the mixture is blended.
4. Set out a deep baking dish. Dip ladyfingers in coffee mixture until each is moist, but not soaked. Place each dipped ladyfinger into the baking dish until ½ the ladyfingers have been used. You should have an even layer of ladyfingers at the bottom of the dish. Spread ½ the mascarpone mixture over the ladyfingers. Sprinkle with ⅓ of the chocolate. Repeat process with another layer of dipped ladyfingers and the rest of the mascarpone, plus another⅓ of the chocolate. Carefully cover dish and refrigerate until chilled.
5. When it's time to serve the tiramisu, combine espresso powder and cream in a bowl. Stir until coffee begins to dissolve. Add sugar and beat with a mixer on high speed until stiff peaks form. Spread whipped cream over tiramisu and sprinkle with the rest of the chocolate. Cut with a sharp knife or spatula to serve.

Play-Offs Boiled Beef Pot Fondue

Whether you and your friends are glued to the big screen television for the Super Bowl run-up or March Madness, this menu of hearty, simple flavors will satisfy.

Menu

Chopped Salad

Boiled Beef Pot Fondue

Potatoes, Carrots, Parsnips, and Cabbage

Horseradish Sauce

Hard Rolls and Parsley Butter

Stout Beer and Burgundy

Easy Carrot Cake

Coffee

Chopped Salad

Serves 8

1 head Romaine lettuce,
    finely chopped
1 small head purple cabbage, trimmed
    and finely chopped
1½ cups carrots, chopped
1 yellow bell pepper, chopped
1 cup radishes, finely chopped
1 cup celery, finely chopped
1 cup black olives, chopped
1½ cups artichoke bottoms, chopped
1½ cups chickpeas
2 cups Cheddar-jack cheese, shredded
1 cup olive oil
⅔ cup balsamic vinegar
1 teaspoon Dijon mustard
1 clove garlic, pressed
¼ teaspoon oregano

> Serve this colorful, layered salad in a large glass trifle dish or punch bowl for optimum effect.

1. In a large glass bowl, layer first ten ingredients.
2. Whisk together olive oil, balsamic vinegar, mustard, garlic, and oregano.
3. Drizzle dressing over salad just before serving.

Substantial Salads

To make this salad a main dish, simply add two more layers to the mix—one layer of diced chicken and one layer of diced ham or salami. Adding a sprinkle of chopped egg or crumbled bacon couldn't hurt.

Boiled Beef Pot Fondue

Serves 8

4 pounds boneless prime rib roast
2 tablespoons butter
2 large onions, chopped
1 leek, cleaned and sliced
1 teaspoon Worcestershire sauce
½ teaspoon Tabasco
8 cups strong beef broth
16 large red potatoes

The classic cut for boiled beef would be brisket or chuck roast. But shaved prime rib roast offers tender meat without hours of cooking.

4 parsnips
4 carrots
8 baby turnips
1 green cabbage

1. Trim roast and slice in very thin slices. (Ask meat department staff to do this step, if possible.) Roll slices of raw beef, sprinkle with black pepper, cover, and refrigerate.
2. In a large kettle, melt butter over medium-high heat. Add onions and leeks and sauté until onions become soft and translucent. Add Worcestershire sauce, Tabasco, and beef broth. Bring to a boil, reduce heat to medium-low, and simmer for 15 minutes.
3. Fill another large pot with water and bring to a boil. Trim and quarter potatoes, and cut parsnips and carrots into 4 pieces. Trim turnips. Drop vegetables into the boiling water and parboil for 10 minutes. Drain and arrange on serving platters. Cut cabbage into small wedges and place on serving plates.
4. Remove beef from refrigerator and place the beef rolls on a serving platter. Pour simmering beef stock into 1 or more fondue pots and place on heating source. Keep leftover broth warm on the stove.
5. Provide guests with shallow bowls and forks or skewers. Have them cook beef to desired doneness in simmering broth and finish cooking root vegetables. Cabbage wedges should be dipped in broth last, and cooked just until warmed, and crisp and tender. Broth can be ladled into bowls after cooking. Pass the horseradish sauce.

Easy Carrot Cake

Serves 10

1 10-ounce package frozen
    carrots in butter sauce
1 cup raisins
2 cups all-purpose flour
2 cups sugar
1 teaspoon baking powder
1 teaspoon baking soda
1½ teaspoons cinnamon
1 teaspoon salt
1 cup plus 2 tablespoons
    vegetable oil

4 eggs
½ cup butter, softened
8 ounces cream cheese, softened
1 pound confectioners' sugar, sifted
½ teaspoon vanilla extract
1½ cups pecans, chopped

> This homemade carrot cake can be thrown together quickly and served from the baking pan.

1. Thaw carrots in butter sauce. Place in a food processor work bowl along with raisins. Pulse until mixture is finely chopped.
2. Combine flour, sugar, baking powder, baking soda, cinnamon, and salt in a large bowl. Whisk to remove any lumps.
3. Add oil and beat with mixer on medium speed until blended. Add eggs 1 at a time and mix until batter is creamy. Pour into greased 9" x 13" pan and bake at 350°F for 40 minutes. Cool completely.
4. To make frosting, mix together cream cheese and butter, beating until smooth. Slowly add sifted confectioners' sugar, beating until mixture is fluffy and all sugar is blended. Add vanilla. Frost cooled cake and sprinkle chopped pecans over the frosting.

. . . .

Casual Cakes

Sure, a mousse cake or genoise torte will wow your dinner party guests. But for casual get-togethers, don't bother. Homemade sheet cakes taste fabulous, are easy to serve, and are usually quite easy to make. The more you do to make entertaining stress-free, the more likely you are to enjoy the party.

Patio Luncheon Fish Fondue

Maybe you can't schedule that cruise to Cancun just yet.
But you can always invite a few friends over for a south-of-
the-border coastal fondue feast.

MENU

ooooooooooooooo

Chilled Avocado Bisque

Grouper Vera Cruz Fondue

Yellow Rice

Black Beans

Chardonnay or Dry Riesling

Flan

Iced Cinnamon Coffee

Chilled Avocado Bisque

Serves 6

4 ripe avocados
2 cups chicken broth, room temperature
¼ cup plus 1 tablespoon lime juice
1 cup sour cream
¼ cup onion, chopped
1 clove garlic, minced
¼ cup plus 1 tablespoon cilantro, finely chopped
Salt and pepper to taste
2 plum tomatoes, finely diced
1 cucumber, seeded and diced
1 green onion, minced
1 jalapeño pepper, minced
1 teaspoon lime zest, grated

Serve small portions of this rich, but still refreshing, soup as a culinary scene setter for a tropical menu.

1. Peel and seed avocados. Place in a blender with chicken broth, ¼ cup lime juice, sour cream, onion, garlic, and ¼ cup cilantro. Blend until mixture is puréed.
2. Season soup with salt and pepper, cover, and refrigerate until chilled.
3. Combine tomatoes, cucumber, green onion, jalapeño, and lime zest. Add remaining lime juice and cilantro and toss to mix. Serve the bisque in cups or small bowls and garnish each with a tablespoon of tomato-cucumber salsa.

Cold Comfort

Chilled soups can jumpstart summer meals by immersing guests in one or more of the essential flavors of the season. Creamy, cold asparagus, cucumber, or tomato soup—accented with a drizzle of hot pepper oil, a shaving of Parmesan cheese, or a dollop of chutney—can take the place of salad or offer an appetizer when salad is the main event. Oh, and don't forget balsamic vinegar-spiked berry soups with a small berg of vanilla ice cream or frozen yogurt for dessert.

Grouper Vera Cruz Fondue

Serves 6

2 cups fish or seafood broth

4 cups tomato juice

1 cup dry white wine

1 tablespoon lemon juice

4 bay leaves

3 tablespoons olive oil

2 cups tomatoes, diced

1 cup onions, finely chopped

2 cloves garlic, minced

1 jalapeño pepper, minced

½ cup green olives with pimientos, sliced

¼ cup black olives, sliced

2 tablespoons capers

1 teaspoon lemon zest, grated

¼ teaspoon thyme leaves

¼ cup fresh parsley, minced

2½ pounds grouper fillets, cut in 1-inch dice

Fresh grouper is a firm, mild-tasting fish prized for its texture. However, any white fish can be used in this recipe.

1. Bring broth, tomato juice, wine, lemon juice, and bay leaves to a boil in a large saucepan. Reduce heat and simmer for 10 minutes.
2. In a deep skillet, heat olive oil over medium-high heat. Add tomatoes, onions, garlic, and jalapeño. Cook, stirring constantly, for 3 minutes or until tomatoes begin to soften. Reduce heat to medium and add olives, capers, lemon zest, thyme, and parsley. Simmer for 5 minutes, stirring often. Add a little fondue broth if mixture becomes too dry.
3. Pour broth and tomato juice mixture into 1 or more fondue pots and place over heating source. Arrange raw grouper on a serving platter and ladle tomato-olive sauce mixture into individual bowls. Guests can skewer grouper pieces and cook them until opaque in fondue broth, then dip in Vera Cruz sauce or ladle it on.

Flan

Serves 6

1 ¼ cup sugar
2½ cups half-and-half
2 teaspoons vanilla extract
1 teaspoon almond extract
3 eggs
3 egg yolks

This classic Spanish dessert has many cousins, including crème brûlée and crème caramel. Serve flan simply, with berries and fruit on the side.

1. In a saucepan over medium heat, cook ½ cup sugar, stirring constantly, until it liquefies and turns a golden shade. Pour the caramelized sugar into a heat-safe flan mold or soufflé dish. Carefully swirl the liquid around to coat the bottom and sides of the dish.
2. Pour half-and-half into a saucepan and heat until steamy, but not boiling. Add vanilla and almond extracts. In a large bowl, beat eggs, egg yolks, and sugar until light-colored and fluffy. While beating, slowly pour in warm half-and-half. Mix until combined.
3. Pour egg mixture into flan dish. Place in a baking pan with water coming halfway up the sides of the flan dish. Bake at 350°F until firm, about 1 hour. (Make sure water in baking pan doesn't evaporate.) Cool in refrigerator and serve with berries.

Not-so-Tricky Custards

Once you get the hang of it, making smooth flans and crème brûlées is quite simple. First, always add hot mixtures to eggs slowly, while beating the eggs. Or, beat in a small amount of a hot liquid to warm the eggs, then whisk the eggs into the hot mixture. This will keep the eggs from cooking. Also, custards should be baked in a very moist, humid oven. A water bath will keep the custard from cooking too quickly, which could result in a lumpy dessert.

Sweet Sixteen
Tropical Chicken Curry

Serve this menu to your teen queen and her friends. It's exotic enough to be memorable, but doesn't stray too far outside most comfort zones.

MENU

◇◇◇◇◇◇◇◇◇◇◇◇◇◇

Fresh Spinach-Mandarin Salad

Chicken in Pineapple-Orange Curry Fondue

Almond Basmati Rice Pilaf

Sugar Snap Peas

Fresh Peach Chutney

Macadamia Brittle Ice Cream

Coconut Macaroons

Non-Alcoholic Piña Coladas

Chicken in Pineapple-Orange Curry Fondue

Serves 8

2 cups chicken broth

2 cups orange juice

2 cups pineapple juice

1 10-ounce can coconut milk

1 tablespoon Thai Massaman curry paste

1 teaspoon soy sauce

8 chicken breast halves

3 green bell peppers

1 fresh pineapple

1 large onion

> This fondue smells heavenly while cooking, plus it isn't too spicy for young, but discerning, palates.

1. In a large saucepan over medium heat, bring chicken broth, orange juice, pineapple juice, curry paste, and soy sauce to a boil. Stir until paste is dissolved and let simmer for 3 minutes. Reduce heat slightly and add coconut milk. Simmer for 10 minutes.
2. Cut chicken breasts, bell peppers, pineapple, and onions into uniform, bite-sized pieces. Thread ingredients onto skewers, alternating chicken and pineapple with vegetables. Place skewers on a serving platter.
3. Pour hot curry mixture into 1 or more fondue pots and place pots over heating sources. Have guests hold skewers in the hot curry broth until chicken is opaque and cooked through. Serve with soy sauce and chutney.

A Cache of Curries

Curry isn't really a spice—it's a type of dish. Known throughout the Middle East, Africa, and Asia, curries are actually stews that may or may not include meats. Curry seasonings—which can be powders or pastes—are handed down from one generation to the next and vary widely in composition. The spice most Americans and Europeans know as curry powder usually contains coriander, cumin, turmeric, cardamom, cloves, cinnamon, mustard, and possibly red pepper.

Almond-Basmati Rice Pilaf

Serves 8

2 cups Basmati rice
2½ cups water
1 teaspoon salt
4 tablespoons butter
½ teaspoon almond extract
1 tablespoon soy sauce
1½ cups slivered almonds
1 cup green peas
1 cup raisins
⅓ cup green onion, minced
Salt and pepper to taste

> Basmati rice has a nutty, sweet fragrance and fine texture that makes it perfect for pilafs and rice salads.

1. In a heavy saucepan with a lid, combine rice, water, and salt. Bring to a boil, then cover and reduce to medium-low. Cook, covered, for 20 minutes.
2. In a large skillet or wok, melt butter over medium-high heat. Add almond extract, soy sauce, and slivered almonds. Sauté, stirring frequently, for 2 minutes. Add peas and raisins.
3. Spoon rice into skillet and toss until ingredients are blended. Season with salt and pepper to taste.

Pick Your Pilaf

Any mixture of grains, nuts, seeds, vegetables, or fruits can qualify as a pilaf. Add meats or seafood to the mix, and you have a main dish pilaf and a close cousin to the jambalayas of the American South.

Fresh Peach Chutney

Serves 8

6 peaches, peeled and diced
½ cup dried cranberries
1 cup red onion, finely chopped
2 tablespoons fresh ginger, grated
1 tablespoon lemon juice
⅓ cup apple cider vinegar

⅓ cup sugar
Salt and pepper to taste

This quick-fix chutney has a nice fresh flavor and makes a great accompaniment to poultry and pork dishes.

1. Mix peaches with cranberries, onion, ginger, and lemon juice.
2. Whisk together apple cider vinegar and sugar, stirring until sugar dissolves. Add to peach mixture.
3. Season with salt and pepper. Serve as a condiment.

Coconut Macaroons

Serves 10–12

1 cup sweetened condensed milk
3 cups frozen or fresh coconut, grated
2 tablespoons corn syrup
1 egg white
1 teaspoon almond extract
2 teaspoons vanilla extract

To make these really special, dip them in melted chocolate. Or just set out a pot of chocolate fondue!

1. In a large bowl, combine all ingredients and stir until blended.
2. Drop mixture by heaping tablespoons onto a greased cookie sheet, making about 30 large cookies.
3. Bake at 350°F for 10–12 minutes. Remove from baking sheet and cool.

Chapter 7

Asian Fondues: Hot Stuff from Hot Pots

Mongolian Hot Pot Affair

Clear the coffee table. Serve this basic northern Chinese fondue when the gang arrives to watch the last episode of your favorite television show.

MENU

Sweet and Sour Cucumber Salad

Mongolian Hot Pot Broth

Beef and Lamb

Chinese Cabbage, Green Onions, and Snow Peas

Hoisin Sauce

Hot Mustard Sauce

Bean Thread Noodles

Orange Ice

Hot and Iced Green Tea

Sweet and Sour Cucumber Salad

Serves 8

1 cup white vinegar
1 cup water
1 cup sugar
1½ teaspoons salt
Juice of 1 lime
4 large cucumbers
1 small red onion, minced
⅓ cup cilantro, minced

This super-simple vegetable salad makes a great accompaniment to any Asian hot pot meal.

1. In a saucepan, combine vinegar, water, sugar, and salt. Bring to a boil, stirring. Cook just until sugar has dissolved. Remove from heat and stir in lime juice. Cool slightly.
2. Pour dressing into a glass container, cover, and refrigerate until chilled.
3. About a ½ hour before serving, peel and slice cucumbers. Combine cucumbers, onion, and dressing in a shallow glass dish. To serve, remove from dressing to serving bowl and sprinkle with cilantro.

Fresh Pickles

A basic sweet-sour dressing of sugar, water, and vinegar can be flavored with herbs or citrus, then used to create a variety of marinated salads. Lightly blanched broccoli, cauliflower, and carrots soak up dressing very well. Marinated onions, radishes, celery, and jicama can be mixed into creamy potato and egg salads to add a zippy crunch.

Mongolian Hot Pot Broth

Serves 8

2 pounds beef flank steak

2 pounds boneless lamb loin

½ cup plus 2 tablespoons soy sauce

⅓ cup dark sesame oil

1 tablespoon lemon juice

1 teaspoon ginger, grated

1 teaspoon sesame seeds

2 cups snow peas, trimmed

16 green onions, cleaned and trimmed

1 large head Chinese cabbage, coarsely shredded

8 cups strong beef broth

3 cloves garlic, pressed

¼ cup sake or white wine

1 teaspoon vinegar

1 pound bean thread noodles

This dish pays homage to the nomads of northern China who, according to legend, invented the hot pot as a way to cook hot meals over a campfire. If you prefer, chicken or venison can be substituted for the lamb.

1. Thinly slice steak and lamb. Whisk together ½ cup soy sauce, sesame oil, lemon juice, ginger, and sesame seeds. Separately, toss beef and lamb in the marinade and arrange meats on a serving platter. Cover and refrigerate until ready to serve.

2. Arrange snow peas, green onions, and cabbage on a separate platter. Cover until ready to serve.

3. In a saucepan, combine broth, garlic, wine, remaining soy sauce, and vinegar. Bring to a boil over medium-high heat. Reduce heat and simmer for 10 minutes. Pour broth into 1 or more fondue pots and place over heating sources. Keep leftover broth warm on the stove. Have guests use chopsticks or hot pot strainers to cook meats and vegetables in fondue.

4. Soak bean threads in hot water for 10 minutes. When guests have cooked meats and veggies, add softened noodles to hot broth. Serve broth and noodles to guests in soup bowls.

Orange Ice

Serves 8

2 cups sugar

2 cups water

Juice of 2 lemons

½ teaspoon vanilla extract

6 cups fresh-squeezed orange juice

1 tablespoon orange zest, grated

This recipe also can be used to make strawberry, pineapple, or watermelon ice from puréed and strained fruit.

1. Combine sugar and water in a saucepan. Bring to a boil, stirring often. Reduce heat and simmer until sugar has dissolved. Remove from heat, cool slightly, then place in refrigerator to chill.
2. Mix lemon juice, vanilla, orange juice, and zest with sugar syrup.
3. Process in a sorbet or ice cream maker according to manufacturer's directions. Or freeze in a shallow pan in the freezer, break up into chunks when frozen, and pulse chunks in a food processor to make a coarse ice.

Kitchen Essentials

The newest ice cream and sorbet makers work with improved frozen cylinders that eliminate the messy business of salt, ice, and brine buckets. The down side—you have to freeze the cylinders for 8–24 hours before using. The up side—no mess, and if you do a little planning, you can have homemade ices and ice creams any weeknight.

Spicy Summer Soiree

Rich coconut milk and fragrant lemongrass make this Thai seafood boil memorable. Throw an early summer social to reconnect with friends before the vacation travel season starts.

Menu

Minted Melon Balls

Thai Seafood Hot Pot Broth

Shrimp, Scallops, and Mussels

Eggplant, Zucchini, and Peppers

Hot Chili Paste

Peanuts

Jasmine Rice

Cold Asian Beer

Thai Iced Coffee or Thai Iced Tea

Almond Cookies

Thai Seafood Hot Pot Broth

Serves 8

1 tablespoon vegetable oil

1 tablespoon green Thai curry
   paste

6 cups fish or chicken stock

2 cups coconut milk

1 onion, sliced

4 cloves garlic, minced

1 stalk lemongrass,
   cut in 1-inch pieces

Juice of 2 limes

1 teaspoon lime zest

⅓ cup fresh basil ribbons

3 pounds shrimp, peeled

1 pound scallops

1 pound sea bass fillets,
   cut in 1-inch cubes

2 pounds cleaned baby mussels

2 cups eggplant, diced

2 cups zucchini, diced

2 cups red bell pepper, cut in strips

½ cup cilantro, chopped

> This fragrant broth resembles a thin Thai curry, with lemongrass and lime simmering in rich coconut milk.

1. In a large saucepan, heat vegetable oil over medium-high heat. Add curry paste and cook, stirring constantly, for 1 minute. Add stock, coconut milk, onion, garlic, lemongrass, limes, lime zest, and basil. Stir well to dissolve curry paste.
2. Bring to a boil, then quickly reduce heat to medium-low. Simmer for 10–15 minutes.
3. Arrange shrimp, scallops, and sea bass on a platter. Place mussels in the shells in a bowl. Arrange eggplant, zucchini, and bell pepper on another platter. Sprinkle chopped cilantro over the seafood and veggie platters.
4. Ladle hot coconut milk broth into 1 or more fondue pots. Provide guests with wire strainers for dipping seafood and veggies in the broth. Fish and shellfish should be cooked briefly, just until the outside becomes opaque. Serve with jasmine rice.

Thai Iced Coffee

Serves 8

10 cups strong brewed coffee
½ teaspoon cardamom
1 cup sweetened condensed milk
½ cup cold half-and-half

This coffee drink is more dessert than beverage. Serve it with almond cookies or coconut macaroons for a perfectly cool finish to a hot pot meal.

1. Make coffee using French roast or espresso roast coffee beans. Stir in cardamom and remove from heat to cool.
2. Fill 8 tall glasses with ice. Pour 2 tablespoons sweetened condensed milk into each glass and pour coffee on top. Stir well, then pour a small amount of half-and-half on top of each glass.
3. Serve with straws.

Thai Iced Tea

Serves 8

10 cups strong brewed Thai tea
1 cup sugar
1 cup evaporated milk
8 cinnamon sticks

Thai tea is available at coffee shops, specialty food stores, and some large supermarkets. If you can't find it, add licorice-flavored star anise to regular black tea while it's steeping.

1. Mix sugar with brewed tea. Fill 8 glasses with ice. Pour sweetened tea over each glass, leaving a ½-inch space at the top.
2. Swirl 2 tablespoons evaporated milk into each glass and add 1 cinnamon stick to each.

Beefy Hot Pot Potluck

The potluck portion of this casual dinner party menu is the dessert. Encourage guests to each bring a special dessert to share after the dipping is done.

MENU

Herb and Boston Lettuce Salad

Vietnamese Lau Broth

Sliced Tenderloin and Sweet Onions

Rice Noodles

Nuac Cham Dipping Sauce

Orange Soy Dipping Sauce

Pineapple Spears

Cold Asian Beer

Potluck Desserts

French Roast Coffee

Herb and Boston Lettuce Salad

Serves 8

1 cup fresh cilantro
1 cup fresh basil
1 cup fresh parsley
½ cup fresh mint
1 cup torn radicchio
8 cups Boston lettuce
1 cup vegetable oil
½ cup lime juice
¼ cup rice wine vinegar
2 cloves garlic
1 dried red chili pepper
1 green onion, trimmed
1 tablespoon brown sugar

Flavor-packed fresh herbs are celebrated in this chili-lime seasoned salad. For variety, feel free to toss a little diced cucumber or melon into the mix.

1. Wash and spin-dry herbs, radicchio, and lettuce. In a large bowl, toss together cilantro, basil, parsley, mint, radicchio, and Boston lettuce.
2. In a blender, combine oil, lime juice, vinegar, garlic, red chili pepper, onion, and sugar. Pulse until ingredients are puréed and blended.
3. Toss salad with ½ of the dressing, turning until everything is lightly coated. Serve with remaining dressing on the side.

Handwrapped Spring Rolls

Sometimes Vietnamese Lau ingredients are cooked and immediately rolled into soft rice paper wrappers. A salad of herbs and Boston-type lettuce, plus bean sprouts, would be tucked into the wrappers first, with the freshly cooked meat dropped on top. Diners roll up the wrapper, dip it in sauce, and munch away.

Vietnamese Lau Broth

Serves 8

3 pounds beef tenderloin
1 large sweet onion
1 cup plus 2 tablespoons rice vinegar
2 tablespoons dark sesame oil
Fresh-ground black pepper
6 cups beef broth
1 tablespoon ginger, grated
4 cloves garlic, pressed
1 stalk lemongrass, cut in 4 pieces

¼ cup sugar
1½ pounds rice noodles
Chopped peanuts

Some cooks make Lau with water instead of beef broth. Try this version, and serve the broth in small portions as a hot and sour soup.

1. Slice the tenderloin in paper-thin slices and arrange on 2 serving platters. Thinly slice onion and toss slices in 2 tablespoons rice vinegar. Drizzle sesame oil over beef and sprinkle with fresh-ground black pepper. Drain vinegar from the onions and arrange over the beef.
2. In a saucepan, combine 1 cup rice vinegar, beef broth, ginger, garlic, lemongrass, salt, and sugar. Bring to a boil, then reduce heat and simmer for 10 minutes. Pour broth into 1 or more fondue pots, then place pots over heating sources. Place beef platters near pots and have guests cook beef in the hot broth.
3. Soak rice noodles in hot water for 10 minutes to soften. When beef has been cooked, drop noodles in the hot broth until cooked. Sprinkle with black pepper and ladle into bowls for guests. Pass peanuts as garnish.

. . . .

Food to Go

Hot pot, or Lau, is very popular in Vietnam, both as a street food and as upscale restaurant fare. Feel free to vary your Lau to include seafood, chicken, tofu, and a range of vegetables.

Nuac Cham Dipping Sauce

Serves 8

This zippy sauce will have your taste buds dancing.

1 cup lime juice
⅔ cup Asian fish sauce
⅓ cup sugar
3 cloves garlic, pressed
1 jalapeño pepper, minced
1 tablespoon cilantro, minced

1. Whisk together all ingredients, cover, and refrigerate overnight.
2. Serve as a dipping sauce with hot pots.

Orange Soy Dipping Sauce

Serves 8

Fresh-squeezed orange juice gives this aromatic sauce a wonderful flavor.

1 cup orange juice
1 cup soy sauce
½ cup sake
2 tablespoons dark sesame oil
2 tablespoons rice wine vinegar
1 tablespoon ginger, minced

1. Whisk together all ingredients, cover, and refrigerate until chilled.
2. Serve as a dipping sauce with hot pots.

Asian New Year Dumpling Fete

Tender meat, seafood, and vegetable-filled dumplings are found in most Asian cuisines. They're a fun food and a very important part of the New Year or Spring Festival menu in many regions.

MENU

Vegetable Platter with Yin-Yang Dips

Chicken Hot Pot Broth

Cilantro Chicken Dumplings

Ginger Pork Dumplings

Shrimp and Green Onion Dumplings

Duck and Mushroom Dumplings

Vinegar Soy Sauce

Moon Cakes

Tangerine Slices

Hot or Iced Jasmine Tea

Champagne

Chicken Hot Pot Broth

Serves 8

8 cups chicken broth
2 tablespoons ginger, minced
4 green onions, chopped
64 assorted dumplings
  (see pages 209–211)
Vinegar Soy Sauce
Sweet-and-Sour Sauce

Buy ready-made wonton wrappers in your supermarket produce or refrigerator case to make wontons stuffed with your favorite fillings. The dumpling recipes that follow make 2 of each variety for a total of 8 dumplings per guest. For more, the recipes can be doubled.

1. Bring strong chicken broth to a boil over medium-high heat. Add ginger and green onions. Reduce heat and simmer 10 minutes.
2. Arrange dumplings in shallow serving bowls. Give guests individual dipping bowls for sauces.
3. Pour hot broth into 1 or more fondue pots. Place pots over heating sources and have guests use chopsticks or mesh strainers to warm dumplings.

. . . .

The Best Chicken Broth

In a large soup pot, place 1 stewing chicken plus 3 pounds of chicken backs, 2 chopped large onions, 3 chopped stalks celery, parsley sprigs, and 4 chopped carrots. Add enough water to cover, at least 1 gallon. Bring to a boil, reduce heat, and simmer for 1 hour. Carefully cut chicken breast meat from stewing chicken and set aside for other use. Return remainder of chicken to the pot and continue simmering for 3 hours. Strain broth into a bowl and refrigerate. Before using broth, scrape off congealed fat at the top.

Cilantro Chicken Dumplings

Serves 8

16 *wonton wrappers*

1 *cup chicken, finely minced*
   or ground

⅓ *cup cilantro, minced*

1 *green onion, minced*

1 *tablespoon soy sauce*

1 *tablespoon ginger, grated*

2 *tablespoons sesame oil*

2 *cloves garlic, minced*

2 *tablespoons white wine or broth*

Salt and pepper to taste

> Since dumplings contain raw meat, it's best to cook them before your fondue party. In fact, the dumplings can be made hours in advance and refrigerated. The fondue broth will warm and flavor the dumplings.

1. Lay out ½ of the wonton wrappers on a cookie sheet and cover with waxed paper.
2. Combine chicken and remaining ingredients in a bowl. Mix lightly with fingers until blended. Place a generous tablespoon of chicken mixture into the center of each wonton wrapper. Wet edges of wrappers. Fold wrappers over filling diagonally and press edges together to seal. Trim edges to achieve half-moon shape. Repeat with remaining wonton wrappers.
3. Bring a pot of water to a boil. Add a few dumplings at a time to the pot, then reduce heat to simmering. Cook for 5–7 minutes or until dumplings turn translucent. With a slotted spoon, remove to a bowl and set aside. Dumplings will be warmed in fondue bowls.

Dumplings of All Shapes

Although most dumplings are made in the traditional half-moon shape, sometimes Chinese cooks make dumplings in a round, beggar's-purse shape with the edges gathered at the top of the dumpling. Round dumplings are easier to arrange in bamboo baskets made for dumplings that are steamed, rather than boiled.

Ginger Pork Dumplings

Serves 8

1 cup pork
½ cup bok choy
2 tablespoons ginger
2 tablespoons Ginger Soy Sauce
1 teaspoon sesame oil
2 cloves garlic, minced
2 tablespoons wine or broth
Salt and pepper to taste

Pork is a traditional filling for dumplings and pot stickers. If you can't find lean ground pork at the supermarket, buy a lean cut and ask to have it finely ground.

1. Combine all ingredients in a bowl. Mix lightly with fingers until thoroughly combined.
2. Fill 16 wonton wrappers as directed in recipe on page 209. Boil as directed and serve with fondue broth.

Shrimp and Green Onion Dumplings

Serves 8

1 cup shrimp, finely chopped
½ cup Chinese cabbage, minced
2 green onions, minced
2 tablespoons soy sauce
1 teaspoon sesame oil
2 cloves garlic, minced
2 tablespoons wine or broth
Salt and pepper to taste

Minced scallops or lobster can be substituted for shrimp in this recipe.

1. Combine all ingredients in a bowl. Mix lightly with fingers until thoroughly combined.
2. Fill 16 wonton wrappers as directed in recipe on page 209. Boil as directed and serve with fondue broth.

Duck and Mushroom Dumplings

Serves 8

1 cup duck breast, minced or ground
½ cup shiitake mushrooms, minced
2 tablespoons parsley, minced
2 cloves garlic, minced
1 tablespoon soy sauce
1 teaspoon truffle oil
2 tablespoons wine or broth
Salt and pepper to taste

Truffle oil isn't a common ingredient in Chinese food, but it enhances the mushroom flavor in this stuffing and makes the dumplings quite scrumptious.

1. Combine all ingredients in a bowl. Mix lightly with fingers until thoroughly combined.
2. Fill 16 wonton wrappers as directed in recipe on page 209. Boil as directed and serve with fondue broth.

Vinegar Soy Sauce

Serves 8

1½ cups soy sauce
1 cup rice wine vinegar
1 tablespoon ginger, shredded
2 cloves garlic, pressed
1 green onion, thinly sliced
1 teaspoon red pepper flakes (optional)

This is a classic dumpling dipping sauce. But, don't be afraid to experiment. Black bean sauce, spicy pepper sauce, hoisin sauce, or even balsamic vinegar make nice complements.

1. Combine all ingredients with a whisk. Cover and refrigerate.
2. To serve, whisk ingredients again. Divide sauce into dipping bowls, 1 for each guest.

Moon Cakes

Serves 8

2 cups all-purpose flour
½ cup sugar
Pinch of salt
1 cup butter, softened
2 egg yolks
2 cups sweet red bean paste
(see below)

There are dozens of recipes for moon cakes, a sweet traditionally served at festivals in China. This easy version resembles thumbprint cookies.

1. In a bowl, combine flour, sugar, and salt. Add softened butter and blend mixture with 2 knives or a pastry blender. Add egg yolks and mix well.
2. Roll dough into a ball and cover with plastic wrap. Refrigerate 1 hour.
3. Remove dough from refrigerator. With hands, remove small pieces of dough and roll into 36 balls. Place balls on greased cookie sheets. Flatten each in the center with the back of a teaspoon. Fill each indentation with red bean paste. Bake at 350°F for 20 minutes or until cakes turn light brown.

. . . .

Sweet Bean Paste

Tiny red adzuki beans find their way into many desserts in Asia. You can buy the paste in cans or make your own. Purée 2 cups of cooked beans with 1/3 cup of raisins, then combine in a saucepan with ½ cup water, 4 tablespoons of butter and a ½ cup of sugar. Simmer for 20–30 minutes or until mixture forms a thick paste. Add 1 teaspoon of vanilla extract, cool, and refrigerate until needed.

Shabu-Shabu to Share

Shabu-Shabu means "swish-swish" in Japanese—a reference to the sound of the beef being stirred quickly in simmering water. To make this dinner party menu really special, buy Kobe or Waygu beef, a tender treat now available outside of Japan.

MENU

Shabu-Shabu

Assorted Sushi Rolls

Sliced Sirloin Steak

Carrots, Leeks, Mushrooms

Tofu and Chinese Cabbage

Ponzu Sauce

Sesame Soy Sauce

Steamed Rice

Strawberries and Cream Puffs

Shabu-Shabu

Serves 6

8 cups water or mild broth

2 6-inch pieces of kombu

2½ pounds sirloin steak

6 leeks or 12 green onions

6 carrots

3 cups button mushrooms

1 head Chinese cabbage

1 pound tofu, rinsed and diced

High-quality ingredients make this dish of few ingredients a standout.

1. In a saucepan, combine water or broth and cleaned kombu. Bring liquid to a boil. Reduce heat and remove kombu. Maintain liquid at a simmer.
2. Slice sirloin across the grain in paper-thin slices. (Partial freezing can make slicing easier.) Arrange slices on serving platters.
3. Clean and trim leeks or green onions, cut carrots into chunks, and clean and trim mushrooms. Clean and chop cabbage. Place vegetables on serving platters. Place tofu on serving platters.
4. Pour hot broth into 1 or more fondue pots and set pots over heating sources. Have guests use chopsticks to swish beef in broth to cook. Chopsticks or mesh strainers can be used for vegetables. Serve with dipping sauces and rice.

Quick-Fix Sushi

If you haven't practiced your sushi rolling technique, don't worry. Just add a little vinegar and water to cooked rice, spread it over toasted seaweed and tuck slivers of fish, shellfish or veggies in the center. Roll it into a cone shape. Repeat with remaining ingredients and stack rolled cones on a platter.

Ponzu Sauce

Serves 6–8

1 cup soy sauce
½ cup rice vinegar
¼ lemon or lime juice
¼ cup orange juice
1 tablespoon mirin or sherry
1 tablespoon ginger, grated
2 tablespoons sugar
1 green onion, minced

This citrus spiked sauce often finds its way into fusion dishes in upscale restaurants.

1. Whisk together all ingredients, stirring until sugar is dissolved. Divide into serving dishes for guests.

Flakes or No Flakes

Ponzu purists prefer fish-flavored soy sauce for the mixture. Boil soy sauce with a tablespoon of fish flakes, then strain the flakes from the sauce and cool. Use in place of regular soy sauce in Ponzu recipes.

Strawberries and Cream Puffs

Serves 6–8

½ cup butter

1 cup water

Pinch of salt

1 cup all-purpose flour

4 eggs

3 cups pastry cream filling (see below)

2 cups strawberries, sliced

3 tablespoons sugar

Cream puffs happen to be a popular dessert in Japan. They're called shu creams, which sounds a lot like choux pastry and cream.

1. In a saucepan, bring butter and water to a rapid boil. Add flour and salt to saucepan and stir until mixture forms a ball. Remove from heat.
2. Place pastry ball in a large bowl. Add eggs, 1 at a time, beating each in with a mixer on medium speed until blended. With a large spoon, drop 24 mounds of dough on ungreased baking sheets.
3. Bake puffs at 400°F for 20 minutes. Tops should be browned and interiors dry. Let cool completely.
4. Mix strawberries with sugar and set aside for 20–30 minutes. Fill puffs with pastry cream. (Slit puffs with a knife and spoon in filling or use a pastry bag.) Spoon strawberries over puffs and serve.

. . . .

Favorite Pastry Cream

Feel free to use your favorite pudding as a pastry filling. Or, whisk together ½ cup of sugar, ¼ cup of cornstarch, and 6 egg yolks in a saucepan. Very slowly, add 2 cups of scalding milk to the pan, whisking constantly. Keep whisking until the mixture is smooth and very thick. Remove from heat. Slowly stir in 2 tablespoons of butter and 1 teaspoon of vanilla extract. Keep stirring regularly until mixture cools, then cover and chill. Use in pastries. For a lighter filling, fold a cup of whipped cream into the chilled pastry cream.

Harvest Moon Hot Pot Party

In Southern China, Chrysanthemum Hot Pot is served at autumn gatherings. The steamy broth yields all sorts of treasures, including some organ meats and dancing (that is, still alive) seafood. In deference to your less adventurous guests, we've omitted the unfamiliar proteins. But you can still toss edible chrysanthemum petals in the broth just before serving!

MENU

Pear and Spinach Salad

Chrysanthemum Hot Pot Broth

Chicken, Pork, and Shrimp

Snow Peas, Bamboo Shoots, Red Bell Pepper, and Mushrooms

Fine Noodles

Chrysanthemum Petals

Persimmon Sorbet

Hot or Iced Green Tea

Chardonnay or White Merlot

Pear and Spinach Salad

Serves 12

1½ cups vegetable oil
¾ cup apple cider vinegar
3 tablespoons lemon juice
3 tablespoons ginger, minced
1 tablespoon red pepper flakes
1 tablespoon sugar
14 cups baby spinach leaves
2 cups red cabbage, finely shredded
3 cups Asian pears, diced
1 cup dried apricots, chopped
1½ cups cashew nuts

This salad features round, crisp Asian pears and a bracing ginger vinaigrette.

1. Whisk together oil, vinegar, lemon juice, ginger, pepper flakes, and sugar. Set aside until ready to serve salad.
2. In a large salad bowl, combine spinach, cabbage, pears, and apricots. Shake dressing to combine ingredients. Pour over salad and toss until ingredients are lightly coated.
3. Sprinkle cashews over the salad and serve.

Chrysanthemum Hot Pot

Serves 12

12 cups chicken broth

3 cloves garlic, minced

4 slices fresh ginger

½ teaspoon five spice powder

3 pounds shrimp, peeled

2 pounds pork tenderloin

2 pounds chicken breast

3 cups snow peas, trimmed

2 cups bamboo shoots

2 cups red bell pepper strips

2 cups straw mushrooms

2 pounds fine noodles, parboiled

Chrysanthemum petals

This hot pot recipe has universal appeal. It's not too spicy, features popular ingredients, and ends with a comforting dose of chicken soup with noodles.

1. In a large soup pot, combine chicken broth, garlic, ginger, and five spice powder. Bring to a boil, then reduce heat and simmer 10 minutes.
2. Arrange shrimp on 3 or 4 plates. Slice pork in wide matchsticks and cut chicken breasts in strips. Arrange pork and chicken on plates.
3. Arrange snow peas, bamboo shoots, bell pepper strips, and mushrooms on platters.
4. Pour hot broth into several fondue pots and place pots over heating sources. Place food platters near pots and give each guest a wire mesh strainer for dipping and cooking ingredients. When guests have cooked the meats and vegetables, drop noodles into hot broth, sprinkle chrysanthemum petals over the broth, and, once noodles are hot, serve in bowls.

Persimmon Sorbet

Serves 12

2 cups water

3 cups sugar

12 ripe persimmons

1 tablespoon lemon juice

Pinch cinnamon

Persimmons originated in China and are shown prominently in ancient texts and paintings. Both astringent—which must be eaten very soft—and non-astringent varieties grow throughout China, and persimmon wood is used for decorative items and even golf clubs.

1. In a saucepan, bring water and sugar to a boil over medium-high heat. Cook, stirring, until sugar is completely dissolved. Remove from heat and cool completely. Place sugar syrup in refrigerator to chill.
2. Split persimmons and scrape pulp into a bowl.
3. In a blender, purée persimmon pulp, sugar syrup, lemon juice, and cinnamon. Process persimmon purée in a sorbet or ice-cream freezer according to manufacturer's instructions. It may be necessary to make in 2 batches. Just store the first batch in your freezer until the second batch is done.

After Practice Hot Pot

This great little hot pot menu features ingredients mostly prepared in advance. That makes it perfect for after soccer, after play rehearsal, after anything gatherings for your children and their friends. For little ones, substitute plain cabbage or bread-and-butter pickles for the spicy kimchee.

MENU

◇◇◇◇◇◇◇◇◇◇◇◇◇◇

Boiled Eggs

Korean Hot Pot Broth

Beef and Pork Meatballs

Carrots, Daikon Radish, and Mushrooms

Vinegar-Sesame Dipping Sauce

Peanut Sauce

Kimchee

Steamed Rice

Sweet and Crispy Cream Cheese Dumplings

Korean Hot Pot Broth

Serves 6

6 cups beef broth

1 tablespoon rice wine vinegar

½ cup soy sauce

1 pound ground beef

1 pound ground pork

2 eggs

2 teaspoons sesame oil

4 tablespoons fine bread crumbs

Salt and pepper to taste

½ cup pine nuts

½ cup sesame seeds

1 cup sauce and gravy flour

2 cups carrots, thickly sliced

1 cup daikon radish, thickly
  sliced

2 cups white button mushrooms

1. In a heavy saucepan, combine beef broth, rice wine vinegar, and ½ of the soy sauce. Bring to a boil over medium heat, then reduce heat and simmer for 10 minutes.

2. Place ground beef in 1 large bowl and ground pork in another. Break 1 egg into each bowl, add 1 teaspoon sesame oil to each bowl, and divide the remaining soy sauce over each bowl. Knead ingredients in each bowl until very well blended. Add 2 tablespoons of bread crumbs, salt, and pepper to each bowl and continue kneading. (For very fine, dense meatballs, pulse meat in batches in a food processor.)

3. Break off small pieces of meat mixtures and roll into tiny meatballs. You should have 36 beef and 36 pork meatballs. In the center of each pork meatball, insert a pine nut. Lightly roll each beef meatball in sesame seeds. Dust meatballs with sauce and gravy flour and place in separate baking pans. Bake at 350°F for 20 minutes or until meatballs are nicely browned. Cool, then refrigerate until ready to use.

4. Arrange pork and beef meatballs on separate serving platters. Arrange platters of carrots, radishes, and mushrooms. Pour simmering broth into fondue pots and place pots over heating sources. Serve with dipping sauces, kimchee, and rice.

Vinegar-Sesame Dipping Sauce

Serves 6

1 cup soy sauce
⅓ cup rice wine vinegar
1 tablespoon dark sesame oil
¼ cup sesame seeds
1 teaspoon red pepper flakes (optional)
1 green onion, minced

Add green onion to this sauce at the last minute for a fresh, aromatic dipping sauce.

1. Combine all ingredients in a small bowl. Cover and refrigerate until ready to serve.
2. At serving time, whisk ingredients together and pour into individual serving bowls for guests.

Peanut Sauce

Serves 6

If any of your young guests are allergic to peanuts, just skip this sauce and pass a basic Chinese sweet sauce mixed with a little ketchup instead.

1 cup smooth, natural style
  peanut butter
2 tablespoons hot water
2 tablespoons soy sauce
1 tablespoon ketchup
1 tablespoon orange juice

1. Combine peanut butter with hot water and soy sauce. Mix until smooth and blended. Stir in ketchup and orange juice. If peanut butter is stiff, use a food processor.
2. At serving time, spoon sauce into individual serving bowls for guests.

Sweet and Crispy Cream Cheese Dumplings

Serves 6

18 small wonton wrappers
8 ounces cream cheese
1 tablespoon heavy cream
1 cup plus 4 tablespoons confectioners' sugar
1 teaspoon vanilla extract
1 egg white, beaten with 1 teaspoon water
Vegetable oil for frying

> For an extra flourish, drop ½ teaspoon of your favorite cherry jam or orange marmalade into each dumpling.

1. Lay wonton wrappers on a clean, flat surface. In a food processor, combine cream cheese, cream, 4 tablespoons confectioners' sugar, and vanilla. Pulse until smooth.
2. Place a generous teaspoon of cream cheese in the center of each wonton wrapper. Brush edges with egg white mixture and fold wrapper on the diagonal. Press to seal edges.
3. Pour vegetable oil about 3 inches deep in a heavy pot. Heat oil until a drop of water skips across the surface. Drop dumplings into oil a few at a time and fry until golden. Remove to a plate lined with paper towels and sprinkle with confectioners' sugar. Allow to cool slightly before serving.

Chapter 8

Warm and Wonderful Chocolate Fondues

Sophisticates' Chocolate Tasting Menu Fondues

Invite chocolate connoisseurs to write their impressions of these haute chocolate fondues and compare notes.

MENU
◇◇◇◇◇◇◇◇◇◇◇◇

Ghirardelli Fondue

Callebaut Fondue

Valrhona Fondue

Guittard Fondue

Ghirardelli Fondue

Serves 6

1 pound bittersweet
    Ghirardelli Chocolate
²/₃ cup heavy cream
Shortbread cookies
Dried Apricots
Fresh Strawberries

> Ghirardelli Chocolate is the oldest continually operating American fine chocolate manufacturer.

1. Chop chocolate into small pieces. Combine with cream in a saucepan.
2. Over low heat, melt chocolate into cream. Stir constantly until mixture is smooth and thick.
3. Pour chocolate fondue into a fondue pot and place over heating source on lowest setting. Have guests dip cookies and fruit into chocolate and discuss flavors.

Callebaut Fondue

Serves 6

1 pound bittersweet
    Callebaut Chocolate
²/₃ cup heavy cream

Biscotti
Dried mango spears
Apple slices

> Chefs prize the complex, deep-flavored chocolate produced by Barry Callebaut, a Swiss company.

1. Chop chocolate into small pieces. Combine with cream in a saucepan.
2. Over low heat, melt chocolate into cream. Stir constantly until mixture is smooth and thick.
3. Pour chocolate fondue into a fondue pot and place over heating source on lowest setting. Have guests dip biscotti and fruit into chocolate and discuss flavors.

Valrhona Chocolate Fondue

Serves 6

*1 pound bittersweet
    Valrhona Chocolate*
²⁄₃ cup heavy cream
Madeleines

French chocolatier Valrhona always has a major presence at Pastry World Cup competitions.

Dried pineapple rings
Orange slices

1. Chop chocolate into small pieces. Combine with cream in a saucepan.
2. Over low heat, melt chocolate into cream. Stir constantly until mixture is smooth and thick.
3. Pour chocolate fondue into a fondue pot and place over heating source on lowest setting. Have guests dip Madeleines and fruit into chocolate and discuss flavors.

Guittard Fondue

Serves 6

*1 pound bittersweet
    Guittard Chocolate*
²⁄₃ cup heavy cream
Italian ladyfingers
Dried papaya spears
Fresh cherries

This gold rush-era California chocolate company was founded by a Frenchman and still makes European-style chocolate.

1. Chop chocolate into small pieces. Combine with cream in a saucepan.
2. Over low heat, melt chocolate into cream. Stir constantly until mixture is smooth and thick.
3. Pour chocolate fondue into a fondue pot and place over heating source on lowest setting. Have guests dip ladyfingers and fruit into chocolate and discuss flavors.

Box of Chocolates
Fondue Fun Party

This is a great idea for a preteen birthday party or an extended family gathering. Buy good quality supermarket or drugstore chocolates for these recipes.

MENU

◇◇◇◇◇◇◇◇◇◇◇◇

Chocolate Truffles Fondue

Pecan Caramels Chocolate Fondue

Sampler Chocolates Fondue

Chocolate Truffles Fondue

Serves 6

1 pound box of chocolate truffles
⅔ cup heavy cream
Pound cake fingers
Banana slices

Boxes of truffles come in dark, light, or mixed varieties. Pick your favorite and go with it.

1. Combine truffles with cream in a saucepan.
2. Over low heat, melt chocolates into cream. Stir constantly until mixture is smooth and thick.
3. Pour chocolate mixture into a fondue pot and place over heating source on lowest setting. Have guests dip pound cake fingers and banana slices into the fondue.

Pecan Caramels Chocolate Fondue

Serves 6

1 pound box of chocolate-covered
   pecan caramel clusters
1 cup heavy cream
Sugar cookies
Apple chunks

The nuts make a nice surprise in this melted mélange. The caramel takes longer to melt than the chocolate, so stir this fondue carefully.

1. Add chocolate candies to cream in a saucepan.
2. Over low heat, melt chocolates into cream. Stir constantly until mixture is combined and candies have all melted.
3. Pour chocolate mixture into a fondue pot and place over heating source on lowest setting. Serve with sugar cookies and apple chunks.

Sampler Chocolates Fondue

Serves 6

1 pound sampler box of chocolates
1 cup heavy cream
Mini croissants
Pear chunks

Every candy company has a box that contains a mixed bag of treats. Truly, with this fondue, you never know exactly what flavors you're going to get!

1. Combine chocolates with cream in a saucepan.
2. Over low heat, melt candies into cream. Stir constantly until mixture is smooth and thick.
3. Pour chocolate mixture into a fondue pot and place over heating source on lowest setting. Have guests dip croissants and pear chunks into the mix.

. . . .

Double Duty Dippers

When serving a fondue smorgasbord, place all dippers on one or two platters so guests can try them in all the different fondue varieties.

Mocha Madness Fondue Buffet

Lovers of the bean—both coffee and cocoa—will swoon over this dessert party menu.

MENU

◇◇◇◇◇◇◇◇◇◇◇◇

Cinnamon Coco-Latte Fondue

Expressive Espresso Fondue

Mocha-Mocha Java Fondue

Cinnamon Coco-Latte Fondue

Serves 8

1½ pounds milk chocolate
1 cup heavy cream
½ cup cinnamon syrup
½ cup strong brewed coffee
Assorted biscotti

> Cinnamon syrup and other coffee flavorings are available in the coffee aisle of most supermarkets.

1. Combine chocolate with cream in a saucepan.
2. Over low heat, melt chocolate into cream. Stir constantly until mixture is smooth and thick. Add syrup and coffee and stir until completely blended.
3. Pour chocolate mixture into one or more fondue pots and place over heating source on lowest setting. Serve with assorted biscotti.

. . . .

Biscotti

Biscotti get their characteristic crunch from being baked twice. First, the dough is formed into a wide log and baked. Then the log is sliced and the slices are baked again. The resulting cookie is perfect for dunking in coffee or fondue, and will stay fresh in a sealed container for weeks.

Expressive Espresso Fondue

Serves 8

1½ *pounds semisweet chocolate*
½ *cup heavy cream*
1 *cup brewed espresso*
2 *tablespoons Kahlua*
4 *cups lightly sweetened whipped cream*
Biscotti

The whipped cream in this dish starts out icy cold and whipped very stiff. As it melts, it resembles the froth atop a cup of espresso.

1. Combine chocolate with heavy cream in a saucepan.
2. Over low heat, melt chocolate into cream. Stir constantly until mixture is smooth and thick. Stir in espresso and Kahlua. Stir until completely blended.
3. Pour chocolate mixture into 1 or more fondue pots and place over heating source on lowest setting. Ladle a little cold whipped cream over the fondue right before serving with biscotti.

Coffee Options

In a pinch, espresso powder can be used in this dish in place of brewed espresso. Add 1–2 tablespoons of powder and a little more cream to the simmering chocolate. The end product will taste a little different, but still very good.

Mocha-Mocha Java Fondue

Serves 8

1½ pounds semisweet chocolate
1 cup plus 2 tablespoons heavy cream
1 cup brewed Mocha Java coffee
¼ cup Godiva liqueur
¼ pound white chocolate
Biscotti

Try this recipe with your favorite coffee blend.

1. Combine chocolate with 1 cup cream in a saucepan.
2. Over low heat, melt chocolate into cream. Stir constantly until mixture is smooth and thick. Stir in coffee and Godiva liqueur. In a microwave container or a clean saucepan, combine 2 tablespoons heavy cream and white chocolate. Melt over low heat and stir until smooth.
3. Pour dark chocolate mixture into 1 or more fondue pots and place over heating source on lowest setting. With a knife, carefully swirl a little white chocolate into the mixture and serve with biscotti.

. . . .

A Vintage Cup o' Joe

Mocha Java coffee pairs mocha beans from Yemen or Ethiopia with beans grown in Java. The popular blend, with its distinctive smooth-sweet flavor profile, is more than 250 years old. Mocha refers to the name of an ancient Yemeni port.

Favorite Flavors Chocolate Fondues

This dessert party menu features the classic chocolate flavor pairings.

MENU

⟨⟩⟨⟩⟨⟩⟨⟩⟨⟩⟨⟩⟨⟩⟨⟩⟨⟩

Chocolate Mint Fondue

Chocolate Marshmallow Fondue

Chocolate Peanut Butter Fondue

Chocolate Mint Fondue

Serves 6

1 pound semisweet chocolate
⅔ cup heavy cream
½ teaspoon peppermint extract
¼ cup crème de menthe
Chocolate wafers

When serving this fondue to children, look for mint-flavored chocolate bars. Melt the bars with cream and skip the crème de menthe.

1. Combine chocolate and cream in a saucepan over low heat. Heat, stirring constantly, until chocolate is melted and mixture is smooth.
2. Stir in peppermint extract and crème de menthe.
3. Pour chocolate mixture into fondue pots and place over heating source on lowest setting. Serve with chocolate wafers.

Chocolate Marshmallow Fondue

Serves 6

1 pound semisweet chocolate
1 cup heavy cream
2 cups miniature marshmallows
1 teaspoon vanilla extract
2 tablespoons vanilla liqueur
Graham cracker sticks

Sprinkle a few unmelted marshmallows over the top of this fondue for garnish.

1. Combine chocolate and cream in a saucepan over low heat. Heat, stirring constantly, until chocolate is melted and mixture is smooth.
2. Stir in marshmallows, vanilla, and liqueur. Mix until blended.
3. Pour chocolate mixture into 1 or more fondue pots and place over heating source. Serve with graham cracker sticks.

Chocolate Peanut Butter Fondue

Serves 6

1 pound milk chocolate
1 cup creamy peanut butter
1 tablespoon butter
1 cup heavy cream
1 cup peanuts, chopped
Pretzel rods
Fingerling bananas

For variety, consider switching peanut butter with cashew butter or almond butter.

1. Combine chocolate, peanut butter, butter, and cream in a saucepan over low heat. Heat, stirring constantly, until chocolate is melted and mixture is smooth.
2. Pour chocolate-peanut butter mixture into 1 or more fondue pots and place over heating source on lowest setting.
3. Sprinkle peanuts over the top of the fondue. Serve with thick pretzels and small bananas.

. . . .

Peanut Butter au Naturel

It's best to use a natural peanut butter in most recipes. Commercial brands have emulsifiers that may affect melting ability. Be sure to stir natural nut butters well to blend oils that may have separated.

Dipping and Dunking
Fondue Party

This dessert party is strictly kids' stuff. They'll love all the toppings and sprinkles!

MENU

◊◊◊◊◊◊◊◊◊◊◊◊◊◊

Colorful Kisses Fondue

My Favorite Things Fondue

Chocolate, Chocolate, Chocolate Fondue

Colorful Kisses Fondue

Serves 8

1½ pounds of milk chocolate
1 cup heavy cream
4 cups Hershey's Kissables, mini-M&Ms,
    or Reese's Pieces
Large marshmallows
24–32 miniature cupcakes, unfrosted
Large pretzel sticks

1. Combine chocolate and cream in a saucepan over low heat. Warm, stirring constantly, until chocolate is melted and mixture is smooth.
2. Divide candies over 8 dipping bowls.
3. Pour dark chocolate mixture into 1 or more fondue pots and place over heating source. Place marshmallows, cupcakes, and pretzels on serving platters. Allow guests to coat dippers with fondue and roll in candies to coat.

My Favorite Things Fondue

Serves 8

1½ pounds milk chocolate with
    almonds
1 cup heavy cream
2 cups flaked coconut
2 cups multicolored sprinkles
Oreos
Rice Krispy Treats, quartered
Cake donut holes
Large marshmallows

Small children love this dish—but be careful, they usually spend more time dunking and rolling than eating.

1. Combine chocolate and cream in a saucepan over low heat. Warm, stirring constantly, until chocolate is melted and mixture is creamy.
2. Divide coconut into 8 dipping bowls and do the same with sprinkles.
3. Pour dark chocolate mixture into 1 or more fondue pots and place over heating source on lowest setting. Allow guests to dip Oreos, Treats, donuts, and marshmallows in chocolate, then roll dippers in coconut or sprinkles.

Kid-safe Fondue

Chocolate stays melted for a good while. If you're hosting a party of very small children, consider dividing the chocolate fondue among several microwave-safe bowls. You'll eliminate the stress of having an open flame on the table. Let them dunk away and if the chocolate starts to stiffen, just pop it in the microwave for a few seconds.

Chocolate, Chocolate, Chocolate Fondue

Serves 8

1 pound milk chocolate
1 cup heavy cream
2 cups semi-sweet chocolate chips
1 cup white chocolate chips
Angel food cake
Sugar cookies

> The best way to serve this fondue is with gravy ladles and bowls.

1. Combine milk chocolate and cream in a saucepan over low heat. Warm, stirring constantly, until chocolate is melted and mixture is smooth. Remove from heat and stir in semi-sweet and white chocolate chips.
2. At this point, mixture can be divided over 1 or more fondue pots and placed on heat-safe table pads. Allow guests to ladle a small amount of fondue, including chips, into individual serving bowls.
3. Pass a platter of angel food cake cubes and sugar cookies for dunking.

. . . .

In the Chips

Supermarket shelves boast peanut butter chips, butterscotch chips, mint chips, orange chips and several shades of chocolate chips. Candy chips melt very slowly—they're designed to hold their shape—which makes them tricky for fondue. It's best to use them as flavor chips in a smooth fondue of melted chocolate.

Favorite Fruits Chocolate Fondue

These fondues offer sophisticated flavors, perfect for an after theater dessert party.

MENU

◇◇◇◇◇◇◇◇◇◇◇◇◇◇◇

White Chocolate Raspberry Fondue

Bittersweet Chocolate Orange Fondue

Chocolate Cherry Cordial Fondue

White Chocolate Raspberry Fondue

Serves 6

½ cup sugar

½ cup water

2 cups fresh or frozen raspberries

1 pound white chocolate

⅔ cup heavy cream

¼ cup Chambord liqueur

Dark chocolate pound cake, cubed

Look for a quality chocolate brand when shopping for white chocolate.

1. In a saucepan, mix sugar and water. Cook over medium heat, stirring, until sugar is dissolved and mixture begins to boil. Remove from heat and cool slightly. In a blender, combine sugar-water mixture with raspberries. Pulse to purée.
2. Combine white chocolate and cream in a saucepan over low heat. Warm, stirring constantly, until chocolate is melted and mixture is smooth. Pour raspberry purée through a strainer into the white chocolate mixture. Add Chambord and stir well.
3. Warm until white chocolate-raspberry mixture is hot. Pour into 1 or more fondue pots and place over heating source. Serve with chocolate pound cake cubes.

. . . .

Chocolate by Any Other Name

White chocolate, sometimes called confectionery coating, is made from processed cocoa butter without the cocoa solids. Many aficionados and even regulatory agencies don't consider it a true chocolate. However, there's a big flavor difference between real cocoa butter-based white chocolate and white candy coating made with shortening and flavorings. Look for a product with a high cocoa butter content.

Bittersweet Chocolate Orange Fondue

Serves 6

1 pound bittersweet chocolate
⅔ cup heavy cream
2 tablespoons orange zest
¼ cup Grand Marnier liqueur
1 cup slivered almonds
Stemmed strawberries
Shortbread cookies

Orange zest adds a heavenly citrus scent to this dark chocolate fondue.

1. Combine chocolate and cream in a saucepan over low heat. Warm, stirring constantly, until chocolate is melted and mixture is smooth.
2. Stir in orange zest and Grand Marnier.
3. Pour chocolate mixture into 1 or more fondue pots and place over heating source on lowest setting. Sprinkle almonds over the top for garnish. Serve with strawberries and shortbread cookies.

. . . .

Getting Zesty

Citrus zest is the colored, outer part of the fruit peel. The white pith, just beneath the zest, is bitter and should not be added to dessert recipes.

Chocolate Cherry Cordial Fondue

Serves 6

Flavor-infused cream gives this fondue a rich cherry flavor.

1 cup heavy cream
1 cup fresh or frozen sweet cherries, pitted
1 pound semisweet chocolate, chopped
2 tablespoons Kirsch
Stemmed cherries
Biscotti

1. Combine cream and cherries in a blender. Pulse until mixture is blended and cherries are puréed. Strain cherry-flavored cream into a saucepan and heat until just bubbling.
2. Reduce heat and add chopped chocolate. Stir constantly until chocolate is melted and mixture is smooth. Add Kirsch and stir.
3. Pour chocolate mixture into 1 or more fondue pots and place over heating source on lowest setting. Serve with stemmed cherries and biscotti.

A Bowl of Cherries

Most fresh cherries on the market are sweet cherries. Tart cherries turn up in jams and jellies, and occasionally as frozen cherries. Maraschino cherries aren't a type of cherry at all. They're sweet cherries that have been soaked in sugar syrup, flavored with a touch of almond and dyed red.

Chocolate Candy-Making Party

Next time you volunteer to provide the dessert for a charity event, or just want to stock up on treats for the holidays, invite a few friends over to share in the work and the rewards.

MENU

Chocolate Butter Truffles

Chocolate Butter Rum Truffles

Chocolate Orange Truffles

Chocolate Raspberry Truffles

Chocolate Espresso Truffles

Chocolate Mint Truffles

Chocolate Coconut Truffles

Chocolate Cherry BonBons

Chocolate Peanut Butter BonBons

Chocolate Macadamia BonBons

Chocolate Butter Truffles

Makes 5 dozen

1 cup heavy cream
⅓ cup sugar
Pinch of salt
1 teaspoon vanilla
½ pound high quality dark chocolate
½ pound high quality milk chocolate
1¼ cups unsalted butter
Choice of chocolate fondue for dipping
Cocoa powder for coating

This melt-in-your-mouth center is the simplest of all truffle fillings. Be sure to keep the centers very cold until they're dipped.

1. Combine cream, sugar, salt, and vanilla in a medium saucepan. Bring mixture to a boil, stirring often. Finely chop dark and milk chocolate. Remove cream mixture from heat and stir in chopped chocolate. Stir resulting ganache until melted and smooth.
2. Pour chocolate ganache into a glass mixing bowl and allow to cool. Cream butter. Whisk into chocolate ganache a spoonful at a time until mixture is creamy and well-blended.
3. Spoon small dollops of mixture onto a baking sheet lined with waxed paper. Or, place mixture in a pastry bag and pipe balls of ganache onto the sheet. Refrigerate for at least 2 hours or until centers have hardened.
4. Using a wooden skewer or fondue forks, dip the centers into chocolate fondue to coat. Allow excess chocolate to drip off, then roll truffle in the cocoa powder and set on wax paper-lined baking sheet to set. Keep truffles cool until ready to package or serve.

Chocolate Butter Rum Truffles

Makes 5 dozen

1 cup heavy cream
⅓ cup sugar
Pinch of salt
1 teaspoon vanilla
½ pound high quality dark chocolate
½ pound high quality milk chocolate
1¼ cups unsalted butter
3 tablespoons dark rum or 1 teaspoon rum extract
Choice of chocolate fondue for dipping
Confectioners' sugar for coating

> Real rum makes theses candies an adult treat. However, if you prefer a non-alcoholic version, substitute rum extract for the real thing.

1. Combine cream, sugar, salt and vanilla n a medium saucepan. Bring mixture to a boil, stirring often. Finely chop dark and milk chocolate. Remove cream mixture from heat and stir in chopped chocolate. Stir resulting ganache until melted and smooth.
2. Pour chocolate ganache into a glass mixing bowl and allow to cool. Cream butter with dark rum or rum extract. Whisk into chocolate ganache a spoonful at a time until mixture is creamy and well-blended.
3. Spoon small dollops of mixture onto a baking sheet lined with waxed paper. Or, place mixture in a pastry bag and pipe balls of ganache onto the sheet. Refrigerate for at least 2 hours or until centers have hardened.
4. Using a wooden skewer or fondue forks, dip the centers into chocolate fondue to coat. Allow excess chocolate to drip off, then roll truffle in the confectioners' sugar and set on wax paper-lined baking sheet to set. Keep truffles cool until ready to package or serve.

Chocolate Orange Truffles

Makes 5 dozen

²/₃ cup cream
²/₃ cup sugar
3 tablespoons corn syrup
1 pound good quality dark chocolate
2 tablespoons Grand Marnier
1 teaspoon grated orange zest
1¼ cups unsalted butter

Choice of chocolate fondue for
    dipping
Orange buttercream for garnish

> Chocolate and orange combine to make one of nature's most heavenly flavor combinations. If you prefer a perfectly smooth truffle center, skip the grated orange zest.

1. In a medium saucepan, bring cream and sugar to a boil, stirring constantly. Whisk in corn syrup. Remove cream from heat. Finely chop chocolate and add to hot cream a small amount at a time, stirring until completely melted.

2. Cool chocolate mixture completely. In a large bowl, cream softened butter with Grand Marnier and orange zest. Slowly whisk cooled chocolate into butter mixture until smooth and creamy.

3. Using a spoon or a pastry bag, place dollops of chocolate-orange mixture onto a parchment or waxed paper-lined baking sheet. Refrigerate until hardened, at least 2 hours.

4. Using fondue forks or wooden skewers, dip truffle centers into dark or light chocolate fondue. Drizzle a little orange buttercream over the top for garnish. Keep cool until ready to package or serve.

. . . .

A Touch of Color

An icing drizzle or a small bit of candied peel can make your truffles more appealing and help you keep track of which flavor is which. Make a thin, easy buttercream by creaming ½ cup of butter with two cups of sifted confectioners' sugar. Add ¼ teaspoon of orange extract and, if desired, a hint of orange (combine yellow and red) food coloring. If mixture is too stiff, thin with heavy cream. Drizzle a zigzag line of buttercream over the top of truffles. Vary extracts and colorings for other truffle flavors.

Chocolate Raspberry Truffles

Makes 5 dozen

⅔ cup cream

⅔ cup sugar

3 tablespoons corn syrup

½ pound good quality dark chocolate

½ pound good quality milk chocolate

1 tablespoon Framboise

2 tablespoons raspberry syrup

1¼ cup unsalted butter

Choice of chocolate fondue for dipping

Raspberry buttercream for garnish

If raspberries are in season and you're planning to serve these truffles for a same-day dessert, go ahead and place a single raspberry in the center of each of the truffle fillings. Think of it as ultra-chocolate dipped berries.

1. In a medium saucepan, bring cream and sugar to a boil, stirring constantly. Whisk in corn syrup. Remove cream from heat. Finely chop chocolate and add to hot cream a small amount at a time, stirring until completely melted. Cool chocolate mixture completely.

2. Make raspberry syrup. Puree a cup of raspberries and strain liquid into a saucepan. Bring to a boil, then reduce heat. Cook until liquid has reduced by half. Cool completely.

3. In a large bowl, cream softened butter with Framboise and raspberry syrup. Slowly whisk cooled chocolate into butter mixture until smooth and creamy.

4. Using a spoon or a pastry bag, place dollops of chocolate-raspberry mixture onto a parchment or waxed paper-lined baking sheet. Refrigerate until hardened, at least 2 hours.

5. Using fondue forks or wooden skewers, dip truffle centers into dark or light chocolate fondue. Drizzle a little raspberry buttercream over the top for garnish. Keep cool until ready to package or serve.

Chocolate Espresso Truffles

Makes 5 dozen

⅔ cup cream

⅔ cup sugar

2 tablespoons espresso powder or
    instant coffee

3 tablespoons corn syrup

1 pound good quality dark chocolate

1 teaspoon vanilla

1¼ cups unsalted butter

Choice of chocolate fondue for dipping

Mixture of cocoa powder and espresso powder (2 to 1) for coating

These little pick-me-ups call for a coating of cocoa and espresso powder. Espresso powder is extremely fine-ground and usually carried in specialty stores and some supermarkets. Do not substitute regular instant coffee for the coating.

1. In a medium saucepan, bring cream and sugar to a boil, stirring constantly. Whisk in espresso or coffee powder, and stir until dissolved. Whisk in corn syrup. Remove cream from heat. Finely chop chocolate and add to hot cream a small amount at a time, stirring until completely melted.
2. Cool chocolate-coffee mixture completely. In a large bowl, cream softened butter with vanilla. Slowly whisk cooled chocolate-coffee into butter mixture until smooth and creamy.
3. Using a spoon or a pastry bag, place dollops of chocolate-coffee mixture onto a parchment or waxed paper-lined baking sheet. Refrigerate until hardened, at least ¼ hours.
4. Using fondue forks or wooden skewers, dip truffle centers into dark or light chocolate fondue. Combine cocoa and espresso. Roll dipped truffles into powder mixture and place on a baking sheet. Keep cool until ready to package or serve.

Chocolate Mint Truffles

Makes 5 dozen

²/₃ cup cream

²/₃ cup sugar

3 tablespoons corn syrup

1 pound good quality dark or milk chocolate

½ teaspoon peppermint extract

¼ teaspoon vanilla

1¼ cups unsalted butter

White or dark chocolate fondue for dipping

Crushed peppermints for coating

To really gild the lily, try mounding these truffle centers on top of small, thin chocolate wafers. Dip the whole thing in chocolate fondue for a truffle with a crunchy surprise.

1. In a medium saucepan, bring cream and sugar to a boil, stirring constantly. Whisk in corn syrup. Remove cream from heat. Finely chop chocolate and add to hot cream a small amount at a time, stirring until completely melted.
2. Cool chocolate mixture completely. In a large bowl, cream softened butter with peppermint extract and vanilla. Slowly whisk cooled chocolate into butter mixture until smooth and creamy.
3. Using a spoon or a pastry bag, place dollops of chocolate-mint mixture onto a parchment or waxed paper-lined baking sheet. Refrigerate until hardened, at least 2 hours.
4. Using fondue forks or wooden skewers, dip truffle centers into dark or white chocolate fondue. Crush peppermint candies. Roll dipped truffles into candy and place on a baking sheet. Keep cool until ready to package or serve.

Mmmm, minty

Mint truffles also can be made with 3 tablespoons of Crème de Menthe mixed into the butter. This version skips the alcohol, making the candies suitable for holiday parties where children will undoubtedly be drawn to the truffle dish.

Chocolate Coconut Truffles

Makes 5 dozen

⅔ cup cream

⅔ cup sugar

3 tablespoons corn syrup

1 pound good quality milk or
    white chocolate

1 teaspoon coconut extract

2 tablespoons cream of coconut

1 ¼ cup unsalted butter

White chocolate fondue for dipping

Flaked or toasted coconut

You can use plain white coconut from a bag or box to give these truffles a snowball look. Or toast flaked coconut in the oven just until lightly browned, then chop finely in a food processor.

1. In a medium saucepan, bring cream and sugar to a boil, stirring constantly. Whisk in corn syrup. Remove cream from heat. Finely chop chocolate and add to hot cream a small amount at a time, stirring until completely melted.
2. Cool chocolate mixture completely. In a large bowl, cream softened butter with coconut extract and cream of coconut. Slowly whisk cooled chocolate into butter mixture until smooth and creamy.
3. Using a spoon or a pastry bag, place dollops of chocolate-coconut mixture onto a parchment or waxed paper-lined baking sheet. Refrigerate until hardened, at least 2 hours.
4. Using fondue forks or wooden skewers, dip truffle centers into white chocolate fondue. Roll dipped truffles into coconut and place on a baking sheet. Keep cool until ready to package or serve.

Chocolate Cherry BonBons

Makes 5 dozen

1 pound almond paste

2 cups confectioners' sugar

*1 cup finely chopped maraschino
    cherries*

1–2 tablespoons liquid from cherries

Choice of chocolate fondue for dipping

Commercial cherry cordials are made through a complicated process that includes enzymes that create the liquid cherry center. These candies have a firm center and sweet cherry flavor.

1. In a bowl, use 2 knives or a pastry blender to combine confectioners' sugar and almond paste. Work in chopped cherries until ingredients are evenly distributed. Add cherry liquid if paste seems too stiff.
2. On a board floured with confectioners' sugar, roll cherry-almond mixture into a rectangle ¾ inch thick. Cut the rectangle diagonally in each direction to make small diamonds.
3. Dip centers into dark or light chocolate fondue and place on a waxed paper or parchment-lined baking sheet to set. Keep cool until ready to serve or package.

. . . .

Versatile Almond Paste

Almond paste is made of ground almonds mixed with a hint—no more than 35 percent—of sugar, processed to a super-fine, soft consistency. The delicate almond flavor can be showcased by enrobing almond paste in chocolate, or it can form the basis for a variety of candy centers. However, pure almond paste is very soft. To make it workable for most cooks—particularly when dipping it in melted chocolate—it must be stiffened with the addition of confectioners' sugar. Try making candy centers with almond paste and finely chopped dried fruits like apricots.

Chocolate Peanut Butter BonBons

Makes 5 dozen

2 cups smooth peanut butter

2 cups confectioners' sugar

½ cup butter, melted

1 tablespoon cocoa powder

Milk or dark chocolate fondue coating

Crushed peanuts (optional)

These candies are incredibly easy to make and very popular. Before serving to a crowd, make sure to either garnish the candies with peanuts or tell everyone what's inside. Peanut allergies are serious business.

1. In a large mixing bowl, combine peanut butter, confectioners' sugar, melted butter, and cocoa powder. Beat with an electric mixer until well combined and smooth.
2. Cover and refrigerate for at least 1 hour. Form mixture into balls and place on a waxed paper-lined baking sheet. Refrigerate until ready to dip.
3. Using wooden skewers or fondue forks, dip peanut butter centers into milk or dark chocolate fondue. Shake off excess chocolate and roll in crushed peanuts if desired.

. . . .

Do-it-Yourself Peanut Butter

To control the amount of salt and sugar in peanut butter, just make your own. All it takes is fresh, blanched, roasted peanuts and a food processor. Place peanuts in the bowl and pulse until mixture is smooth. If peanut butter seems dry, drizzle a little peanut oil into the paste. Use as is or add a little salt or sugar to taste.

Chocolate Macadamia BonBons

Makes 5 dozen

Almond paste makes these macadamia treats simple and simply delicious.

1 pound almond paste
4 ounces milk chocolate, melted
3 tablespoons confectioners' sugar
2 cups coarsely chopped unsalted macadamia nuts
Dark or light chocolate fondue for dipping
Finely chopped macadamia nuts (optional)

1. Blend melted chocolate with almond paste and sugar. Mix until smooth and chocolate is evenly distributed. Stir in chopped macadamia nuts.
2. Spoon small mounds of mixture onto a waxed paper-lined baking sheet. Refrigerate 30 minutes or until mounds harden slightly.
3. Using wooden skewers or a fondue fork, dip centers into light or dark chocolate and, if desired, coat with finely chopped macadamia nuts.

- -

Macadamia Madness

Though native to Australia, macadamia nuts were introduced to Hawaii in the late 1800s and represent a major export from that state. Long considered a luxury food, the cost of the macadamia is in part related to the difficulty in harvesting these hard-shelled nuts. Macadamias have an 80 percent fat content, making them popular with low-carb dieters.

Tri-Chocolate Fondue for Candy

Coats 15 dozen candies

1½ pounds white chocolate, finely chopped
1½ pounds semi-sweet or dark chocolate, finely chopped
1½ pounds milk chocolate, finely chopped

1. In the top of a double boiler, melt ½ pound of finely chopped white chocolate, stirring constantly. Add the remaining chocolate in 4 batches, waiting until chocolate is melted to add the next batch. Pour the chocolate into a glass bowl. As it begins to set around the edges, stir the set chocolate into the melted chocolate.
2. Repeat process with semi-sweet chocolate and with milk chocolate.
3. Pour different fondues into 3 fondue pots and place pots over heating elements on low settings. Allow chocolates to melt fully and begin dipping.

. . . .

Only the Best

When making candy, buy the best chocolate you can find and treat it gently. To make things easier for guests, be sure to have small plates of shredded coconut, cocoa powder, confectioners' sugar, chopped nuts, and other coatings near each place so no one has to reach. Consider buying pretty foil-lined boxes or tins for guests to take home a sampling of the evening's handiwork.

Chapter 9

**Dessert Party Fondues:
Beyond Chocolate**

Sweet Southern Nights

This dessert party menu showcases the rich, comforting flavors of Latin America and the American South. Serve these sugary fondues with tart fruit and barely-sweet pastries or after a simple meal.

MENU

Dulce de Leche Fondue

Louisiana Butter Pecan Fondue

Bourbon and Butterscotch Fondue

Dulce de Leche Fondue

Serves 6

½ gallon whole milk
2 cups sugar
1 vanilla bean, split
½ cup heavy cream
3 starfruits, sliced
2 papayas, sliced
3 bananas, sliced
Shortbread cookies

> Dulce de Leche—literally sweet milk—is one of the prized flavors of Latin America.

1. In a nonreactive soup pot, combine milk, sugar, and vanilla bean. Cook over medium heat, stirring constantly, until mixture begins to bubble around the edges. Lower heat to medium-low and cook, stirring often, for 2 hours. Mixture should be thick, caramel-colored, and reduced to about 2 cups.
2. Remove vanilla bean from mixture and add heavy cream. Stir well.
3. Pour mixture into a fondue pot and place over a heating source. Serve with tropical fruits and cookies.

Timesaving Tip

Homemade Dulce de Leche is a tasty treat. But if you don't have time to make it, just pour 3 cans of the ready-made version from your supermarket into a saucepan. Add a little vanilla extract and heavy cream and heat to a simmer. Pour into a fondue pot and dip away.

Louisiana Butter Pecan Fondue

Serves 6

Think of this as pecan pie in fondue form!

2 cups pecan halves
½ cup butter
1 cup brown sugar, packed
½ cup corn syrup
2 cups heavy cream
1 teaspoon vanilla extract
Shortbread cookies

1. In a heavy Dutch oven, combine pecans with the butter. Cook over medium heat, stirring frequently, until pecans are toasted.
2. Stir in brown sugar and corn syrup. Cook until sugar is melted and mixture is bubbly. Add cream and bring to a boil. Reduce heat and simmer for 2 minutes. Add vanilla.
3. Pour pecan mixture into 1 or more fondue pots. Set over heating source and serve with shortbread cookies.

. . . .

Nuts to You!

Nuts are high in healthy fats. That makes them good for you, but also makes them perishable. Store nuts in airtight bags in the freezer to keep flavor.

Bourbon and Butterscotch Fondue

Serves 6

2 cups sugar
2/3 cup water
1 tablespoon lemon juice
1/2 cup butter
1 cup heavy cream
1/4 cup bourbon
Pound cake cubes

> To make this without alcohol, increase the amount of cream and add a teaspoon of vanilla or rum extract.

1. In a large, heavy saucepan, combine sugar, water, and lemon juice. Cook over medium heat, stirring until sugar has dissolved. Increase heat to medium high and cook, stirring often, until mixture is golden.
2. Remove pot from heat and carefully add butter. Stir in cream a little at a time. When cream is thoroughly blended, allow mixture to cool slightly. When fondue is no longer bubbling, stir in bourbon.
3. Transfer butterscotch mixture to 1 or more fondue pots and place over heating source. Serve with pound cake cubes.

. . . .

Spirited Fondue

High-proof alcohol can be added to cheese and dessert fondues in small amounts. However, you should never substitute spirits for wine in a Bacchus fondue. At high temperatures, whisky and other spirits are inflammable.

Fruity Brunch Fondues

This menu can be served with scones, muffins, or breakfast breads for a wonderfully unique brunch offering.

MENU

◇◇◇◇◇◇◇◇◇◇◇◇◇

Sweet Apricot Jam Melt

Warm Berry Compote Fondue

Butter Maple Raisin Sauce

Sweet Apricot Jam Melt

Serves 6

2 cups fresh or frozen apricot halves
1 tablespoon lemon juice
1 cup plus 1 tablespoon water
1 cup sugar
1 teaspoon cornstarch
1½ cups apricot jam
Scones

Guests can dip their scones into this sweet fondue, or just spoon some over a split scone.

1. Place apricots, lemon juice, and 1 cup water in a blender or food processor. Pulse until puréed. Strain the apricots into a heavy saucepan over medium heat. Add the sugar. Bring to a boil, stirring frequently.
2. Dissolve cornstarch in 1 tablespoon of water and add to the boiling mixture. Stir until blended and slightly thickened. Add apricot jam and whisk until jam has melted and is completely blended.
3. Pour apricot mixture into 1 or more fondue pots and set over heating source. Serve with scones.

. . . .

Jammin' in the Kitchen

Jams and jellies make excellent timesavers. In a pinch, quality jams can serve as cake fillings, while melted jellies are perfect for glazes and flavoring sugar syrups.

Warm Berry Compote Fondue

Serves 6–8

1 cup cherries, pitted
1 cup blueberries
1 cup blackberries
1 cup raspberries
1½ cups sugar
½ cup water
1 tablespoon cornstarch
2 tablespoons Grand Marnier
Croissants
Biscuits

If fresh berries aren't in season, don't hesitate to use frozen ones in this dish.

1. Combine berries, sugar, and water in a heavy saucepan. Cook over medium heat, stirring often, until sugar is dissolved and mixture is beginning to bubble. Reduce heat slightly and simmer for 15 minutes.
2. Dissolve cornstarch in Grand Marnier. Increase heat on berries and bring to a boil. Add cornstarch and cook, stirring constantly, until mixture is thickened.
3. Pour berries into 1 or more fondue pots and place over heating source. Serve with croissants and biscuits.

. . . .

Bountiful Berries

This compote can be ladled over ice cream as a topping or used as a sauce for sponge cakes and pound cakes. Just add whipped cream.

Butter Maple Raisin Sauce

Serves 6

½ cup butter
1 teaspoon cinnamon
1½ cups raisins
2 cups maple syrup
¼ cup water
French toast sticks
Waffle pieces

Kids absolutely love this fondue. Serve it with mini waffles on a winter morning.

1. Combine butter and cinnamon in a saucepan over medium heat. Stir until butter is melted and cinnamon is blended. Add raisins, syrup, and water. Bring to a boil, then remove from heat.
2. Pour maple sauce into 1 or more fondue pots. Place over heating source and serve with French toast and waffle pieces.

Sap Lovers

Authentic maple syrup—the kind distilled from maple tree sap—is a gourmet gift from nature. It's considerably more expensive than maple-flavored corn syrup, but worth the price. You'll appreciate the complex flavors in fondues and other dishes.

Creamy, Dreamy Fondue Desserts

Just because a dessert isn't dripping with chocolate doesn't mean it isn't decadent. Here are a few show-stoppers to brighten any dessert buffet.

MENU

◇◇◇◇◇◇◇◇◇◇◇◇◇

Crème Anglaise Fondue

Mascarpone and Calvados Fondue

Coconut Milk and Macadamia Nut Fondue

Crème Anglaise Fondue

Serves 6

6 egg yolks
½ cup sugar
2 cups heavy cream
1 cup milk
1 teaspoon vanilla extract
2 tablespoons Irish Cream liqueur
Quartered fresh peaches
Stemmed strawberries

You'll have to stop your guests from taking out a spoon and slurping this luscious cream.

1. In a large bowl, whisk together egg yolks and sugar until light yellow and thick.
2. Pour cream and milk into a saucepan and cook over medium heat until just scalded. Slowly pour hot cream mixture into the egg mixture, whisking constantly to keep cream from cooking the eggs.
3. Pour eggs and cream into a saucepan and cook over medium heat, stirring constantly, until mixture is thick enough to coat a spoon. Stir in vanilla and liqueur. Pour sauce into 1 or more fondue pots and place over heating source. Serve with peaches and strawberries.

Mascarpone and Calvados Fondue

Serves 6

2 cups mascarpone cheese
½ cup heavy cream
¼ cup Calvados
1 teaspoon vanilla extract
¼ teaspoon nutmeg
Tart and sweet apple, sliced

> Mascarpone, a creamy fresh cheese, stars in the Italian dessert tiramisu. But it's also very tasty in other desserts!

1. In a saucepan, combine mascarpone and cream. Cook over medium heat, stirring constantly, until cheese is melted and mixture is bubbly.
2. Stir in Calvados, vanilla, and nutmeg. Remove from heat. Pour into 1 or more fondue pots and place over heating source.
3. Serve with apple slices.

. . . .

Eau de Vie

Dozens of different varieties of apples go into the production of Calvados, an oak barrel-aged brandy that originated in the Normandy region of France. Other clear fruit brandies, such as pear or plum, can be added to dessert sauces or even cheese fondue.

Coconut Milk and Macadamia Nut Fondue

Serves 6

1 cup sweetened condensed milk

2 cups coconut milk

½ teaspoon coconut extract

1 tablespoon macadamia nut butter

2 tablespoons macadamia nut liqueur

2 cups macadamia nuts, chopped

2 cups coconut

Pineapple spears

Chocolate pound cake cubes

> Coconut milk in cans tends to separate into heavy cream and thin liquid. Make sure to stir the milk before measuring.

1. Place condensed milk, coconut milk, coconut extract, and macadamia nut butter in a blender. Blend until smooth. Pour into a saucepan and heat until mixture is bubbling.
2. Add liqueur to saucepan and stir well. Remove from heat and pour mixture into 1 or more fondue pots. Set over heating source.
3. Divide nuts and coconut into individual dipping dishes. Encourage guests to dip pineapple and pound cake cubes, then coat them with nuts or coconut.

. . . .

Do-it-Yourself Nut Butter

Specialty shops carry a range of nut butters. To make your own, simply pour a cup of macadamia nuts into a food processor with a metal blade. Drizzle a few drops of almond oil into the bowl and pulse until nuts are creamy. Add salt if desired.

Fondue Shortcake Dessert Party

Everybody loves berry shortcakes, with tart berries nestling into sweet pastry and cream. This refreshing cold fondue menu brings together all those flavors.

MENU

◇◇◇◇◇◇◇◇◇◇◇◇

Strawberry Shortcake Fondue

Blueberry Shortcake Fondue

White Peach Shortcake Fondue

Sweet Shortcake Biscuits

Strawberry Shortcake Fondue

Serves 6

6 cups strawberries, sliced

1 cup superfine sugar

1 tablespoon amaretto

6 cups sweetened whipped cream

½ cup strawberry syrup or chocolate sauce

2 dozen ladyfingers

> Instead of fondue forks, you may want to give guests long-handled ice tea spoons for this dish.

1. Combine strawberries and sugar in a bowl. Toss well. Pour into a glass baking dish or shallow serving bowl. Cover and refrigerate for at least 1 hour. Remove from refrigerator, sprinkle amaretto over the berries, and stir well.
2. Smooth the top of the berries, then pile on the whipped cream, covering the berries. Drizzle strawberry syrup or chocolate sauce over whipped cream mounds.
3. Serve with spoons and ladyfingers.

Sugar Soak

Sprinkling sugar over peeled fruit draws liquid from the fruit, which dissolves the sugar. The resulting sugar syrup softens and flavors the fruit.

Blueberry Shortcake Fondue

Serves 6

This recipe is almost too easy—but your guests will love it.

3 pints vanilla ice cream, softened
1½ cups prepared Caramel Fruit Dip
2 cups fresh blueberries
6 cups lightly sweetened whipped cream
12 sponge cake cups

1. Spread ice cream evenly in the bottom of a shallow 2-quart casserole dish. Cover dish and return to freezer for at least 1 hour.
2. Spread caramel dip over the top of the ice cream. Sprinkle blueberries over the top and lightly press into the caramel. Mound whipped cream over all.
3. Serve with long spoons and sponge cake cups.

. . . .

Baked Alaska Fondue

If you're feeling adventurous, make a batch of meringue (4 egg whites, cup superfine sugar, ½ teaspoon cream of tartar, and 1 teaspoon of vanilla extract, all beaten stiff) and mound that over the blueberry-topped ice cream instead of whipped cream. Bake at 375°F for 10 minutes or until nicely browned.

White Peach Shortcake Fondue

Serves 6

4 cups Crème Anglaise Fondue
   (page 269), chilled
6 cups white peaches, sliced
6 cups lightly sweetened whipped cream
12 sweet shortcake biscuits (page 276)

Southerners favor sweet biscuits, rather than sponge cake, for shortcakes.

1. Pour chilled Crème Anglaise into 1 or 2 serving bowls. Place a shallow bowl or glass pie plate of fresh peach slices next to each bowl.
2. Divide whipped cream into dipping bowls for each guest.
3. Split warm biscuits and place on serving platters. Encourage guests to dip peaches in Crème Anglaise, dip in whipped cream, and enjoy with bites of warm biscuits.

. . . .

The Rose of Fruits

Peaches are members of the rose family, which may explain their wonderful fragrance. White peaches have less acidity than yellow peaches, and therefore, taste sweeter than their more colorful cousins.

Sweet Shortcake Biscuits

Serves 6

3 cups all-purpose flour
⅓ cup sugar
4 teaspoons baking powder
½ teaspoon salt
¾ cup shortening or butter, chilled
1½ cups heavy cream
1 teaspoon almond extract

If you're pressed for time, skip the rolling and cutting. Just drop generous teaspoon-size balls of dough onto a greased cookie sheet.

1. In a large bowl, combine flour, sugar, baking powder, and salt. Whisk to blend and remove any clumps.
2. Add shortening and cut in with 2 knives or a pastry blender until mixture resembles coarse meal.
3. Add almond extract to cream and stir into flour mixture. Use moistened fingers to blend dough and work it into a ball. Cover and refrigerate until chilled.
4. Press dough into a 1-inch thick square. With a small biscuit cutter, cut 12 circles. Place on a greased cookie sheet. Bake at 400°F until nicely browned, about 15 minutes. Serve warm.

Dessert Fondue for Two

Sometimes you just want the taste of something sweet. Here are three options for ending a romantic meal on the right note.

MENU

◇◇◇◇◇◇◇◇◇◇◇◇

Crème Caramel Fondue

Key Lime Pie Fondue

Pumpkin Cheesecake Fondue

Crème Caramel Fondue

Serves 2

10 *caramel candies*
½ *cup heavy cream*
1 *tablespoon brandy*
1 *tablespoon brown sugar*
Apple slices
Dried apricots
Banana slices

To make this non-alcoholic, just omit the brandy and add ½ teaspoon of vanilla extract.

1. In a heavy saucepan, combine the cream and caramels. Cook over medium-low heat, stirring, until caramels are melted and mixture is bubbly. Add brandy.
2. Pour mixture into a fondue pot and place over heating source. Sprinkle brown sugar on top.
3. Enjoy with sliced fruit.

Key Lime Pie Fondue

Serves 2

½ *cup sweetened condensed milk*
½ *cup Key lime juice*
½ *cup heavy cream*
½ *teaspoon vanilla extract*
Graham crackers

This mixture can also be chilled and served as a cold fondue.

1. In a heavy saucepan, combine condensed milk and Key lime juice. Heat, whisking constantly, until mixture is bubbly. Slowly whisk in heavy cream and vanilla.
2. Pour into a fondue pot and set over heating source.
3. Enjoy with graham crackers.

Pumpkin Cheesecake Fondue

Serves 2

¹/₃ cup canned pumpkin
3 ounces cream cheese
¹/₃ cup heavy cream
2 tablespoons sugar
1 teaspoon pumpkin pie spice
Shortbread cookies
Almond biscotti

Make a larger batch of this recipe for an unexpected Thanksgiving dessert.

1. In a saucepan, combine pumpkin, cream cheese, heavy cream, and sugar. Cook over medium heat, stirring constantly.
2. When cream cheese has melted, stir in spice. Heat mixture until bubbly, then pour into a fondue pot. Place over heating source and enjoy with shortbread cookies and biscotti.

Cheese Course Fondue

Elaborate French menus often include a cheese course served between the entrée and dessert. The slightly amended version of the practice places the cheese course as the meal finale, in place of dessert. Either way, this fondue cheese course menu is perfect for socializing at home after a light restaurant meal or other outing.

MENU

Explorateur Cheese Fondue

Cherry Mascarpone Fondue

Havarti with Stilton Swirl Fondue

Platter of Apples, Pears, Dried Apricots, Walnut Halves, Ladyfingers and Shortbread Cookies

Explorateur Cheese Fondue

Serves 6

1 cup white dessert wine

Juice of 1 lemon

1 pound Explorateur cheese,
   rind removed

½ pound cream cheese

1½ tablespoons cornstarch

3 tablespoons pear eau de vie

½ teaspoon vanilla extract

> Explorateur is a triple-cream cheese with a high fat content and a buttery flavor. Like Brie, it has an edible rind. However, the rind is best removed before melting for a smooth fondue.

1. Pour wine into heavy saucepan over medium heat. Add lemon juice to wine. Bring mixture to a simmer.
2. Break Explorateur and cream cheese into pieces. Add ¼ of the cheese to the simmering liquid and stir in a figure-eight pattern. Once that cheese has melted, add another ¼ to the saucepan. Keep stirring. Repeat until all cheese is melted and mixture is hot, but not boiling.
3. Dissolve cornstarch in eau de vie. Stir into cheese mixture. Cook until just bubbly, then reduce heat and simmer for 1 additional minute. Stir in vanilla.
4. Pour liquid into 1 or more fondue pots and keep warm over heat source. Serve with fruit, shortbread, nuts, and ladyfingers.

Cherry Mascarpone Fondue

Serves 6

1 pound Mascarpone cheese

¼ cup Kirsch

1 tablespoon cornstarch

3 tablespoons confectioners' sugar

3 eggs

1 cup cherries, chopped and pitted

> Mascarpone is the ultimate dessert cheese, with the texture of a soft, silky cream cheese and slightly tart, clean flavor.

1. In a double boiler over simmering water, whisk together cheese, Kirsch, cornstarch, and confectioners' sugar.
2. In a bowl, whip eggs with a mixer on medium speed until eggs are light and frothy.
3. When mascarpone cheese is melted and mixture is hot, slowly pour a ladle of the hot cheese into the eggs while beating the eggs. Pour the eggs into the double boiler and whisk together briskly. Stir in cherries.
4. Pour mixture into 1 or more fondue pots and place over heat source. Serve with fruit, shortbread, and crisp ladyfingers.

. . . .

Temper, Temper

Eggs must be warmed slightly and quickly before being whisked into hot liquid. Otherwise, you'll have bits of hard, cooked egg in your mixture. It takes practice, but the trick is to add hot liquid slowly while keeping the eggs moving.

Havarti with Stilton Swirl Fondue

Serves 6

1½ cups white dessert wine
Juice of 1 lemon
1 pound Havarti cheese,
    rind removed
1½ tablespoons cornstarch
3 tablespoons apple brandy
½ pound Stilton cheese, crumbled

Crumbled blue-veined Stilton is stirred into this creamy Havarti fondue just before serving, giving the resulting fondue an interesting color and texture.

1. Pour wine into heavy saucepan over medium heat. Add lemon juice to wine. Bring mixture to a simmer.
2. Grate Havarti in a food processor. Add ¼ of the grated cheese to the simmering liquid and stir in a figure-eight pattern. Once that cheese has melted, add another ¼ to the saucepan. Keep stirring. Repeat until all Havarti is melted and mixture is hot, but not boiling.
3. Dissolve cornstarch in apple brandy. Stir into Havarti mixture. Cook until just bubbly, then reduce heat and simmer for 1 additional minute.
5. Pour liquid into 1 or more fondue pots. Swirl crumbled Stilton into the fondue and keep warm over heat source. Serve with fruit, shortbread, nuts, and ladyfingers.

Chapter 10

Good Carbs, Good Fats, Great
Fondue: Healthy Celebrations

Game Night Supper Fondue

On a cold winter evening, invite friends to sit by the fire, play team Scrabble, and enjoy a simple meal built around a mellow, reduced-fat cheese fondue.

MENU

Dijon Salmon Roll-Ups

Tapenade-Stuffed Celery

Roasted Tomato Soup

Cheddar-Blue Fondue

Whole Grain Breads

Vegetable Platter

Baked Apple Crisp

Fume Blanc

Dijon Salmon Roll-Ups

Serves 8

4 cups salmon, poached
*   and flaked*
1 cup cucumber, finely diced
½ cup celery, finely diced
1 green onion, minced
1 cup plain yogurt
½ cup canola mayonnaise
½ cup Dijon mustard
2 packets artificial sweetener
2 tablespoons fresh dill, minced
4 12-inch whole wheat flatbreads or wraps
Salt and pepper to taste

> Middle Eastern bakeries often sell large airy flatbreads that resemble giant pitas without the pocket. If you can't find soft flatbread, use whole grain tortilla wraps.

1. In a large bowl, combine salmon, cucumber, celery, and green onion.
2. In a separate bowl, whisk together yogurt, mayonnaise, mustard, sweetener, and dill. Fold Dijon dressing into salmon mixture. Divide salmon over flatbreads and sprinkle with salt and pepper to taste.
3. Roll flatbreads firmly and slice into 1-inch thick pinwheels. Place on a platter and serve.

Fish Flakes

Leftover cooked fish makes a great starting point for salads. Rather than reach for canned tuna for lunch, try cooking a little extra salmon, snapper, or fresh tuna the next time you serve fish. Chill the leftovers, remove bones and skin, and combine with chopped egg whites and your favorite dressing.

Tapenade-Stuffed Celery

Serves 8

2 cups pitted Kalamata olives

6 anchovy fillets

3 tablespoons capers

1 teaspoon lemon juice

1 teaspoon fresh thyme leaves

¼ teaspoon black pepper

2 tablespoons olive oil

8 celery stalks, trimmed and washed

Dark, intensely flavorful tapenade can be served as a dip or spread. Omit the anchovies, if you like, and substitute a few sun-dried tomatoes.

1. Place olives, anchovies, capers, lemon juice, and thyme in a food processor. Pulse until just chopped.
2. Add pepper and olive oil and process until mixture forms a coarse purée. Cut celery stalks in half horizontally to make 16 pieces. Spoon tapenade into celery pieces or serve with whole grain crackers.

. . . .

A Sea of Olives

Virtually every country around the Mediterranean grows a few signature varieties of olives, from the tiny picholine olives of France to the large hondroelia olives of Greece. Olives range from bright green to purple to black and can be cured in lye, water, brine, salt, or oil. The type of olive and the curing process affect the flavor and texture of the olives, which can be predominantly tart, salty, flowery, bitter, or buttery. Most supermarkets today carry an extensive selection of olives in the deli department.

Roasted Tomato Soup

Serves 8

6 pounds plum tomatoes

16 cloves garlic, peeled

⅓ cup plus 1 tablespoon olive oil

1 small onion, minced

8 cups chicken broth or tomato juice

¼ cup fresh basil, minced

1 teaspoon fresh oregano, minced

1 teaspoon Worcestershire sauce

1 tablespoon orange zest

If you've never had the pleasure of home-made tomato soup, this recipe is a great introduction.

1. Cut tomatoes in half lengthwise. Combine with garlic and ⅓ cup olive oil in a baking dish. Toss to coat well and bake at 375°F for 45 minutes or until tomatoes are tender and slightly browned. Set aside.

2. In a soup kettle, combine onion with 1 tablespoon olive oil. Sauté over medium-high heat until onion has softened. Add chicken broth or tomato juice, basil, oregano, and Worcestershire sauce. Bring mixture to a boil.

3. Pour roasted tomatoes and garlic—in batches if necessary—into a food processor. Pulse until tomatoes are puréed. Add tomato mixture to the soup kettle and simmer for 30 minutes. Stir in orange zest and serve.

Cheddar-Blue Fondue

Serves 8

2 cups dry white wine

2 small cloves garlic

Juice of 2 lemons

¼ pound blue cheese, crumbled

½ pound reduced-fat Cheddar cheese, shredded

1 pound reduced-fat cream cheese, cubed

1½ tablespoons cornstarch

3 tablespoons skim milk

½ teaspoon white pepper

¼ cup parsley, minced

½ teaspoon nutmeg

6 cups cubed bread, including whole wheat French,
   country rye, and multi-grain

> Substitute evaporated skimmed milk for the wine if you'd prefer a non-alcoholic fondue.

1. Bring wine, garlic, and lemon juice to a boil in a saucepan. Reduce heat to simmer and add blue cheese and ½ the Cheddar. Stir in a figure-eight motion until cheese is melted. Add remaining Cheddar, stir until melted, and then add all of the cream cheese.
2. Simmer mixture and stir frequently until the cream cheese is melted and the fondue is bubbly. Dissolve cornstarch in milk. Stir into cheese. Add pepper, parsley, and nutmeg.
3. Pour hot mixture into 1 or more fondue pots. Place over heating source and serve with cubed bread.

. . . .

Little Fat, Big Flavor

Use a small amount of high-impact cheeses, like Gorgonzola, Blue, and Romano, to give presence to low-fat fondues. Reduced-fat cream cheese, skim milk ricotta, and cottage cheese can give reduced-fat fondues a creamy texture.

Baked Apple Crisp

Serves 8

6 cups apples, peeled and chopped

1 teaspoon lemon juice

Sugar substitute equal to
    ½ cup brown sugar

1 teaspoon cinnamon

¼ teaspoon ginger

⅛ teaspoon cloves

⅓ cup whole wheat pastry flour

½ cup canola oil margarine, very chilled

⅓ cup rolled oats

Sugar substitute equal to ⅓ cup white sugar

½ cup pecans, chopped

> Who says you have to skimp on dessert when you're eating well? Serve this dish warm, with a soupçon of lightly sweetened cream.

1. In a bowl, toss apples with lemon juice. Mix together brown sugar substitute, cinnamon, ginger, and cloves. Toss with apples.
2. Pour apples into an oblong baking dish.
3. Combine pastry flour and margarine in a bowl and work together with a pastry blender or 2 knives. Cut in oats and white sugar substitute and mix until crumbly. Mix in pecans.
4. Sprinkle crumb mixture evenly over apples. Bake at 350°F for 30–40 minutes, or until apples are tender and topping is browned.

. . . .

Good and Crunchy

Trying to avoid white flour? Aside from whole wheat flours, consider using wheat germ, wheat berries, oats, chopped nuts and seeds in recipes. For savory casserole toppings, crumbled whole grain crackers or cereals might do the trick.

Olé Mole Fondue

Don't save the chocolate for dessert. This festive fiesta menu features a fondue of chocolate-rich mole sauce. Invite your dinner club over for a Mexican feast.

MENU

∞∞∞∞∞∞∞∞∞∞

Tilapia Ceviche Over Baby Lettuces

Turkey Mole Fondue

Beans and Brown Rice

Sautéed Baby Patty Pan Squash

Whole Grain Flour Tortillas

Pumpkin Cheesecake

Light Mexican Beer

Tilapia Ceviche

Serves 8

6 tilapia fillets
Juice of 5 limes
1 teaspoon red pepper flakes
⅓ cup green onion, minced
⅓ cup cilantro, minced
2 cloves garlic, minced
1 cup tomatoes, diced
1 whole lime
8 cups baby lettuce leaves

This recipe serves 8 appetizer portions of ceviche (also spelled Seviche). To serve 8 as a main course, marinate 8 fillets and increase other ingredients accordingly.

1. Rinse, dry, and dice tilapia fillets. Place in a large, shallow dish and toss with lime juice. Cover and allow fish to marinate in refrigerator for 4 hours.
2. Drain fish and discard juice. Combine fish with pepper flakes, cilantro, garlic, and tomatoes. Squeeze juice of ½ a lime over fish mixture.
3. Line salad plates or bowls with lettuce. Gently toss fish to mix well, then pile on top of lettuce leaves.
4. Thinly slice remaining lime half and use slices as garnish. Serve immediately.

Pucker Up

The acidity in the limes affects the proteins in the fish much the same way heating does. Raw fish or shellfish becomes firm and opaque, as well as flavored by the juice. Any acidic juice or combination of juices can be used to make ceviche, and many South American countries have signature marinade recipes. Marinating doesn't kill parasites (although freezing raw fish does). If you're squeamish about eating uncooked fish, go ahead and cook the fish, then marinate it briefly for the ceviche.

Turkey Mole Fondue

Serves 8

12 ancho chilies
5 New Mexico chilies
4 pasilla chilies
3 tomatoes, peeled
⅓ cup almonds
¼ cup pumpkin seeds
1 teaspoon coriander seeds
1 teaspoon cumin seeds
1 tablespoon sesame seeds
2 tablespoons canola oil
1 tablespoon dried oregano

2 cloves
1 1-inch cinnamon stick
1 large onion, chopped
3 cloves garlic, chopped
⅓ cup raisins
2 ounces unsweetened chocolate, chopped
1 cup chicken broth or water
6–8 cups turkey breast, cooked and diced

1. Split dried chilies, and remove seeds and stems. In a heavy skillet over medium-high heat, toast chilies until just fragrant and slightly browned. Move chilies to a bowl and cover with hot water. Set aside.
2. Put tomatoes in a large blender container and pulse. In the skillet, lightly toast almonds, pumpkin, coriander, cumin, and sesame seeds. Add to blender.
3. Add canola oil to skillet along with oregano, cloves, cinnamon stick, onion, and garlic. Sauté for 5 minutes or until onion softens. Spoon skillet contents into blender container. Add raisins to chilies and soaking liquid. Pulse until mixture is smooth.
4. Strain blender contents into the skillet, pressing against solids with a spoon to extract all liquids. Heat until mixture is bubbly and add chocolate. Stir until chocolate melts. Thin with chicken broth and simmer for 30 minutes, stirring often.
5. Let mole sauce stand for 1 hour for flavors to meld. Before serving, bring to a simmer over medium heat. Transfer sauce to 1 or more fondue pots and place over heating sources. Have guests spear turkey cubes and dip in mole sauce to warm and coat the turkey.

Beans and Brown Rice

Serves 8

3 tablespoons olive oil

1 onion, diced

1 green bell pepper, diced

1 jalapeño pepper, minced

3 cloves garlic, minced

1 cup lean ham, diced

2 tomatoes, diced

½ teaspoon cumin

3 cups red kidney beans, cooked

½ cup bean cooking liquid or broth

5 cups brown basmati rice, cooked

⅓ cup cilantro, minced

Salt and pepper to taste

This classic combination can serve as an entrée. In this version, we turn it into a pilaf side dish.

1. In a large saucepan or Dutch oven, heat olive oil over medium-high heat. Add onion, bell pepper, jalapeno, and garlic. Sauté for 5 minutes, stirring often. Add ham and cook 1 minute longer.

2. Add tomatoes and cook, stirring, for 3 minutes. Sprinkle in cumin.

3. Add kidney beans to liquid and bring mixture to a boil. Turn off heat and fold in rice, cilantro, salt, and pepper to taste.

Pumpkin Cheesecake

Serves 8

12 *large whole wheat crackers*

1 *cup pecans*

Sugar substitute equal to ¼ cup sugar

4 8-ounce packages light cream cheese, softened

Sugar substitute equal to 1 cup brown sugar

3 eggs plus 2 egg whites

1 *teaspoon vanilla extract*

2 cups canned pumpkin

3 tablespoons all-purpose flour

2 teaspoons pumpkin pie spice

> This reduced-fat cheesecake has only the suggestion of a crust, but we promise your guests won't miss it.

1. Place crackers, pecans, and sugar substitute into a food processor. Pulse until ground. Sprinkle over the bottom of a greased 9-inch deep dish pie plate or a springform pan.
2. In a bowl, combine cream cheese and brown sugar substitute. Beat with a mixer until smooth. Add eggs and egg whites one at a time, beating until mixture is fluffy.
3. Add vanilla, pumpkin, flour, and spice. Beat on medium-high speed until everything is blended and smooth.
4. Carefully pour cream cheese mixture over crumbs in pan. Bake at 325°F for 1 hour 45 minutes or until firm. Cool pie, then refrigerate. Serve chilled.

. . . .

Happy Indulgences

Creamy, satisfying desserts can be made with skim ricotta cheese, farmer cheese, and yogurt cheese (made from plain yogurt that's been allowed to drain in a sieve), as well as reduced-fat cream cheese. Just remember that these substitutions have more moisture than regular cream cheese, and adjust your recipe accordingly.

Cine-Fest Fondue di Napoli

Meaty tuna steaks cook in an olive-rich sauce made famous by Naples's ladies of the evening. Invite two couples over for a Fellini film festival and enjoy.

MENU

Mozzarella and Tomato Salad

Pomegranate Granita

Pesce Puttanesca Fondue

Whole Wheat Tortellini

Sautéed Rapini with Pine Nuts

Multi Grain Asiago Garlic Toast

Pinot Grigio

Mozzarella and Tomato Salad

Serves 6

1 pound fresh buffalo mozzarella
3 sun-ripened tomatoes
¼ cup extra-virgin olive oil
¼ cup fresh basil ribbons
Cracked black pepper to taste

This simple dish shines with creamy, fresh mozzarella and juicy ripe tomatoes. If you can't find either, you're better off serving a different salad.

1. Slice the mozzarella into thin disks. Trim and slice the tomatoes.
2. On a serving platter, arrange the tomato and mozzarella slices in a circle, alternating and overlapping, to make a red and white pinwheel. Drizzle olive oil over the dish and sprinkle with basil ribbons. Grind black pepper to taste over all and serve.

Pomegranate Granita

Serves 6

1 cup water
Sugar substitute equivalent
    to ⅔ cup sugar
5 cups pomegranate juice

Mystifying pomegranates are an ancient fruit. The treat is in the tiny juice-filled seeds inside the unassuming looking skin. Use fresh or bottled juice for this recipe.

1. In a saucepan, bring water to a boil. Add sugar substitute and stir briskly until dissolved. Add juice and remove from heat.
2. Cool mixture completely, then pour into a shallow baking pan. Place in the freezer. Starting 30 minutes after placing in freezer, take a fork and begin scraping ice crystals into the center of the dish. Return to the freezer and scrape more ice crystals every hour or so until dish is a mass of ice crystals.
3. Cover until ready to serve. Serve in sherbet or martini glasses.

Pesce Puttanesca Fondue

Serves 6

¼ cup olive oil

6 cups ripe tomatoes, diced

6 anchovies, chopped

1 large onion, minced

4 cloves garlic, minced

1 cup Kalamata olives, chopped or sliced

¼ cup small capers

1 teaspoon red pepper flakes

1 teaspoon dried oregano

3 tablespoons tomato paste

1 cup dry white wine

1 cup water or broth

1 tablespoon fresh basil, chopped

⅓ cup fresh parsley, chopped

Salt to taste

6 fresh sushi-grade tuna steaks, cut into 1-inch cubes

The tomato paste here gives the sauce extra body, making it better for dipping and swirling ingredients in the fondue pot.

1. In a large, heavy saucepan, heat olive oil over medium-high heat. Add tomatoes and sauté, stirring often, for 3 minutes. Add anchovies, onion, garlic, olives, and capers. Reduce heat to medium and cook, stirring occasionally, until onion is soft.
2. Add pepper flakes, oregano, tomato paste, wine, and broth. Stir until blended. Bring mixture to a boil. Reduce heat and simmer for 15 minutes. Add salt to taste.
3. Pour hot sauce into one or more fondue pots and place over heating source.
4. Have guests skewer tuna cubes and cook in the hot sauce until the fish is cooked as desired. Encourage diners to scoop tomatoes and olive up with their fish.

Sautéed Rapini with Pine Nuts

Serves 6

1½ pounds rapini
1 cup pine nuts
⅓ cup olive oil
3 cloves garlic, sliced
Salt and pepper to taste

Rapini, a leggy, slightly bitter green that's very popular in Italy, is a close relative of broccoli and is sometimes called broccoli raab.

1. Wash rapini and trim about 1 inch from the stem ends. Cut remaining stalks into 2- or 3-inch lengths. Bring a large kettle of water to a boil. Blanche rapini for 1 minute or until stalks turn bright green. Drain in a large colander.
2. In a large, heavy saucepan, toast pine nuts until fragrant and just turning brown. Move to a plate. Add olive oil to saucepan. Swirl over medium high heat until sizzling. Carefully add garlic and rapini to saucepan and sauté, turning to coat well, for 2 minutes or until rapini is just tender.
3. Add pine nuts and season with salt and pepper. Serve immediately.

. . . .

Hearty Garlic Bread

Slice crusty country-style multigrain loaves on a diagonal. Press 2 or 3 cloves of garlic into olive oil or melted butter. Brush bread with garlic mixture and toast in a 350°F oven for 3–5 minutes or until lightly toasted. Carefully sprinkle slices with grated Asiago cheese and return to oven until cheese is bubbly and browned.

After-Hours Ginger Lemongrass Hot Pot

This broth-based fondue brings a steamy cloud of aromatic herbs and flavorings to the table. It's perfect for a light, late-night supper.

MENU

◇◇◇◇◇◇◇◇◇◇◇

Endive with Pear Salad

Ginger Lemongrass Hot Pot
with Chicken, Turkey Sausage, and
Mushroom Skewers

Baby Bok Choy

Sesame Soba Noodles

Clementine Orange Slices

Dry Sake and Iced Green Tea

Endive with Pear Salad

Serves 6

24 *large endive leaves, trimmed*
6 *ripe pears, seeded and diced*
1 *rib celery, thinly sliced*
1 *jalapeño pepper, minced*
⅓ *cup green onion, minced*
1 *teaspoon fresh ginger, grated*
½ *teaspoon Singapore curry oil*
¼ *cup sherry vinegar*
¼ *cup canola oil*
Black and white sesame seeds (optional)

A kiss of Singapore curry oil gives this sweet-and-spicy salad a unique flavor. For a less spicy salad, substitute basil oil for the curry oil and bell pepper for the jalapeño.

1. Spread endive leaves, edges up, on a serving platter.
2. In a bowl, toss together celery, jalapeño pepper, green onion, and ginger.
3. In a small bowl, whisk together curry oil, vinegar, and canola oil. Drizzle over pear mixture and toss well.
4. Spoon pear mixture into endive leaves. Sprinkle with sesame seeds, if desired, and serve.

- -

Pear Varieties

Six to ten different types of pears can be found in supermarkets at any given time. Asian pears make a good choice for salads because they're crisp and don't brown as quickly as other pears. Firm and fragrant Anjou pears or meaty Bosc pears are also good choices. Kieffer pears, which grow in many backyards in the American South, don't ripen to a soft consistency and must be cooked before being eaten.

Ginger Lemongrass Hot Pot

Serves 6

6 cups strong chicken broth

1 lime, washed and sliced

2 stalks lemongrass

6 slices fresh ginger

3 cloves garlic, pressed

⅓ cup basil, chopped

1 onion, chopped

4 chicken breast halves, diced

4 turkey sausage links, cut in 1-inch slices

18 button mushrooms

Hot pot strainers or skewers can be used to simmer combinations of meats and veggies in this flavorful broth.

1. Combine chicken broth, lime slices, lemongrass, ginger, garlic, basil, and onion in a saucepan. Bring mixture to a boil, reduce heat, and simmer for 10 minutes.
2. Ladle broth into 1 or more hot pots or fondue pots and place over heating source.
3. Thread skewers with chicken breast cubes, turkey sausage, and button mushrooms. Have guests cook skewers in simmering broth.

Hot Pot Veggies

If you're skilled with chopsticks, heads of baby bok choy and chunks of eggplant or summer squash can be dropped into a hot pot and retrieved when tender. Otherwise, try strainers or slotted spoons.

Sesame Soba Noodles

Serves 6

1 pound soba noodles

⅓ cup dark sesame oil

2 tablespoons vegetable oil

½ cup soy sauce

1 tablespoon garlic hot pepper paste

2 tablespoons sushi vinegar or apple cider vinegar

¼ cup green onion, minced

3 tablespoons toasted sesame seeds

Salt and pepper to taste

> Nutty soba noodles are made from buckwheat. They're a high-fiber, high-nutrient pasta that actually tastes good.

1. Bring a large kettle of water to a boil. Add soba noodles and cook until al dente, about 6–8 minutes. Drain in a colander.
2. Whisk together sesame oil, vegetable oil, soy sauce, garlic pepper paste, and vinegar. Place in warm pasta kettle and add noodles. Toss until noodles are completely coated with sauce. Add green onion, sesame seeds, salt, and pepper to taste. Serve hot or make in advance and serve chilled.

Rustic Impromptu Fondue Dinner Party

Nothing about this menu is difficult or complicated, and the ingredients can be grabbed at the supermarket on your way home from work.

MENU

Gorgonzola-Topped Portobello Mushrooms

Truffle-Scented Oil Fondue with Pork Tenderloin

Ratatouille

Warm Sweet Potato Salad

Whole Wheat Baguettes

Bittersweet Chocolates and Fresh Fruit

Sangiovese or Barolo

Dark Roast Coffee

Gorgonzola-Topped Portobello Mushrooms

Serves 8

¼ cup olive oil
1 clove garlic, pressed
8 large portobello mushroom caps
½ pound Gorgonzola cheese
¼ cup fresh basil, chopped
Fresh-ground black pepper to taste

If you have an outdoor grill handy, a quick turn over the coals is a great way to handle portobello caps. Otherwise, just grill in a skillet.

1. In a small saucepan, warm olive oil and garlic. Wash mushroom caps and pat dry. Brush mushroom caps on both sides with olive oil mixture and grill, 1–2 at a time, in a heavy nonstick skillet. Cook mushrooms for 30 seconds on each side.
2. Place mushrooms, top side down, on non-stick aluminum foil on a baking sheet. Brush tops with any remaining garlic oil.
3. Sprinkle Gorgonzola over mushroom caps, followed by basil. Season with fresh-ground black pepper.
4. Bake at 400°F until cheese is bubbly and lightly browned, about 5–7 minutes.

. . . .

Mighty Mushrooms

Portobellos, brown beauties with saucer-sized caps, are closely related to ordinary white mushrooms and can be used interchangeably in recipes. However, the meaty texture of portobellos—largely attributed to the reduced moisture in the caps—makes them excellent candidates for grilling and baking. Try chicken or steak on a portobello platter, or grill and slice portobellos for veggie sandwiches.

Truffle-Scented Oil Fondue with Pork Tenderloin

Serves 8

5 cups olive or canola oil
¼ cup truffle oil
3 pounds pork tenderloin, cut in 1-inch cubes
1 teaspoon salt
½ teaspoon black pepper
2 cups roasted red peppers
1 teaspoon basil, minced

Truffle oil is a great way to offer your friends the luxury of truffle flavor, without the huge price tag of fresh truffles

1. Heat olive or canola oil in a saucepan until hot, but not smoking. Remove from heat and stir in truffle oil. Carefully ladle oil into one or more fondue pots. Place over heating source.
2. Season pork cubes with salt and pepper and place on a platter beside fondue pot.
3. Warm roasted red peppers (prepared peppers from a jar are fine) with basil. Purée in a blender. Strain into sauce dishes.
4. Have guests cook pork tenderloin in hot oil and, if desired, dip in pepper sauce.

. . . .

Savory Oils

Flavored oils—available in flavors ranging from curry to pumpkin to basil-garlic to mushrooms—can add complexity and interest to sauces and dressings. The flavor compounds tend to be volatile and begin to dissipate when heated. That's why it's best to add these oils right before serving a dish.

Ratatouille

Serves 8

2 tablespoons olive oil

2 cloves garlic, minced

1½ cups Japanese eggplant,
    halved and sliced

1½ cups zucchini, halved and sliced

1½ cups yellow squash, halved and sliced

1 cup mushrooms, sliced

2 cups plum tomatoes, diced

½ teaspoon dried thyme leaves

¼ cup parsley, minced

Salt and pepper to taste

> The classic version of this Provençal dish is very soupy, great for serving over couscous and with pasta. This recipe makes more of a ratatouille sauté.

1. In a large saucepan, heat olive oil. Add garlic and sauté over medium-high heat for 1 minute.
2. Add eggplant, zucchini, squash, mushrooms, and tomatoes. Sauté, stirring often, until vegetables are crisp and tender and tomatoes are soft, about 6–8 minutes.
3. Season with thyme, parsley, salt, and pepper and serve.

· ·

Eggplant Shopping

Japanese eggplant is long, thin, and usually less bitter than its egg-shaped European cousin. When buying any type of eggplant, look for unblemished vegetables that seem heavy for their size. Eggplants with a lot of dark seeds inside are likely to be more bitter than white-seeded eggplants. Salting eggplant slices and letting them drain for 30 minutes will extract some bitter liquid. Just remember to rinse the slices before cooking.

Warm Sweet Potato Salad

Serves 8

4 *large sweet potatoes*
1 *cup toasted pecans*
½ *cup celery, sliced*
⅓ *cup olive oil*
1 *sweet onion, minced*
1 *red bell pepper, seeded and diced*
⅓ *cup balsamic vinegar*
Salt and pepper to taste

Sweet potatoes, which are often incorrectly confused with yams, are a great source of beta-carotene and fiber. Serve this dish as an alternative to all those candied recipes.

1. Boil sweet potatoes until just tender, about 30–40 minutes. Carefully peel and dice. Combine in a bowl with pecans and celery.
2. In a saucepan, heat olive oil. Sauté onion over medium-high heat for 2 minutes. Add red bell pepper and sauté for 1 minute longer. Add vinegar and swirl until warmed and combined with oil.
3. Drizzle dressing over sweet potatoes. Toss well and serve.

Bloody Mary Brunch Fondue

Who says a Bloody Mary has to be a cocktail? This eye-opening brunch fondue uses the spicy drink as a hot broth for dipping vegetables and whole grain bread. Pull this menu out during busy months when you need an alternative to evening socializing.

MENU

Bloody Mary Fondue

Raw and Blanched Vegetable Assortment

7-Grain Bread Cubes

Mushroom Egg Casserole

Sweet Potato Kugel

Oat Bran Muffins

Carrot Muffins

No Sugar Added Preserves

Champagne and Fruit Juice Spritzers

Dark Roast Coffee

Bloody Mary Fondue

Serves 8

6 cups tomato or mixed
    vegetable juice
⅔ cup vodka
Juice of 2 limes
Juice of 1 lemon
½ cup horseradish
1 tablespoon Tabasco sauce
1 tablespoon Worcestershire sauce
2 bay leaves

> This twist on the favorite brunch beverage makes a fragrant, colorful fondue course. The vodka adds a little kick to the mix, but if you'd rather have a non-alcoholic dish, just substitute broth or more vegetable juice.

1. In a large saucepan, whisk together all ingredients until well blended. Bring to a boil. Reduce heat and simmer for 3 minutes.
2. Pour into 1 or more fondue pots. Place pot over heat source and serve with vegetable platter and 7-grain bread cubes.

. . . .

Variations on the Bloody Mary Theme

This vegetarian-with-a-kick fondue broth can be used for poaching mild fish or warming boiled potatoes. The broth also can be made with the addition of clam juice, a few crushed garlic cloves, a spike of chili powder, or a few tablespoons of minced fresh basil or oregano for added interest.

Raw and Blanched Vegetable Assortment for Fondue

Serves 8

1 stalk celery

4 seedless cucumbers

4 yellow bell peppers

4 large zucchini

8 cups baby carrots

4 cups whole green beans

48 asparagus spears

4 cups grape tomatoes

Some vegetables can be served raw with the Bloody Mary Fondue, while others should be blanched slightly for best flavor and ease in dipping. This recipe divides ingredients between two platters for easy access. Depending on your table layout, you may choose to use more platters.

1. Cut base from celery stalk, removing about 2 inches from the ribs. Separate ribs, wash well, and remove any discolored leaves. Cut ribs in half vertically and horizontally and divide over 2 platters.

2. Wash cucumbers well and trim off ends. Cut cucumbers in half horizontally, then cut each half into 6–8 spears. Divide spears over 2 platters, creating a spoke pattern next to the celery.

3. Cut bell peppers in half. Remove seeds, stems and inside ribs. Cut pepper halves into strips and divide over 2 platters, making another spoke in the pattern.

4. Trim the ends from the zucchini. Slice diagonally across, making large oval-shaped slices. Place the slices overlapping on the platters, adding to the spoke pattern.

5. Bring a large pot of water to a rolling boil. Using a metal strainer, blanch carrots in the water for 2 minutes, then rinse in cold water and drain well. Arrange carrots in a spoke on the platters. Trim green beans and repeat the process. Trim asparagus and blanch asparagus in the same way, but only for 1 minute. Add to the platter.

6. Wash and drain grape tomatoes and place in the center of the platters. Serve with skewers or small-tined fondue forks.

Mushroom Egg Casserole

Serves 8

2 tablespoons olive oil

1 pound white or baby Portobello
    mushrooms, sliced

1 shallot, minced

2 cloves garlic, minced

⅓ cup minced fresh herbs

1 cup crumbled farmer's cheese

1 cup sharp Cheddar cheese, shredded

1 dozen eggs

1 cup low-fat evaporated milk

Salt and pepper to taste

> This crustless quiche is super easy to make. Use fresh, cageless, or brown eggs for best flavor and color.

1. In a heavy saucepan, heat olive oil until sizzling. Add mushrooms, shallot, and garlic and sauté until mushrooms are tender, about 3 minutes. Add fresh herbs and remove from heat.
2. Spread mushrooms over the bottom of a non-stick oblong baking dish or a casserole coated with cooking spray. Sprinkle farmer cheese over mushrooms, followed by Cheddar cheese.
3. In a blender, combine eggs, evaporated milk, and salt and pepper. Pulse until well blended. Pour over mushrooms and cheese. Bake at 325°F for 25 minutes or until sides are puffy and center is set. Let stand 10 minutes before cutting.

· ·

Eggsactly!

Eggs are a good source of high-quality protein and contain only 70 calories each. Although a large egg contains 213 milligrams of cholesterol, nutritionists generally agree that whole eggs, in moderation, can be part of a healthy diet. Egg whites have no cholesterol and can be eaten frequently.

Sweet Potato Kugel

Serves 8

6 medium sweet potatoes

1 cup sultanas

2 egg whites

2 eggs

1 teaspoon cinnamon

½ cup orange juice

⅔ cup matzo meal or fine bread crumbs

Sweet potatoes are a great source of vitamin A and also offer vitamin C, calcium, fiber, and protein. They're also a New World native plant and were sustaining Native Americans when Columbus arrived.

1. Carefully peel sweet potatoes. Grate the potatoes in a food processor and place shreds in a large bowl. Toss with sultanas.
2. Whisk together egg whites, eggs, cinnamon, and orange juice. Pour over sweet potatoes and mix well. Sprinkle matzo meal over mixture and toss well.
3. Pour mixture in a casserole sprayed with cooking spray. Bake at 350°F for 45 minutes or until sweet potatoes are tender and kugel top is crisp and browned.

Oat Bran Muffins

Serves 8

4 cups oat bran
⅓ cup unbleached or
    whole wheat flour
1 teaspoon baking soda
1 teaspoon baking powder
1 teaspoon cinnamon
¼ cup sugar or sugar equivalent
2¼ cups skim milk

> This recipe can be made completely fat free by omitting the canola oil and increasing the applesauce by 2 tablespoons.

3 tablespoons canola oil
4 egg whites
1 cup applesauce
1 cup raisins

1. In a large bowl, combine oat bran, flour, baking soda, baking powder, cinnamon, and sugar or sugar equivalent. Stir with a whisk to remove any lumps.
2. In another bowl, whisk together milk, oil, egg whites, and applesauce. Pour wet mixture into dry mixture, and stir until dry ingredients are moistened. Stir in raisins.
3. Divide mixture into 2 dozen non-stick muffin cups. Bake at 350°F for 20 minutes or until nicely browned. Let stand in muffin pans for a few minutes before removing.

- -

Sugar, Sugar

Ask any dentist or nutritionist and you'll likely hear that we're all eating too much sugar, which has little nutritional value. Getting sugar out of your diet is easier said than done, since so many commercially prepared foods and baked goods contain this flavor enhancer. Baking your own treats with little or no sugar is one way to cut back. But remember: In baking, sugar acts as a liquid, adding moisture as well as flavor. Sugar substitutes can help replace the sweet taste of sugar, but to keep baked goods moist, add a little extra liquid to recipes.

Carrot Muffins

Serves 8

3 cups whole wheat pastry flour

½ cup wheat or oat bran

1 teaspoon baking soda

1 teaspoon baking powder

1 teaspoon cinnamon

½ teaspoon ginger

½ cup brown sugar

2 cups plain yogurt

⅓ cup canola oil

4 egg whites

2 cups shredded carrots

1 cup finely chopped dried apricots

Grated carrots give these whole grain muffins color as well as texture. Try baking them in "muffin top" pans for shallow, domed-top muffins everyone will love.

1. In a large bowl, combine flour, bran, baking soda, baking powder, cinnamon, ginger, and brown sugar or sugar equivalent. Stir with a whisk to remove any lumps.
2. In another bowl, whisk together yogurt, oil, and egg whites. Pour wet mixture into dry mixture, and stir until dry ingredients are moistened. Stir in carrots and apricots.
3. Divide mixture into 2 dozen non-stick muffin cups. Bake at 350°F for 20 minutes or until nicely browned. Let stand in muffin pans for a few minutes before removing.

Paper Mart

www.papermart.com

Check out the wonderful selection of favor boxes, including gold and silver chest-type boxes, pastel Chinese food cartons, and heart-covered purse-style boxes. The company also sells a full assortment of organza, silk, and woven bags.

The Stationery Studio

www.thestationerystudio.com

This online merchant offers invitations, printed napkins, coasters, fanciful letterhead designs, stamps, gifts, and gift bags to fit any occasion—formal or casual.

Paper Direct

www.paperdirect.com

Long popular with self-employed consultants and corporate event planners, Paper Direct now offers plenty of themed papers, cards, and letterhead stock to appeal to the home party maven. Whether you're hosting a bridal shower, wine club party, Earth Day celebration, or soccer club bash, you'll find designs to enhance the experience.

Kate's Paperie

www.katespaperie.com

The legendary New York stationer is online, with a full range of handmade papers, wire-and-fringe ribbons, "crystal" tissue, and handmade paper-covered gift boxes. Peruse the shaped paper punches and scrapbook accessories, in addition to the beautiful wax stamps.

Bags & Bows

www.bagsandbowsonline.com

Yes, this online retailer has a vast selection of frosted and patterned take-out boxes and gabled boxes. But don't miss the great leopard-print gift boxes, floral tissues, and neon jelly bags.

The Invitation Source

www.theinvitationsource.com

Give your guests personalized, white chocolate-dipped cookies as favors. Or decorate your dining room with light-up balloons. The Invitation Source offers a wide range of products, including letterhead and invitations from a range of designers.

Mulberry Invitations

www.mulberryinvitations.com

Peruse this vendor's selection of beautiful paper flowers—perfect for laying across a plate or tucking into an unusual centerpiece. Heart-shaped favor boxes, translucent leaves, and Chinese message cards are also eye-catching.

Artisanal Cheese Producers

Specialty cheeses can make fondues a widely varying taste treat. Don't be afraid to experiment with an herb-laced Cheddar or an organic Chevre from a boutique cheese maker. Even if you're serving broth or oil fondue, you can pique palates with an interesting hors d'oeuvres tray of cheeses and crusty breads.

Cowgirl Creamery

www.cowgirlcreamery.com

Two former chefs from San Francisco founded this female-owned creamery in Point Reyes Station, CA. Products are available at a few California retailers, or directly from the company online. Try the triple-cream Red Hawk or the extraordinary Frommage Blanc.

Bellwether Farms Artisan Creamery

www.bellwetherfarms.com

Aside from wine, Sonoma County agribusiness also yields great cheeses. Try the Carmody Reserve from Bellwether Farms, a semi-hard, rich, buttery cheese that—depending on your perspective—tastes like a mellow Cheddar or a slightly-sharp Gouda. White slabs of Crescenza will make you want to take a break from Brie.

Vella Cheese Co.

www.vellacheese.com

This hundred-year-old artisan cheese producer turns out extraordinary Monterey Jack cheeses from its Sonoma, California creamery. If your only acquaintance with this delicious cheese is from mass-market brands, do try the Mezzo Secco (partially dry) jack or flavored jack varieties from Vella.

Grafton Village Cheese Company

www.graftonvillagecheese.com

Cheddar is the mainstay here. Try the crumbling, melt-in-your-mouth Five Star Cheddar for eating out of hand. Then experiment with the smoked, sage, or garlic-flavored Cheddars in fondue.

Old Chatham Sheepherding Company

www.blacksheepcheese.com

Order the sublime Hudson Valley Camembert, made from a combination of goat's milk and cow's milk, or the Ewe's Blue, a sheep's milk Roquefort that can give a little kick to any salad or fondue.

Meister Cheese Co.

www.meistercheese.com

This Muscoda, Wisconsin, producer makes an unusual, delicious Morel jack cheese with an earthy mushroom flavor and a tomato-basil Cheddar to spice up your favorite fondue blend.

Widmer Cheese Cellars

www.widmerscheese.com

Cheesemaking in the Swiss tradition occurs at this Wisconsin creamery that's known for its washed-rind Brick cheeses, flavored Bricks and Colbys, and aged Cheddars. For a real treat, order a package of soft, fresh Cheddar curds.

Sugarbush Farm

www.sugarbushfarm.com

Vermont cheese makers are known for fine, firm Cheddar and this Woodstock producer is one of the best. Order a five-pound wheel of extra-sharp aged Cheddar and start slicing, crumbling, and melting.

Index

alcoholic beverages. *See* drinks
American traditions, 3
Antipasto Roll-Ups, 108
apples: Apple and Rutabaga Salad, 165;
    Baked Apple Crisp, 291; Charosets in
    Orange Shells, 175; Cranberry Apple Tart
    with Cinnamon Cream, 18; Green Apple
    Salad, 50
artichokes: Artichoke and Oyster Soup, 157;
    Artichoke Bottoms with Chicken Salad,
    78; Sautéed Baby Artichokes, 41
Asian traditions, 2
asparagus: Cucumber and Asparagus
    Salad, 124; Steamed Red Potatoes with
    Asparagus and Peppers, 25
avocados: Chilled Avocado Bisque, 188;
    Gazpacho, 141

beans: Beans and Brown Rice, 295; Black-
    and-White Bean Salsa, 129; Ranch Beans,
    74
beef: Boiled Beef Pot Fondue, 185; Cocktail
    Meatballs, 89; Corned Beef Hash Cakes
    with Eggs, 48; Fajita Beef, 66; Fondue
    Bourguignon, 102; Korean Hot Pot
    Broth, 222; Marinated Lamb or Beef
    Kebab Fondue, 133; Mongolian Hot Pot
    Broth, 198; Queso Chili Con Carne, 64;
    Rice Dressing, 160; Shabu-Shabu, 214;
    Vietnamese Lau Broth, 205
Beer Fondue, Mixed Sausages with Red
    Pearl Onions in, 166
beverages. *See* drinks
bisques. *See* soups and bisques
Bloody Mary Fondue, 311
Blueberry Shortcake Fondue, 274
bonbons, 255–257
bouquet garni, 154
Bread Pudding, 53
breads, 6, 13, 89; Currant Scones, 51;
    Focaccia, 37; Irish Brown Soda Bread, 47;
    Tomato Bruschetta, 153
broth-based fondues: Boiled Beef Pot
    Fondue, 185; Chicken Hot Pot Broth,
    208; Chicken in Pineapple-Orange Curry
    Fondue, 192; Chrysanthemum Hot
    Pot, 219; Court Bouillon Seafood Boil,
    171; Ginger Lemongrass Hot Pot, 303;
    Grouper Vera Cruz Fondue, 189; Korean
    Hot Pot Broth, 222; Matzo Ball Fondue
    with Chicken, 176; Mongolian Hot Pot
    Broth, 198; Pesce Puttanesca Fondue,
    299; Shabu Shabu, 214; Thai Seafood

Hot Pot Broth, 201; Turkey Mole Fondue,
    294; Vietnamese Lau Broth, 205
Bruschetta, Tomato, 153

cabbage: Coleslaw, 115; Pepper Slaw, 59;
    Sautéed Cabbage with Bacon and Parlsey,
    49
cakes: *See also* cheesecake; Black Forest
    Cherry Cupcakes, 167; Easy Carrot Cake,
    186; King Cake, 163; Lemon Pound Cake,
    117; Moon Cakes, 212; Rum Cake with
    Guava Glaze, 131; Texas Sheet Cake, 75
candies. *See* bonbons; chocolate; truffles
caquelon, 3–4
caramel: Crème Caramel Fondue, 278; Pecan
    Caramels Chocolate Fondue, 230
carrot: Carrot Muffins, 316; Easy Carrot
    Cake, 186
Celery, Tapenade-Stuffed, 288
ceramic pots, 3–4
Charosets in Orange Shells, 175
cheesecake: Amaretto Cheesecake with
    Sliced Peaches, 42; Pumpkin Cheesecake,
    296; Pumpkin Cheesecake Fondue, 279
cheese fondues, 5; Ale-Spiked Cheddar
    Fondue, 71; Appenzeller Cider Fondue,
    20; Cajun Hot Pepper Cheese Fondue,
    92; Carrigaline-Blue Fondue, 46;
    Cheddar-ama Fondue, 82; Cheddar-
    Bleu Fondue, 290; Cherry Mascarpone
    Fondue, 282; Cup Cheese Fondue,
    56; Dubliner Cheddar Fondue, 45;
    Explorateur Cheese Fondue, 281;
    Favorite Ro-Tel Dip, 64; French Brie
    Fondue, 32; Frobourg-Style Fondue, 24;
    Garlicky Vaud Fondue, 16; Geneva-Style
    Fondue, 27; Gorgonzola Fondue, 96;
    Havarti with Stilton Swirl Fondue, 283;
    Kaasdoop, 34; Lump Crab and Cream
    Cheese Fondue, 77; Neufchatel Cheese
    Fondue, 13; Northern Italian Fonduta,
    36; Queso Chili Con Carne, 64; Queso
    Fundido, 63; Rosy Alfredo Fondue, 88;
    Spiced Feta-Spinach Fondue, 94; Welsh
    Rarebit, 33
cheeses, selecting, 2, 155
cherry: Black Forest Cherry Cupcakes, 167;
    Cherry Mascarpone Fondue, 282
chicken: Artichoke Bottoms with Chicken
    Salad, 78; Baked Chicken Fingers, 83;
    Chicken Hot Pot Broth, 208; Chicken
    in Pineapple-Orange Curry Fondue,
    192; Chicken-Spinach Croquettes, 40;
    Chrysanthemum Hot Pot, 219; Cilantro

Chicken Dumplings, 209; Fajita Chicken, 65; Ginger Lemongrass Hot Pot, 303; Jerk Shrimp, Pork, and Chicken, 127; Matzo Ball Fondue with Chicken, 176; Rosemary Roasted Chicken, 57; Sherry-Poached Chicken and Veal Fondue, 142

chick peas: Falafel Fondue, 123; Hummus, 136

chocolate: Black Forest Cherry Cupcakes, 167; bonbons, 255–257; Chocolate Chip Marshmallow Fluff Cookie Sandwiches, 86; Chocolate Shortbread, 105; Hot Chocolate, 86; truffles, 248–254

chocolate fondues, 3, 5; Bittersweet Chocolate Orange Fondue, 245; Callebaut Fondue, 227; Chocolate, Chocolate, Chocolate Fondue, 242; Chocolate Cherry Cordial Fondue, 246; Chocolate Marshmallow Fondue, 237; Chocolate Mint Fondue, 237; Chocolate Peanut Butter Fondue, 238; Chocolate Truffles Fondue, 230; Cinnamon Coco-Latte Fondue, 233; Colorful Kisses Fondue, 240; Expressive Espresso Fondue, 234; Ghirardelli Fondue, 227; Guittard Fondue, 228; Mocha-Mocha Java Fondue, 235; My Favorite Things Fondue, 241; Pecan Caramels Chocolate Fondue, 230; Sampler Chocolates Fondue, 231; Tri-Chocolate Fondue for Candy, 258; Valrhona Chocolate Fondue, 228; White Chocolate Raspberry Fondue, 244

Chutney, Fresh Peach, 194

coffee: Cinnamon Coco-Latte Fondue, 233; Coffee Crème Brûlée, 104; Expressive Espresso Fondue, 234; Irish Coffee, 54; Mocha-Mocha Java Fondue, 235; Thai Iced Coffee, 202

Coleslaw, 115

cooking liquids, 6

corn: Corn Salad, 59; Corn Salsa, 113; Roasted Corn Salsa, 67

Crab and Cream Cheese Fondue, 77

Crawfish Balls, 93

Crème Fraiche, 120

cucumber: Cucumber and Asparagus Salad, 124; Raita Sauce, 134; Sweet and Sour Cucumber Salad, 197

dessert fondues: See also chocolate fondues; Baked Alaska Fondue, 274; Blueberry Shortcake Fondue, 274; Bourbon and Butterscotch Fondue, 263; Butter Maple Raisin Sauce, 267; Cherry Mascarpone Fondue, 282; Coconut Milk and Macadamia Nut Fondue, 271; Crème Anglaise Fondue, 269; Crème Caramel Fondue, 278; Dulce de Leche Fondue,

261; Explorateur Cheese Fondue, 281; Havarti with Stilton Swirl Fondue, 283; Key Lime Pie Fondue, 278; Louisiana Butter Pecan Fondue, 262; Mascarpone and Calvados Fondue, 270; Pumpkin Cheesecake Fondue, 279; Strawberry Shortcake Fondue, 273; Sweet Apricot Jam Melt, 265; Warm Berry Compote Fondue, 266; White Peach Shortcake Fondue, 275

desserts: See also cakes; cheesecake; chocolate; chocolate fondues; Baked Apple Crisp, 291; Bread Pudding, 53; Coconut Macaroons, 194; Coeur a la Crème with Berries, 151; Coffee Crème Brûlée, 104; Cranberry Apple Tart with Cinnamon Cream, 18; Flan, 190; Guava and Pineapple Petit Fours, 69; Lemon Curd, 52; Lemon Squares, 173; Mango Sorbet, 178; Meringue Tarts, 80; Miniature White Peach Tarts, 110; Old School Pie Crust, 61; Orange Ice, 199; Persimmon Sorbet, 220; Raspberry Jelly Roll, 22; Shoo-Fly Pie, 60; Strawberries and Cream Puffs, 216; Sweet Shortcake Biscuits, 276; Tiramisu, 182

dippers, 6–7

dips, 5–6

dressings: Creamy Vidalia Dressing, 172; Raspberry Vinaigrette, 21; Tangerine Vinaigrette, 149

drinks: Classic Martini, 30; Easy Frozen Margaritas, 68; Flavored Martini, 30; Hot Chocolate, 86; Irish Coffee, 54; to serve with fondues, 7–8; Thai Iced Coffee, 202; Thai Iced Tea, 202

duck: Duck and Mushroom Dumplings, 211; Duck Breast and Chutney Pinwheels, 28

dumplings: Cilantro Chicken Dumplings, 209; Duck and Mushroom Dumplings, 211; Ginger Pork Dumplings, 210; Shrimp and Green Onion Dumplings, 210; Sweet and Crispy Cream Cheese Dumplings, 224

egg dishes: Corned Beef Hash Cakes with Eggs, 48; Mini Spinach Quiches, 79; Mushroom Egg Casserole, 313; Potato Tortilla, 144

endive: Endive Stuffed with Salmon Tartare, 101; Endive with Pear Salad, 302

European traditions, 1–2

firepot, 2; See also broth-based fondues

fish, 6–7; See also seafood; Bagna Cauda Fondue, 107; Endive Stuffed with Salmon Tartare, 101; Fried Fish Fondue, 112; Grouper Vera Cruz Fondue, 189; Halibut and Lobster Tail Wine Fondue, 154;

Pesce Puttanesca Fondue, 299; Seared Tuna Bites, 97; Smoked Fish Dip, 158; Smoked Salmon and Dilled Cream Cheese, 29; Tilapia Ceviche, 293
Flan, 190
Focaccia, 37
fondue pots, 3–4
fruits: *See also* dessert fondues; specific types; Charosets in Orange Shells, 175; Coeur a la Crème with Berries, 151; Guava and Pineapple Petit Fours, 69

Gazpacho, 141
Gnochi, 38
Grouper Vera Cruz Fondue, 189

Halibut and Lobster Tail Wine Fondue, 154
ham: Ham Croquettes, 145; Mixed Beggar's Purses in Burgundy Fondue, 159
health and safety tips, 8–9
history of fondue, 1–3
hot pot, 2; *See also* broth-based fondues
Hummus, 136

Irish Coffee, 54

lamb: Grilled Lamb Bites, 95; Marinated Lamb or Beef Kebab Fondue, 133; Mongolian Hot Pot Broth, 198
Lemon Curd, 52
Lobster Tail Wine Fondue, Halibut and, 154

mango: Mango Salsa, 67; Mango Sorbet, 178
margaritas, 68
martinis, 30
matzo balls: Matzo Ball Fondue with Chicken, 176; Mini Matzo Balls, 177
meats, 6–7; *See also* specific types
Meringue Tarts, 80
metal pots, 4
muffins: Carrot Muffins, 316; Cheesy Corn Bread Muffins, 116; Oat Bran Muffins, 315
mushrooms: Duck and Mushroom Dumplings, 211; Gorgonzola-Topped Portobello Mushrooms, 306; Mushroom Egg Casserole, 313

Neuchâtel, 1
Noodles, Sesame Soba, 304

oil-based fondues: Bagna Cauda Fondue, 107; Falafel Fondue, 123; Fondue Bourguignon, 102; Fried Fish Fondue, 112; Jerk Shrimp, Pork, and Chicken, 127; Marinated Lamb or Beef Kebab Fondue, 133; Tempura Veggie Skewers with Ginger-Soy Sauce, 119; Truffle-Scented Oil Fondue with Pork Tenderloin, 307

olives: Creole-Italian Olive Salad, 162; Hot Peppered, 109; Tapenade-Stuffed Celery, 288
orange: Bittersweet Chocolate Orange Fondue, 245; Charosets in Orange Shells, 175; Chicken in Pineapple-Orange Curry Fondue, 192
Orzo Walnut Sultana Salad, 155

peaches: Fresh Peach Chutney, 194; Miniature White Peach Tarts, 110; White Peach Shortcake Fondue, 275
pears: Endive with Pear Salad, 302; Pear and Spinach Salad, 218
peppers: Pepper Slaw, 59; Red Pepper Rouille, 172; Steamed Red Potatoes with Asparagus and Peppers, 25; Zucchini and Peppers Fondue, 150
pies. *See* desserts
pineapple: Chicken in Pineapple-Orange Curry Fondue, 192; Guava and Pineapple Petit Fours, 69; Pineapple Salsa, 128
Pomegranate Granita, 298
pork: *See also* ham; sausage; Chrysanthemum Hot Pot, 219; Cocktail Meatballs, 89; Ginger Pork Dumplings, 210; Jerk Shrimp, Pork, and Chicken, 127; Korean Hot Pot Broth, 222; Rice Dressing, 160; Truffle-Scented Oil Fondue with Pork Tenderloin, 307
potatoes: Baked Potato Wedges, 84; German-Style Potato Salad, 73; Gnochi, 38; Potato Salad, 58; Potato Tortilla, 144; Roasted Fingerling Potatoes with Garlic and Rosemary, 103; Spicy Boiled Potatoes, 114; Steamed Red Potatoes with Asparagus and Peppers, 25; Sweet Potato Kugel, 314; Swiss Potato Balls with Herbed Crème Fraiche, 120; Warm Sweet Potato Salad, 309
pumpkin: Pumpkin Cheesecake, 296; Pumpkin Cheesecake Fondue, 279

Rapini with Pine Nuts, Sautéed, 300
raspberry: Chocolate Raspberry Truffles, 251; Raspberry Jelly Roll, 22; Raspberry Vinaigrette, 21; White Chocolate Raspberry Fondue, 244
Ratatouille, 308
rice: Almond-Basmati Rice Pilaf, 193; Beans and Brown Rice, 295; Coconut Rice, 128; Rice Dressing, 160

safety tips, 8–9
salads: Apple and Rutabaga Salad, 165; Artichoke Bottoms with Chicken Salad, 78; Chopped Salad, 126, 184; Coleslaw, 115; Corn Salad, 59; Creole-Italian Olive Salad, 162; Cucumber and Asparagus

Salad, 124; Endive with Pear Salad, 302; German-Style Potato Salad, 73; Green Apple Salad, 50; Herb and Boston Lettuce Salad, 204; Mozzarella and Tomato Salad, 298; Orzo Walnut Sultana Salad, 155; Pear and Spinach Salad, 218; Pepper Slaw, 59; Potato Salad, 58; Radish Slaw with Balsamic Dressing, 17; Red Hat Salad, 21; Sweet and Sour Cucumber Salad, 197; Tabbouleh, 135; Warm Sweet Potato Salad, 309

salmon: Endive Stuffed with Salmon Tartare, 101; Smoked Salmon and Dilled Cream Cheese, 29

salsa: Black-and-White Bean Salsa, 129; Corn Salsa, 113; Fresh Heirloom Tomato and Lime Salsa, 129; Fresh Tomato Salsa, 68; Mango Salsa, 67; Pineapple Salsa, 128; Roasted Corn Salsa, 67; Roasted Tomato Salsa, 130

Sandwiches, Mini Muffuletta, 161

sauces: Bailey's Irish Cream Sauce, 54; Béarnaise Sauce, 102; Crème Fraiche, 120; Custard Sauce, 137; Fritada Sauce, 143; Mojo Verde, 143; Nuac Cham Dipping Sauce, 206; Orange Soy Dipping Sauce, 206; Peanut Sauce, 223; Ponzu Sauce, 215; Raita Sauce, 134; Sicilian Red Gravy Fondue, 180; Tomato Coulis, 122; Vinegar-Sesame Dipping Sauce, 223; Vinegar Soy Sauce, 211; Wasabi Cream, 150

sausage: Court Bouillon Seafood Boil, 171; Ginger Lemongrass Hot Pot, 303; Grilled Bratwurst, 72; Mixed Beggar's Purses in Burgundy Fondue, 159; Mixed Sausage Platter, 17; Mixed Sausages with Red Pearl Onions in Beer Fondue, 166; Pigs in a Blanket, 85

scallops. See seafood

Scones, Currant, 51

seafood, 6–7; See also fish; Artichoke and Oyster Soup, 157; Basil Shrimp, 39; Cold Seafood Platter, 14; Court Bouillon Seafood Boil, 171; Crawfish Balls, 93; Fried Calamari, 181; Garlic Shrimp, 146; Halibut and Lobster Tail Wine Fondue, 154; Lump Crab and Cream Cheese Fondue, 77; Mixed Beggar's Purses in Burgundy Fondue, 159; Pan-Seared Sea Scallops, 24; Savory Scallop and Sake Fondue, 149; Thai Seafood Hot Pot Broth, 201

shrimp. See seafood

soups and bisques: Artichoke and Oyster Soup, 157; Chilled Avocado Bisque, 188; Gazpacho, 141; Roasted Tomato Soup, 289; Tomato-Basil Bisque, 148

spinach: Chicken-Spinach Croquettes, 40; Mini Spinach Quiches, 79; Nutty Spinach Balls with Tomato Coulis, 121; Pear and Spinach Salad, 218; Spiced Feta-Spinach Fondue, 94

Squash, Stir-Fried Pattypan, 98

strawberries: Strawberries and Cream Puffs, 216; Strawberry Shortcake Fondue, 273

Sweet Potato Kugel, 314

Tabbouleh, 135

tahini, 123

Tilapia Ceviche, 293

Tiramisu, 182

tomatoes: Bloody Mary Fondue, 311; Fresh Heirloom Tomato and Lime Salsa, 129; Fresh Tomato Salsa, 68; Fritada Sauce, 143; Gazpacho, 141; Mozzarella and Tomato Salad, 298; Roasted Tomato Salsa, 130; Roasted Tomato Soup, 289; Sicilian Red Gravy Fondue, 180; Tomato-Basil Bisque, 148; Tomato Bruschetta, 153; Tomato Coulis, 122

truffles, 36, 249–254

tuna: Pesce Puttanesca Fondue, 299; Seared Tuna Bites, 97

turkey: Ginger Lemongrass Hot Pot, 303; Turkey Mole Fondue, 294

vanilla extract, 46

Veal Fondue, Sherry Poached Chicken and, 142

vegetables: See also salads; specific types; Ratatouille, 308; Raw and Blanched Vegetable Assortment for Fondue, 312; Tempura Veggie Skewers with Ginger-Soy Sauce, 119

Welsh Rarebit, 33

wine-based fondues: Halibut and Lobster Tail Wine Fondue, 154; Mixed Beggar's Purses in Burgundy Fondue, 159; Savory Scallop and Sake Fondue, 149; Sherry-Poached Chicken and Veal Fondue, 142

wine pairings, 7–8, 97

Zucchini and Peppers Fondue, 150